peter lutz marcel Wanders micky rosen ale(x)
urseanul Kai hollman lars pihl jan söder der
eto gurtner christian köck siv sundfær
blanche van berckel jorge Cosme antoni
navarro carlos couturier moises micla
andrade silva emanuele garosci his nin
Sendlinger silva emanuele garosci claus
berckel nini carlos couturier lars pihl blanch
p gurtner andrade silva siv sundfær ret va
peter lutz Kai Christian köck jan söder et
antonio Kai hollman jorge der li
emanuele navarro marcel nico mer claus sendlinge
c garosci moises celt urseanu
Wanders alex micky rosen
es micha alex micky rosen

lute the pure ger bermühle gastWerk hotel 25
suites roomers the mühle gastWerk hotel 25 ours
25 hours roomers the george 25 hours condesa 2 ours
azucar george hotel sdf life
the franklin nori light rocks resort life
franklin luite hotel fontana medicine
nospes hot te suites nro Palau park resort
maricel de pa del de la mar
palacio o de hde bae za
helbailio Villa de abita sen
amerigo gast del df basico
he george gastWerk hotel Nordic light hotel
roomers the fontanapark Nordic light rocks
azucar adri franklin gerbermühle M resort
basico adrid thepure deseo amerigo life medicine r
25 hours hotel the roomers resort Ndesa df
condesa df

PEOPLE, PLACES & THINGS
---
*A BOOK FEATURING 170 OF THE WORLD'S MOST DISTINCTIVE INDEPENDENT HOTELS … AND THE EVEN MORE DISTINCTIVE, INDEPENDENT PEOPLE BEHIND THEM.*

# TABLE OF
# CONTENTS

*SEE THE DESIGN HOTELS™ ORIGINALS IN ACTION.* LOG ON TO DESIGNHOTELS.COM FOR SHORT FILMS PRESENTING EACH STORY & PROPERTY.

# MEMBER HOTELS
## BY DESTINATION

## *EUROPE*

# *EUROPE*

# HUMAN DESIGN

---

*A new look, a novel concept, a focus on the people who make it happen:*
*Design Hotels™ founder and CEO Claus Sendlinger introduces*
*the firm's next moves.*

Sixteen years ago, Design Hotels™ started off with an unknowingly prescient vision. Realising that more and more hotels would start considering and using good design and architecture – and of course incorporate them into their concepts – we gave our young company the generic name "Design Hotels."

Even then we knew that the choice might be risky, but we gladly jumped at the chance to become a household name once the lifestyle movement took off. And it has, far more than we could have predicted at the time. Today, not only the movement toward smaller, more intimate properties but also the predominance of "design" in larger properties has become more rule than exception.

Different "design hotels" might be all over the place today, but Design Hotels™ remains unique. Since the beginning, we've been the champions of brilliant hotel design and amazing hotel architecture. But we've always thought a few steps ahead of the usual curve and outside the normal box by placing value on intangibles. Like the perfect vibe, the evoked emotion, the story told – and, most of all, the people behind the properties in our portfolio. A hotel that's really going to work absolutely has to have soul. Right now, as "designed" hotels become the norm, the human touch is more important than ever.

This past year, more than 400 hotels applied for Design Hotels™ membership, but we selected only 25 as new members. What makes a good hotel a Design Hotels™ member is a combination of tangibles and intangibles that we look at holistically. Topping the criteria is the hotel's overall concept. Design isn't simply placing a Marcel Wanders lamp or Ron Arad chair in a lobby, or offering the bells and whistles of high-tech gadgets that no one can understand or operate when they're alone in their rooms. It's a cohesive idea as well as an emotion that permeates a property and creates an authentic experience. The second factor is architecture: how public and private spaces feel and how the building functions as an "organism," so to speak. Then comes design, of course. The visual, tactile and sensual elements in furnishings, textiles and materials that come together to create an unusual experience. Some of our most illustrious hoteliers stress the importance of details, and how a great hotel lives not from one idea, but thousands. Yet it should all keep a certain simplicity.

Last but not at all least comes the human capital; the people behind the look and feel of a property as well as the faces guests see when they walk through the front door. What brings the most successful hotel operators and hoteliers together is the desire to do something special that possesses an inherent quality. It's about creating a unique DNA that guests can feel. A truly curated collection, The Design Hotels™ portfolio reflects these things in a myriad of different ways. And it does in even better ways as each year passes.

Those of you who have followed us over the years will notice that this edition of our annual book has a different look than previous editions. It has a larger, coffee-table format, it's less like a catalog, and it's differently

---

CLAUS
SENDLINGER

## AS "DESIGNED" HOTELS BECOME THE NORM, THE HUMAN TOUCH IS MORE IMPORTANT THAN EVER.

---

categorised. Instead of geographical sections, we have divided our member hotels into loose categories based on the experiences guests might have in each of them.

The largest group is based on a reliable but never ever predictable kind of style. The hotels in this group are like signatures – and although a signature might have the power to close a deal or sign off, no two are alike. In these hotels, seamless service, excellent aesthetics and an authentic connection to local culture are the common denominator; the rest as individual as a fingerprint.

A second group is more experimental, alternative and boundary pushing in both design and concept. These hotels take visual and behavioural risks, offering offbeat features like an haute-cuisine breakfast box delivered to your door or striking visuals like Arad's huge silver ring as a reception desk. The third group is the smallest: hotels that take the accoutrements

and service features of a traditional grand hotel but offer them in a more contemporary, casual package. These new groups are where we see the hospitality movement heading today.

The book's second new feature, one we're sure you will have a lot of fun reading, focuses on people. We're proud to introduce some of the outstanding personalities behind our member properties in up-close and personal profiles we are calling "Made by Originals". To produce the stories, we've travelled around the world with writers, photographers, and film crews to finally show you just who's who in the Design Hotels™ world and what interesting tales they have to tell.

These are the motors behind innovative design concepts and revolutionary hospitality ideas. One set of "originals" has kick-started boutique-hotel culture in its home country of Mexico. In Austria, a married couple combines top-notch health care with 21st-century design and spa culture on the forefront of a new movement in hospitality. In the Netherlands, a star designer (okay, it's Marcel Wanders) and an earthy chef have come together to create a property in which down-to-earth values meet over-the-top visuals and drop-dead delicious cuisine. And in Venice, a former racecar driver has captured the decadent, luxurious spirit of mysterious city in a new way, in a property with a history. And there's more.

If you like what you read and would like to see our originals and their unique properties in action, log on to www.designhotels.com to view a series of short films featuring each original in his, her, or their element.

Design, hotels – and our wonderfully generic moniker-slash-household name Design Hotels™ will continue to evolve along with our very original people and their innovative ideas. With people like these, and others to come, good design and exquisite experience will never go out of style.

*Claus Sendlinger*
*Founder and CEO*
*Design Hotels™*

# BUILT TO LAST

Claus Sendlinger, pictured on the previous pages at home in Berlin, Germany, sees a few developments in design that are important right now and will continue to be in the near future. Today's best design uses the finest materials, but not just for their prestige factor or luxurious texture and look. Increasingly, these materials are chosen for their plain and simple durability. Well-designed interiors and objects are made for the long haul. Flooring and surfaces in granite or treated steel, walls in high-quality wood, handmade glass mosaics and other materials offer timeless style that will stay beautiful for years. It is quite the opposite of trendy, planned obsolescence.

Although it has always been an important mark of quality, genuine craftsmanship is also making a major comeback. Outsourced mass production is giving way to meticulously, often locally handcrafted pieces. Perhaps you can call it the return of the masterpiece, but design aficionados are investing in truly unique, limited edition possessions – from the worlds of fashion, furnishing, housewares, textiles and more – that add unlimited intrinsic value, and not only due to the individual energy, skill, and tradition that went into their production.

These movements add up to a kind of sustainability that's a few steps away from the "sustainability" catchphrase that we hear from the Green Police or in the fear-inducing mass media. In a world in which not much is certain, old-fashioned methods and exquisite materials underscore a new development in contemporary design that's brilliantly grounded in tradition, both emotionally and aesthetically. And it's built to last.

MATERIAL WORLD
*Bathroom walls in rusted steel sealed with beeswax.*
*Bathtub by Falper. Stool by E15. Interiors by Armin Fischer,*
*3 Meta, with C. Sendlinger and his wife, Polina.*

DESIGN HOTELS™
PRESENTS

# MADE BY
# *ORIGINALS*

---

EDITED BY KIMBERLY BRADLEY
PHOTOGRAPHY BY KERSTIN ZU PAN
AND PETER LANGER

# KEEPING IT REAL

———

*At Lute Suites, one of the Netherlands' premier hospitality destinations,
star designer Marcel Wanders and celebrated chef Peter Lute have
assembled and prepared exactly the right combination of
ingredients for a one-of-a-kind experience.*

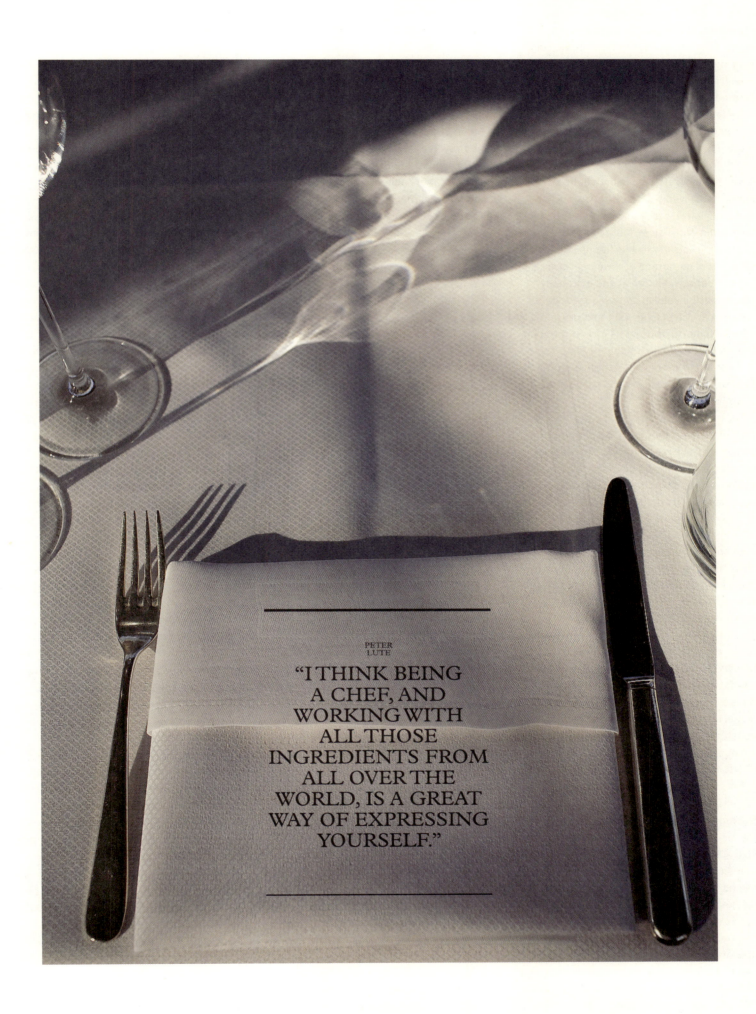

PETER
LUTE

"I THINK BEING
A CHEF, AND
WORKING WITH
ALL THOSE
INGREDIENTS FROM
ALL OVER THE
WORLD, IS A GREAT
WAY OF EXPRESSING
YOURSELF."

When mega-designer Marcel Wanders and acclaimed chef Peter Lute get together, the camaraderie and like-mindedness are obvious. Smiles spread, jokes fly, backs are patted and an almost overwhelming warm-heartedness surrounds anyone who's near them. But it's clear something more than friendship exists here: these two are kindred spirits who share not only an innate drive to innovate, but also an honesty and self-knowledge that are becoming more and more unusual in today's fast-paced world.

It's an honesty reflected in both Lute, Peter's eponymous, wildly successful restaurant, and Lute Suites, the unusual property that is their common creation. More like a collection of design jewels in which to live, the Suites are a mix of quirky and down-home, surprising and serious, historical and extremely avant-garde in seven converted worker's cottages attached to an 18th-century gunpowder factory. "Both of us gave more than 100 percent to make it happen," says Lute. "It's not about money or technical stuff. Of course it's a business, but the feeling of it isn't a business."

On a small road that hugs the shimmering, gentle Amstel river about 15 miles outside Amsterdam in the village of Ouderkerk aan de Amstel, a row of old gabled cottages suddenly appears across from a docked boat on the river's bank. This is Lute Suites.

Turning into the courtyard, it's immediately clear that this is not a "normal" hotel and restaurant combination. There's an inviting dining terrace sheltered under elegant canvas tarps; white geometric chairs are carefully arranged outside. At a right angle to the cottages, the barnlike building that houses the restaurant beckons. Inside is a comfortable lounge area, where Martin Baas's deep, burnt Smoke chairs sit beside Moooi lamps; huge, fluffy area carpets punctuate the rough floor. To the right is the dining room – an open space also dotted with thick carpets – and then a wall of wines, behind which is the perfect kitchen.

But more on that later. We'll start here with the feeling: daylight streams into the open space, slightly illuminating the huge nails that still dot the old-fashioned dark ceiling beams. It's comfortable and kind, and feels a bit like a barn or a cowshed – which, it turns out, is exactly what it once was. With ruffled hair and in a black T-shirt and jeans, Lute appears and mentions that he and his team served a special party the night before – on top of the 110 normal covers they turn over when the restaurant is at capacity. Lute wanders through the restaurant's glass pavilion in

which the party took place, walks out to the lawn and takes a few jumps on a trampoline that his young daughters Sarah and Isabel like to play on. Then he takes a sprig from a planter and sniffs it. He sometimes uses his own herb garden to season his dishes. The restaurant's overall effect is remarkably homey, even if it's filled with high design. And not a bite of food has been tasted – yet.

To watch Lute operate his kitchen during a noon or evening meal is like watching a maestro conduct a well-rehearsed orchestra. The impeccable kitchen is a rectangular stainless-steel machine; Lute stands at the helm and directs perfectly prepared truffle

MARCEL WANDERS FOR MOOOI
CARBON CHAIR

soup in shot glasses, entrees mixing delicate cheek of beef with fresh whole trout that Lute jokes was "illegally caught in the Amstel", and various small courses and desserts to the relaxed waitstaff, which delivers everything to the guests. Each meal comes as a series of five or nine small courses; each dish is a work of art to the eye and an explosion of flavour to the palate. This isn't trendy molecular, but Lute's own take on French-influenced cuisine, a mix of traditional and experimental.

Many dishes feature unusual elements or exotic ingredients like Tahiti vanilla or Parmesan foam, or combine opposing textures, such as homemade crisps served with otherwise smooth desserts and creamy soups. "As a young boy, I was already feeling all the elements and flavours of nature. You want to do something with your senses: everything you see, everything you feel, everything you smell," says the 39-year-old.

"I think being a chef, and working with all those ingredients from all over the world, is a great way of expressing yourself." There's an obvious love for individual expression in the food, the ambience, even the employees' hardworking, jovial team spirit. And in true Dutch tradition, what you see is what you get: there's no secret storeroom for foods and supplies. Each day's ingredients are shipped in fresh early in the morning.

Lute started off in a technical school and worked his way through many of Holland's best kitchens, but always harboured the dream of opening his own restaurant. "I quit my job and took three years off," he says, talking about the genesis of Lute. Finding this factory and securing the permits to have the listed structure converted took time, but the restaurant was very nearly an instant hit.

He likes to tell the story involving a beautiful onion field that transfixed him as a child, and how this memory made him realise that part of what having a successful restaurant is about is evoking – or creating – memories. "My business is bringing back memories. If someone has risotto in my restaurant and thinks of a holiday they had ten years before, I'm happy," he says, mentioning that the guest, not the chef, is the most important element in any successful restaurant. "It's not important to put your name on your chest. What's important is what people feel when they sit in your restaurant."

The Suites themselves are perhaps less about evoking old memories than about generating wildly creative new ones. Although it could be argued that each of the cottages is a modified historical memory in itself. Renovated over the course of two years and then filled with Wanders's powerfully imaginative touches, the Suites are feasts for the eyes; amalgamations of seemingly disparate but intriguingly cohesive ingredients.

All have ten-foot windows that allow spacious views of the Amstel. Tiny details, like ceramic bears, are hidden in corners. Some of the coat hangers are actually white ceramic dishes attached to the wall. Wanders's famous knotted chair crops up as, yes, a chair, but also informs the knotted-rope railing on one suite's very vertical staircase. A grey rug explodes in a fluff of yarn at one edge, on purpose. And in Suite Five – in which both Lute and Wanders simply couldn't sleep, they explain, for all the visual information going on inside – the entire mezzanine floor is a wet room featuring an wall sporting an image printed on tiles, and a bathtub that looks something like an oversize bar of white soap cut in »

"BOTH OF US
GAVE MORE THAN
100 PERCENT TO
MAKE IT HAPPEN.
IT'S A BUSINESS,
BUT THE FEELING
OF IT ISN'T
A BUSINESS."

half and scooped out. Suite Two features a colourful stool in funky mosaics, as well as stacked lamps distributed by Wanders's design firm Moooi. (Mooi means "beautiful" in Dutch; Moooi has an extra "o" for extra beauty.) Suite Seven has a twisting spiral staircase and inlaid floors that look like mother-of-pearl.

All of the spaces feature elements of modern baroque, such as Wanders's famous swirly wallpaper and crocheted couch tables. Along with these come more pragmatic elements, like an enclosed kitchenette (packed, by the way, with designer dishes and accessories) or, well, the unique bars of soap found in the bathrooms. Actually, even these have a hidden meaning – the soaps are shaped like the lute (the instrument, not Peter). "When we were researching names for the project, we realised that Bach was composing the Lute Suites about the same year this factory was built," says Wanders. "It was magical."

Lute Suites was, remarkably, Marcel Wanders's first hotel project. (He's gone on to decorate the ground floor of The Hotel on Rivington in New York and the highly dramatic Mondrian South Beach in Miami.) Now in his mid-forties, the celebrated designer was long the design world's enfant terrible, but he has entered a new, mature era. Back in 1996, the knotted chair – which he designed for the Dutch collective Droog Design – landed in the MoMA collection, but he's since designed pieces for nearly every big-ticket manufacturer, including B&B Italia, Bisazza, Flos, Cappellini and more. His signature fabrics and wallpaper decorate edgy spaces everywhere. Moooi turns over 30 million euros in revenue a year, and there's some talk of designing retail spaces and even museums. Wanders speaks of the difference between creating an object and creating a three-dimensional experience. "The way you design an interior is completely different from how you design an object," he says. "When you design an object, it's like taking a piece of marble and releasing something beautiful inside. But interior design is like writing music, or haikus. Some lines are separate, but somehow they are together. It doesn't live on one idea; it lives on a thousand ideas," he explains.

Lute Suites took a year and a half to create, and it contains many thousands of ideas. As the story goes, the project involved seven drawing boards in the Marcel Wanders studio morphing and shifting as each suite took shape. In the construction site that is now his new offices in Amsterdam (in the past two years or so, Studio Wanders has grown from just a few stalwart assistants to thirty-odd full-time employees), Wanders – traipsing over wildly patterned plaid carpets he designed last year, and wearing a wacky chain of marble-size pearls and shiny metallic shoes – credits Lute for being a remarkable designer. "To work with a chef who's a great designer! It's like making babies: you look for the right woman. We took a huge amount of time for each room, and it was a huge amount of fun."

# THE BEST GUEST LIST IN TOWN

---

*Frankfurt native sons Micky Rosen and Alex Urseanu are entrepreneurs, real-estate pioneers, social impresarios and business partners who have changed the face of their hometown's nightlife and hospitality scenes.*

MADE BY
*ORIGINALS*

---

**MICKY ROSEN &
ALEX URSEANU**

FRANKFURT AM MAIN

High up on a construction site near the central train station in Frankfurt am Main, a pair of raven-haired men in crisp dark suits climb from a dusty ladder onto what will ultimately be the roof terrace of a new hotel's spa. Emerging amazingly dust-free and without a hair out of place, the two are reminiscent of what Batman and Robin might look like if Gotham City's dynamic duo lost their masks and capes. But in terms of innovative hospitality, entertainment, social networking and entrepreneurship, Micky Rosen and Alex Urseanu are the duo extraordinaire of Germany's financial capital.

This construction site will soon be Roomers, Frankfurt's first high-design boutique hotel with five-star services, including a "biorhythm" spa, wraparound-view conference rooms, the city's first member bar, and 117 gorgeously appointed rooms. Scaffolding still envelops the structure – which used to be an office building – but it's already clear that it will be another success in the partners' diverse palette.

It's a palette of hospitality properties that began in 2003 with the Bristol Hotel (not a Design Hotel member hotel, but a start), near the same station. Up the street, in 2005, came The Pure – all in white, a cool urban vision and an instant haven to design-aficionado travellers. More recent additions are the Gerbermühle, an expansive historical property directly on the river Main, and, of course, Roomers. Together, the two men have not only built a hometown mini-empire but have been pioneers in terms of the city's social scene, with two ultrapopular local bars, a satellite of The Pure called The Pure Basement for events, and a positively notorious party series.

Urseanu walks through Roomers' interlocking spaces-in-progress on the ground floor, showing how, in just a few months, the restaurant, members' bar, courtyard lounge and lobby will lead patrons from one mood-infused space to another. He enthusiastically describes colours and lighting, the future menu, the people who'll come here. The thirty-something entrepreneur's eyes shine as his partner Rosen explains their philosophy from behind sleek frameless glasses: "We love new projects, we love production, we love hotels, we love service," he says. "You walk in and it has to have soul. Just name-brand design doesn't do it."

## So what *does* do it? Where does that soul come from, and what's the secret to your success?

**Alex Urseanu:** Capturing a good feeling is what we're trying to do in all of our businesses. It's what makes us different from the large chains. It's a bit like Apple and PCs. Our advantage is that we bring individuality into the properties. You check in and get a nice person in front of you; the lighting, the atmosphere ... it all works.
**Micky Rosen:** We've always made properties in which we feel good. We're also perfectionists. We place high demands on

---

MICKY ROSEN

## "YOU WALK IN AND IT HAS TO HAVE SOUL. JUST NAME-BRAND DESIGN DOESN'T DO IT."

---

ourselves. Well, we're selling a feeling, not [hotel] stars, but then again, we live this way ourselves.
**AU:** You know, you have a good feeling when you go to the concierge and he gets you a table at an amazing restaurant; when you can count on always being hooked up with the best places.

## Are you always a few steps ahead of the rest of the city?

**MR:** I don't know if it's a step ahead ... but we travel and see a lot.
**AU:** Everywhere in the world we're inspired by details, music, people. And then we develop ideas and see what's missing in Frankfurt.

**MR:** The difference is that a lot of people might have an idea, but when we have something in our heads, we do it. We actually dare to do it. Many people don't. We see something ... let's do it.
**AU:** But you also can't overwhelm Frankfurt. It's a little conservative. Sometimes you have good ideas but you're too early with them. Frankfurt is probably the smallest global city or the biggest small town. But we do go against the everyday grey of the city. We've brought some colour into the city with entertainment.

## Your parties have become legendary. How did they start?

**AU:** We wanted to bring local Frankfurt life into the hotels. At first, we invited a few friends to our first hotel. It was great. Then it became 60 to 70, then 200 people. Then it was 300 to 400 people. They kept getting bigger every time. Now we have parties once a month, and they've become a solid element of Frankfurt nightlife. We have them in The Pure Basement; tonight there's a big one in the Gerbermühle. The whole city is buzzing.

## How does it feel to be seen as a kind of social organiser or impresario?

**MR:** Frankfurt has a lot of skyscrapers, but it's still a village. I'm not so sure I like being recognised, but it's nice when the properties are connected to us. It's also nice to see that in a city in which you were born and grew up, that you've become a brand or label. I don't mean to sound arrogant. We just know that when we send an invitation, we don't need to send RSVP cards. We know it's always going to be more than full. That's great, and that's how it has been now for the past six years.

## What makes a good party?

**MR:** It depends on the people. We were always about having a good mix, not just the investment banker with a bottle of champagne. There should also be a funky graffiti sprayer, and then a model and someone from the culinary scene. It's the mix that makes it. »

"WE LIKE TO
GIVE PEOPLE
ANOTHER
REASON TO
COME TO
FRANKFURT."

# "OUR PASSION IS A PART OF US. IT'S OUR CHARACTER – FROM THE FUN, THE WORKING RELATIONSHIP, THE FRIENDSHIP, AND OUR LOVE OF FINE THINGS."

**AU:** It's when a week before the party, women talk about what they'll wear – and the guys are trying to get on the guest list. That's a good party (laughs).

**A lot of Frankfurt's nightlife revolves around your guest list and connecting skills. But you've also been pivotal in revitalising the once-seedy area around the Frankfurt central train station.**

MR: We started with the Bristol six years ago on the north side of the train station; back then, it was slums filled with junkies. But since then we've played a large part in developing the area. Then came The Pure. We know that people like to go to the train station area these days. As a Frankfurt native, it's nice to see this development. The hotels are bringing in other investors and building into the area. This is how an area becomes hip.

**You have another new development near the train station – the Gecko loft. Can this be rented as well?**

MR: Yes, it's an event location but also a hotel room – the new loft is 250 square metres and can be rented for conferences, for meetings, or as a kind of private restaurant for clients who want privacy, or VIPs who need security. This location is meant for these kinds of clients. They book it like a suite.

**It's beautifully designed. It looks like a private apartment.**

MR: I actually live next door in an identical apartment. Even though we're not completely finished with it, we've already had three events here. You know, we have a lot of restaurants and hotels and day rooms; but there aren't so many places that are intimate.
AU: Here's a place where you get your cooks, your service staff – or no one!

**What drives the two of you?**

AU: We get really bored. And of course we want to be really, really rich (laughs all around). No, seriously. We go with the flow. We don't have a solid plan; we're not a management consultancy. But our heads are always working. In a new project like Roomers, when there's a great concept, it's like a puzzle. You develop this kind of passion and challenge, and then you get good people around you and make sure you can communicate everything: that's the drive. It's just really important that you stay open, that you can challenge yourself, that you have a feeling for people. On top of this, our passion is a part of us. It's our character – from the fun, the working relationship, the friendship and our love of fine things.
MR: (smiling) And moving things within the city.
AU: We like to give people another reason to come to Frankfurt.

**Do you think of the business risks?**

MR: Yes, definitely. The projects we do cost huge amounts of money. If it doesn't work we have a problem. But if you don't take a risk, you can't have success – you stay in your little room and you can't grow. You have to be ready to take risks.

**What's the next step?**

MR: We're thinking we could take the Roomers concept to other cities. We still have to find the next location. A Roomers in Frankfurt and a Roomers in Berlin won't look the same, but they'll be parts of a bigger concept. We don't want a museum; we want life! And we've always tried to be exemplary hosts.

**What's a good host … and a good entrepreneur?**

AU: A good entrepreneur is a good host and might earn a little money in the end. For us, it's much, much more important that the guest goes home happy. We might have a little less in our pockets, but that the guest goes home happy – that's our maxim. For us, another big added value is to give people here in the city a bit more quality of life. And you know what? When you give them a little more quality of life, in some way you always get a little bit back. «

*Interview by Kimberly Bradley*

# THE HANSEATIC HOTELIER

Hotel mogul Kai Hollmann has transformed his native city of Hamburg with a new breed of properties that reflects his ease, business savvy and philosophies on hospitality.

Kai Hollmann sweeps his arms across the urban landscape, gesturing towards Hamburg's Alster Lake below. He's standing on the roof terrace of his newest hotel, The George, mysteriously unruffled by the North Sea winds that race across the expansive deck. "Anyone who grew up here needs that wind," he says with a laugh. Like a king surveying his dominion, he leans casually against the railing, chatting with the slew of journalists here to check out the latest addition to the Hamburg hotel scene.

This is his city. Of course, he'd never say as much – no true native would. But the facts speak for themselves. Hollmann was born and raised in Hamburg and has lived here all his life. He's opened four hotels in the city, renovated dozens of landmark-protected buildings and, together with his sister and four brothers, started a local real estate company. He circulates amongst the city's movers and shakers, and clinks glasses with its local business owners. He was voted Hotelier of the Year in 2003 and Hamburg's Businessman of the Year just a few months ago. All the Hanseatic reserve in the world can't conceal the fact that this heavyweight has left his mark on the streets below. The view from up here is magnificent. At six storeys, The George towers over the other buildings in the St. Georg neighbourhood for which it is named. Hollmann's hands move constantly and surely; he could point out buildings all day. "See that?" he asks, pointing to a tall, impressive structure. "That's the hotel we opened a few months ago, the Superbude." And, "Down there is where I did my first hotel apprenticeship." Or, "See that building right there? That's the Alsterperle. Great atmosphere. Perfect place to grab a beer and sit by the water."

It's at first difficult to imagine Hollmann grabbing anything, much less a beer. He holds his tall, slender frame erect in something like a noble stance, just laid-back enough – a hand in the pocket, a slightly bent right knee – to hint of a glamourous bygone age when businessmen were gentlemen and deals were closed over glasses of expensive whiskey. In soft grey trousers and a smart blue blazer, he's the very picture of self-assured elegance. But behind the façade is a surprisingly easygoing fellow. Maybe this has something to do with the simple fact that he's got nothing to prove. When it comes to

hotels, Hollmann knows what he's doing. "I was classically trained," he explains. "I came up through the traditional system and went through all the apprenticeships. I'm a true hotelier." After completing secondary school, the 17-year-old Hollmann, who dreamed of one day opening a restaurant, began a cooking apprenticeship at Hamburg's InterContinental hotel. Next came two years of hotel management training, followed by a move to Willi Bartels's Hotel Hafen Hamburg, where, at age 24, Hollmann became the hotel's youngest assistant director ever. Just one year later, Bartels promoted his protégé to director, making him the youngest in all of Germany.

---

KAI
HOLLMANN

**"I WAS CLASSICALLY TRAINED. I CAME UP THROUGH THE TRADITIONAL SYSTEM AND WENT THROUGH ALL THE APPRENTICESHIPS. I'M A TRUE HOTELIER."**

---

In 2000, after almost two decades of building hotels for his mentor, Hollmann decided to break out on his own. Some years earlier, he and his siblings had founded a real estate company with an inheritance from their grandfather, publishing giant Heinrich Bauer. One of the properties owned by the company was a former municipal gasworks. In its revamped red-brick buildings, Hollmann created Gastwerk, Hamburg's first design hotel. The city had never seen anything like it. The "traditional hotelier," it seemed, had something of the maverick in him after all.

Next came the 25hours hotel in 2004, intended to "make design accessible to those on a smaller budget." The concept was so successful that Hollmann's friends quickly

approached him about transporting it to other cities; soon thereafter, the 25hours Hotel Company was born, and it now has two additional houses in Frankfurt and several others in development. In 2008, Hamburg saw the opening of two further Kai Hollmann creations. The first, Superbude, or "Super Digs," is a hotel/hostel mash-up, a new form of budget boarding house for people of all ages. The second, of course, is The George, a four-star property inspired by traditional English social clubs.

This inspiration is nowhere more evident than in the ground-floor public spaces, particularly the library, where guests can enjoy a spot of afternoon tea in the deep embrace of a warm leather sofa or in one of Mies van der Rohe's famous Barcelona chairs, contributed by Hollmann himself. "Some dealers won't sell to hotels," he chuckles. "These chairs are perfect for sitting in hotel lobbies and people-watching." At the moment, however, Hollmann is leafing through one of the several gorgeous books on the coffee table. "Did you know that [German rock star] Udo Lindenberg also paints?" Hollmann asks. "I ran into him the other day and he gave me this book of his work." The autographed volume is one of The George's many unique pieces personally sourced by Hollmann, who sees guests as friends and is happy to share with them. "This idea of having friends over appeals to me because friends take care of each other. That makes things a lot more fun," he says.

Yet, like a good friend, the guest has a few responsibilities, too. "In my houses," explains Hollmann, "if a guest doesn't behave respectfully, the situation will definitely be addressed." An unusual philosophy in this age of extravagant entitlement. The other side of that, of course, is that at Hollmann's hotels, there is no such thing as no. "If a hungry guest arrives late at night because he was stuck in traffic on the motorway and the kitchen is already closed, we'll have the night porter throw together a sandwich. The idea is, if there's something we can't do, we have to find an alternative."

Hollmann inherited this philosophy from his mentor, Bartels, who was known as the King of St. Pauli. "He was one of those old-timers," remembers Hollmann. "Every city has them – those four or five people whose word »

LIFESTYLE, AS
HOLLMANN SEES IT,
IS ABOUT "STORY."
IN A HOTEL, IT'S
THE GUESTS AND
STAFF WHO WRITE
THE STORY.

matters. He had a real sense of duty. When the tenant came and said, 'I can't pay my rent this month,' the response was, 'Okay, well get to work and pay it as soon as you can.' Those times are over now." Perhaps not entirely. Through Hollmann, Bartels's legacy lives on. "I learned how to conduct a business from him," says Hollmann fondly. "There's always stress when it comes to buildings, but you have to live and let live, and you have to treat one another fairly."

But that doesn't mean he throws pragmatism to the wind. Quite to the contrary, Hollmann is a man who likes to talk numbers. "I'm probably a more sober thinker than other design hotel owners," he explains. "I always see the business side. I couldn't build a hotel without thinking about figures – material costs, personnel costs." You won't see Hollmann building any fantastic, profits-be-damned, purely conceptual masterpieces. He isn't an artist who chooses hotels as his canvas; he's an hotelier who is inspired by art. To him, then, design isn't the be-all and end-all of his vision. "All hotels have design," he explains. "Maybe an ugly design, but still a design. It's the lifestyle my hotels embody that motivates me. Design is just one part of that."

Lifestyle, as Hollmann sees it, is about "story." In a hotel, it's the guests and staff who write the story. Thus, Hollmann sees The George as a place where like-minded people can come together for business or pleasure. Almost all of the property's spaces are open not only to guests but also to neighbourhood locals: an important point for the hotelier, who carefully chose the location. "St. Georg has a heart," he explains. "It has an unbelievable vitality."

Once somewhat seedy, the area has been vamped up in recent years, sprouting dozens of boutique shops, cafés and lively bars. Multifaceted and multicultural, it fits right into Hollmann's vision for The George. "I was inspired by those alleys off Oxford Street in London. The mix there is so exciting. You have so many different kinds of people; a Gucci shop next to a 15-euro T-shirt shop. I love that," he says.

The George intends to provide a similar mix of elements in a kind of members-only club for which membership is not actually required. The idea, as Hollmann puts it, "is to create a new way of meeting" – intimate and privileged without being exclusive. All rooms are available for private hire, including a private dining room, two clubrooms and Hollmann's favourite space, an indoor courtyard with English garden.

"We're aiming for those people who want more than the typical conference room atmosphere." The George, in other words, isn't for large masses running around with name tags. It's for people who want to work with the hotel to create a personalised experience with which both sides are happy. Again, it all comes down to this idea of friendship between hotel and guest.

Hollmann gives himself wholly to that friendship, and it shows. It's the little things that are most revealing – the Italian waiters stirring hot noodles on top of a gigantic round of Parmesan cheese right at your table; the 130 varieties of whiskey available at the bar, served with a smile by an Italian barman named Giovanni who knows his alcohol; the rooftop webcams fed to elevator televisions so that guests can watch sail-boats speed across the Alster in real time. Hollmann has thought of everything.

The sun is setting, and the busy man only has time for one last cigarette. He's promised his daughter that he'll help her with her math homework tonight. He starts pointing out neighbourhood landmarks again, this time from ground level. "You know," he says suddenly, "I couldn't care less if a waiter sets down plates from the left or the right. What's important to me is that he knows what he's serving and likes what he's doing. Guests notice that." Finishing his cigarette, he shakes hands all around and strolls calmly off into the city into which he's poured his heart. «

*Jenna Krumminga*

KAI HOLLMANN

# "St. Georg has a heart. It has an unbelievable vitality."

# NORDIC
# BY NATURE

---

*A unique Scandinavian hotel's brilliant, ever-changing play on lights
takes its inspiration from nature, nurture and designer
Lars Pihl's own personal illumination.*

For designer Lars Pihl, inspiration and creativity are usually accompanied by movement. It might be the momentum of the music coming from the headphones he dons while designing in his office, or it could be the forward drive provided by his bike or even two feet while jogging along some of the 30,000 islands that make up the Stockholm archipelago. It was during the latter activity that the concept for the Swedish capital's premier design hotel came to him like ... a ray of light. Literally.

Pihl recounts a morning he was running in the forest near his home just outside Stockholm in late fall. Coming out of the woods, he found himself confronted with a stunningly beautiful vista: the sea stretched out in front of him was blanketed with a fog that obscured the low-hanging sun. As he watched, the sun's rays broke through the heavy mist, dancing over the water and flooding the landscape with an orange-yellow light. The landscape was transformed, along with Pihl's mood. In a flash of realisation, he decided that future guests at the new hotel he and co-designer Jan Söder were helping to launch should have a similar experience. He decided the focus would be not on sleek, modernist furniture or uncommon textures, but on that most ephemeral of natural phenomena: light.

"Like the Nordic light, I wanted the atmosphere to be changeable, not static," Pihl says. "It should relax people, or surprise them, or nudge them in a certain direction, depending on what mood people want to be in. It may even provoke a mood." The 48-year-old designer, who looks a decade younger, is talking about his inspiration and motivation in the Black Room, a monochromatic chill-out lounge that's suspended over the Nordic Light Hotel's lobby and outfitted with low-slung couches, newspapers and a flat-screen TV. It and the hotel are the result of Pihl's jogging epiphany.

Pihl fits right in with the space's inky interior. His wardrobe tends towards the dark side; a black hat stays perched firmly on his head at all times. A ring made of a few bike-chain links on his right hand, along with chunky pieces of metal on four fingers of his left, make him look like he could inflict some damage in a fist fight. Not that anyone could imagine him involved in any kind of hostility: it's quickly clear that this slightly edgy exterior belies an extremely gentle soul. One with five children at home. »

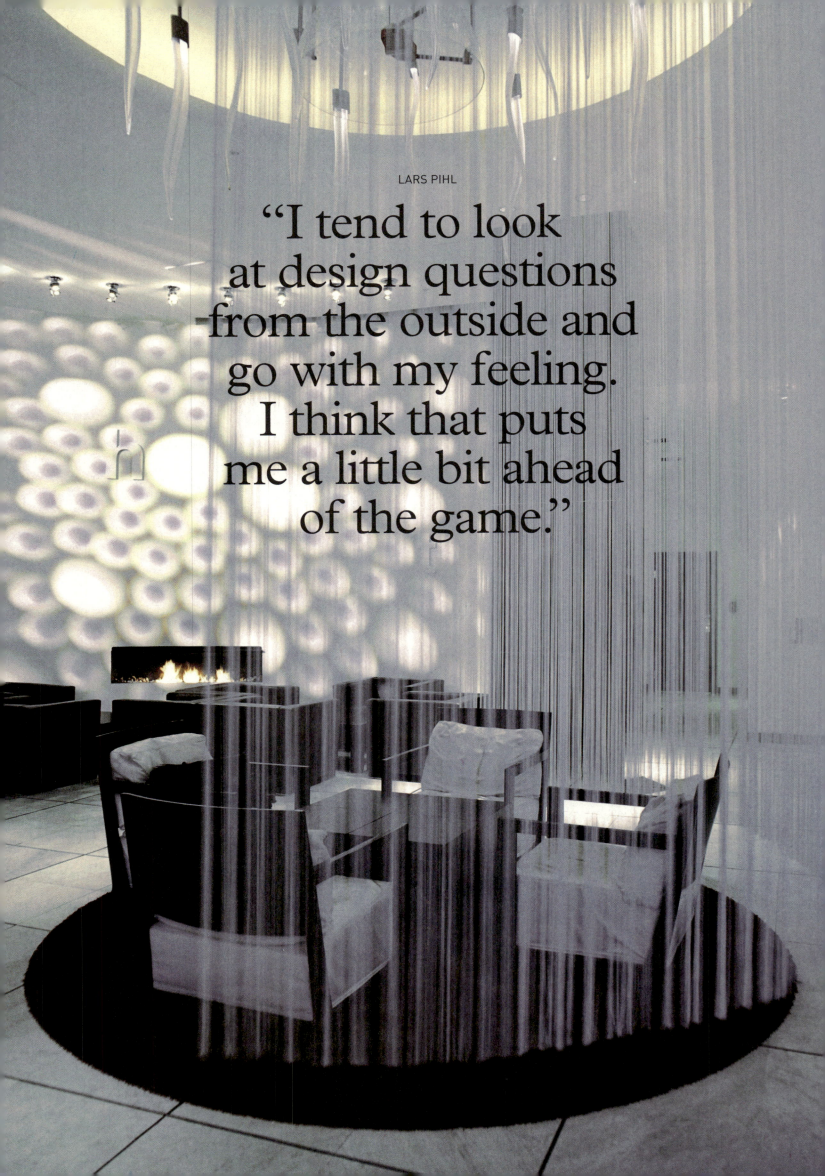

LARS PIHL

"I tend to look
at design questions
from the outside and
go with my feeling.
I think that puts
me a little bit ahead
of the game."

That's why, after spending some time abroad following his schooling, Pihl returned to his native country, needing to get back to the authenticity of the Swedes. It's a culture that's more about coopera-tion and consensus than competition. "They're very honest and you can nearly always rely on them. If they say something, it's generally true." An important factor in Swedish life and the Swedish soul is the quality of local light, or the lack of it. "In the winter, we can be quite silent," he says. "But in the summer, it's a completely different matter." It's that malleable personality that Pihl incorporated into his design. "Just as the light changes over the year, we change the hotel's light with the season, and also over the day," he explains. "We bring the outside light into the hotel when there's a lot of it. When there's not, we help out through electrical means."

The Nordic Light Hotel is a glass-and-steel box constructed in the late 1950s by a Swedish architect in love with the International Style, particularly the Lever House on New York's Park Avenue. Lars Erik Lallerstedt so admired that building that he simply built a copy of it in central Stockholm. For years it housed the U.S. Trade Center; nowadays, the kinds of deals made here are generally between players in the media, fashion, film and design industries. Parties in the lobby have become a magnet for creative types from Sweden, Scandinavia and beyond.

Like it does outside the lobby's floor-to-ceiling windows, the light inside the Nordic Light Hotel fluctuates with the time of day, the season or the guest's mood. The focus is on the slow progression of colour and brightness during a Scandinavian day as the lobby's light settings change over time. As darkness approaches, a fire begins crackling, its warm glow contrasting with the smooth black surfaces around it. "The light interacts with everyone who comes into the hotel and makes them a part of what is going on," says Pihl. "It keeps things interesting."

This constant fluctuation is accomplished not just with dimmer switches and a few well-placed fixtures. Pihl, Söder and a permanent in-house design team remake the lobby four times a year, roughly in keeping with the seasons. The team starts with a story it wants to tell largely through light, and comes up with a design plan, or it works with outside firms that they admire. One recent theme turned the lobby into a Scandinavian forest, and some fifty artificial fir trees were set up on a soft wooden floor. Guests could grab drinks at the hotel's hip destination bar and return to the forest to enjoy them

amidst soft beams of light streaming through the branches, like in the real forests near Pihl's home. A new theme explores the starlit darkness of outer space. "Light Space," a collaboration with the Belgian design group Dark, features large, translucent humanoid figures called "space walkers" hung from the ceiling. The installation is about welcoming the unexpected and involves a great many light bulbs – some 55,350 in the lobby alone.

Then there's the suite of meeting rooms, which uses light and furniture design to keep people productive, not bored. Head to the 175 rooms upstairs and the design experience continues, this time on a more personal level. In the hotel's "Mood Rooms," each bed's headboard is fitted out with fluorescents and more than 250 light-emitting diodes that allow guests to create a multitude of lighting environments. If the goal is to relax after a hard day, turning a dial will bathe both bed and room in soft blue, melting stress away. Another turn will fill the room with an orange or yellow glow, ideal for summoning up energy for productive work, say colour theorists. And if the adrenaline really needs to get pumping, switch the light to red and turn on a programme that will start the light flashing, from slow and sultry to near disco-quick. "Red could be the colour of love for many people, but it can also make you angry if you're in a bad mood," cautions Managing Director Anders Johansson with a smile. "So you have to be a little bit careful with it."

The goal of the Mood Rooms is to put part of the design process in the hands of the guests. "I want them to be a part of what we are trying to create. They should get out of it what they want, not what I want," says Pihl, a man who loves the outdoors, who rides his bike 40 minutes to work in rain or shine and who is planning his wedding in far northern Sweden, in the near-empty wilderness, he and his bride surrounded by a ring of fire. "We wanted that because we like being in nature," he says, giving another glimpse into his personal design philosophy. "It's clean and pure, and there are a lot of stories to be told."

Since change is the watchword at the Nordic Light Hotel, Pihl and Söder haven't been content to rest on their illuminated laurels, which have won them their share of awards and recognition. They're now engaged on a quest for what they're calling "the perfect hotel room," and have begun collaborating with Dutch electronics giant Philips to reach that lofty goal. Called "Prototype Room 602," the experiment is the culmination of research about what hotel guests want in a room. Philips developed the technology and the Nordic Light Hotel staff is » coming up with the design to provide it. "The challenge to us is, can we make life easy and interesting in one little room?" says Jan Söder, who is largely responsible for the room's look. At this stage, it features a state-of-the-art remote control interface for all of the room's electronics, from lighting to the television, stereo and DVD player. The remote has six pre-programmed light scenes to fit varied activities, and the bathroom features a "light shower," high-intensity light therapy to treat the blues that can strike some with ferocity during dark winter days. And the fine-tuning continues.

Originally, Pihl wasn't signed on as the designer for Nordic Light Hotel at all, and, in fact, he isn't even a designer by training. After secondary school, he spent some time in the French Alps as a ski instructor before succumbing to the inexorable call of his beloved native city. The next two decades saw him in the advertising industry, during which time he started working on exhibitions and art direction projects. In 1999, the hotel owners charged Pihl with judging the concepts submitted by Swedish and international design teams for the new hospitality development.

Pihl wasn't satisfied with the ideas coming across his desk. He wanted a place that was firmly set in Stockholm; that captured the Swedish personality as he sees it: a calm, cool exterior hiding fire and determination inside. Then came that run in the forest ...

Pihl told the owners what he was looking for, and they decided to cut out the middleman and ask him to take over the design responsibilities himself. He plunged in and hasn't looked back. He says he doesn't have time to; the hotel eats up 100 percent of his design time. "I don't think I'm like a typical designer. I'm not a high-lifestyle person; in fact, I'm quite modest," he explains. "I tend to look at design questions from the outside and go with my feeling. I think that puts me a little bit ahead of the game." And it can't hurt that Pihl, codesigner Söder and the entire Nordic Light Hotel design team has in its toolbox a palette few other designers can access – the subtle, shifting hues and undulating tones of their native northern light. «

*Kyle James*

LARS PIHL

"The light interacts with everyone
who comes into the hotel and makes
them a part of what's going on."

# ON THE
# ROCKS

---

*On the high-altitude slopes of southeastern Switzerland,
innovative entrepreneur/hotelier Reto Gurtner has
shaped the personality of an entire region.*

Reto Gurtner is a mountain man with a mission. Born and raised in the high Alpine Swiss canton of Grisons, he lived in Los Angeles as a young man, then returned to Switzerland to study business and law. His surroundings and education shaped his boundary-pushing character as well as his intuitive, forward-thinking business savvy.

Gurtner's American experience inspired him to transform the pristine mountain regions around the villages of Laax, Flims and Falera into winter sport wonderlands akin to Colorado's Aspen or Vail. He has definitely succeeded: the award-winning entrepreneur is not only the president and CEO of Weisse Arena, a firm that operates all 29 mountain railways and lifts in the area, but is also a high-tech tourism pioneer, who's been especially groundbreaking around Laax. More than two decades ago, Gurtner led the pack in encouraging snowboarders and freestylers to discover Laax's slopes by offering them half-pipes, lift packages and moderately priced but always very cool hotels. He launched the country's first tourist website (laax.com) in 1995. In 2001, the hotel Riders Palace opened to great acclaim. And now there's the brand new rocksresort.

An innovative mixed-use facility combining sleek condominium units with hotel rooms, rocksresort intends to make mountain culture accessible to visitors from around the world who can book everything, even equipment, online. They can ski in and ski out. They can buy an apartment and have it rented out when they're not there. Or come in summer to hike or golf. The resort's eight blocky freestanding buildings, by Switzerland's Domenig Architects, echo the dramatic rock formations created by a massive landslide that took place 10,000 years ago. Like rough-stone sugar cubes, they're arranged around a kind of "town square" that gives the resort a unique sense of community.

In the meantime, the jovial fifty-something, mustachioed Gurtner continues his quest to infuse Laax with a little fun and a lot of soul. Speaking from atop the eponymous peak, from a helicopter cruising over the source of the Rhine, or from the local quarry that supplied the resort's façade with stone up to 50 million years old, it's clear the mountain man's mission continues.

## Your father operated one of the region's first mountain railways, starting in the 1940s. Is it a family legacy to be ahead of your time?

It was always my desire to try new ways ... and I definitely got this from my father and

family. I had the chance to travel around the world and it challenged me to see what's different. But I always asked myself, why are mountain people always a little bit behind? Mountains are powerful. Why shouldn't we also be ahead of our time, and put the most sophisticated experiences or design into the mountains? My family started by providing air-dried beef to one of the biggest companies in the meat business, and we thought it should be possible to give a new image to the traditional mountain resorts, too. About 23 or 24 years ago, we started the snowboard movement here in Laax.

## So you based your business on a new sport.

It's not a question of which sport you're doing. It's more a question of lifestyle and the way you organise your company. It attracts a certain crowd. I think of how we can empower people. This is a challenge I've been trying to meet for many, many years.

## Is it hard being a visionary in a conservative business?

Yes. When I started with the snowboarding, a lot of the traditional hoteliers said, "Oh, we don't want this crowd because they have no money." I don't care if they have money. I want to have their spirit here. Now it's the second generation. The freestyle movement is a little bit like it was in '68, but that was a political movement and this time it's more a lifestyle movement. They don't want the same Alpine-style hotels you find all over the mountains.

## What's been your recipe for success?

Our idea was to use the raw material from this area. It's like cooking: a cook makes good food with simple ingredients. The same goes for designing a resort. How can you do something that has a lot of value but very few ingredients? We have beautiful nature. It's a bit like a natural arena. Then, what are the best memories that you had in your life? I try to bring my best memories together. Not only mine, but also those of my colleagues, staff and everybody. People work hard, and we want to give them memorable recreation time. So that's the secret.

## Can you explain your role as an online pioneer in Swiss tourism?

My first experience with the Internet was in '95. The first time I heard about it, I knew:

this is the future, we have to go for it. I was the first Swiss company to use the Internet. I couldn't find a provider here in Switzerland so I started my first page, laax.com, in New York. And then in 1996 I built an Internet café before London had one. At that time the providers, like Swisscom, were all monopolised. They charged me 43,000 Swiss francs a year for a 128 kb line – can you imagine that? Having this Internet café was pretty forward-thinking. We were the originals; we started it.

## Another novel concept in the region is rocksresort's apartment ownership model. How does this work?

We're taking the best of a traditional hotel with top service, but also using the advantage of an apartment's privacy. The problem is that an apartment is not served, so we're combining those things. We want to give investors the possibility to purchase an apartment they can occupy whenever they want – three weeks during high season – and the rest of the time we'll rent it out. This is quite unique in Switzerland. We just want to make it as simple as possible for people to book and organise a trip here so we take care of everything. It's absolutely unique in Europe to have everything – from room to snowboard teacher to equipment – in one place, or one click away on the Internet.

## What else is happening in the off-season?

Our main business is in winter. But summer has big potential, too, which is why we're building it up with golfing and biking. The challenge is attracting urban people. You don't want to offer the same life one finds in Berlin, London or New York, but rather take the good ideas found there and transform them into a kind of mountain lifestyle, a future mountain lifestyle.

## And what's that?

It's about taking what you have from tradition and transforming it. To me, tradition means to carry the fire, not the ash. We have 6.8 billion people in the world and only about 40 percent of this population has the power to travel. But now with the opening of the markets you have India and China, which will grow by 1 billion in the next generation. Some of these people are tremendously educated social climbers. They're looking for originals. When they travel, it's not like the people who fly to Hong Kong to buy a fake Louis Vuitton bag or Rolex. No, they want a »

RETO
GURTNER

"THE MORE
EDUCATED
PEOPLE ARE,
THE MORE
THEY TRAVEL,
THE MORE
THEY SEARCH
FOR THE
ORIGINAL."

RETO GURTNER

"You don't want to offer the same life one finds in Berlin, London or New York, but rather take the good ideas found there and transform them into a future mountain lifestyle."

real Rolex, a real Porsche, the real mountains. And most of the highest mountains in the Alps are in Switzerland. It doesn't make sense to copy something and make a fake old chalet. The more educated people are, the more they travel, the more they search for the original. Where do you find something unique, where do you find something original? This is what we're trying to create here.

## This canton is special. It's the only place where the Romansch language is spoken, for example, and the population density is still very low.

Our canton is the biggest in Switzerland but we have the lowest population. So 98 percent of the area is completely nature. We're just concentrated on two percent. We have to make that two percent as dense as possible so you can just walk out of your hotel and be in the middle of nature. That is our philosophy. It also makes ecological, economical and social sense. You create a kind of village, as they've always existed throughout history.

## Yes, the way the resort is organised is like a piazza or square. You've said in the past that rocksresort is like a skyscraper built into the ground. How?

Rocksresort is made with raw materials from the area. You won't see any cars since the parking lot goes four levels into the ground. The structure is high-tech from the engineering side, because of the heavy stone buildings – each uses 500 tons of indigenous stone. We use hydroelectric power to limit our carbon footprint and use our snowmaking system to produce electricity and reuse energy. It came out looking so simple. But the more simple you make it, the more complicated it actually is.

## How do you relax?

I relax best when I learn or see something new. That's why I'm always exploring new countries. To learn the surf lifestyle you have to go to Hawaii; if you want to learn about entertainment, you go to Los Angeles.

## When was your first time on skis?

At about the age of three. I started skiing and after that I explored snowboarding for a while. I started skateboarding while I was a student in the U.S. That was more than 33 years ago. I would say now that Laax is the number one place in Europe for freestylers.

## Do you still ski?

Not as much I used to. I still try to steal an opportunity whenever I have a few hours during the day, just getting out and riding the mountain. It's still fascinating after 30 or 40 years. I really love it. It's my passion.

## And where does your passion come from?

My parents were very demanding. They said, "okay, you can go to university but then you have to become one of the best. Otherwise you can come back to the butcher shop." I learned a lot from my parents because my father was never satisfied with mediocrity.

## How do you avoid mediocrity?

Create a new history, something new, then afterward you can compare it to something. You can either say I love it, I like it or I hate it. You have to do something for your body, your spirit and then for your soul. It's very important. Nobody can define your soul.

## Where does soul come in, in this resort?

The combination of what's good for the soul, spirit, and the body is our daily task. We always have to ask ... are we on the right track? Is our strategy still pure? This is more and more important for the future if you don't want to be one of thousands of hotels around the world. This is also the fascinating thing about Design Hotels™ because its members aren't like a chain. When I go to a traditional hotel chain, I know what to expect because they all look the same, like a McDonald's. But Design Hotels™ has a lot of different characters. It has a good spirit behind it, good people who create and support the brand. «

*Kimberly Bradley*

# HEALING
# BY DESIGN

---

*A couple's unique concept ushers in a mini revolution in health and hotels:
a singular mix of high design, top-notch medical care and a broad array
of wellness offerings has found success in southern Austria.*

"What sums it up between us is qualified experimentation," says Siv Sundfær with an easy laugh. "It's always something new, but we try to make sure that it has some qualified meaning and knowledge behind it."

The "we" here is Sundfær and her husband, Christian Köck, the dynamic duo behind the life medicine RESORT in Bad Gleichenberg, Austria. A cross between traditional five-star luxury hotel and high-tech medical treatment facility, life medicine may just represent the wave of the future in terms of travel destinations. Here is a wellness retreat that marries hospitality and medicine and brings together service-industry standards, old-school European spa culture and modern diagnostic and therapeutic tech-nologies. The result is a visionary resort where guests can come for prevention, diagnosis, treatment, rehabilitation or just plain old relaxation in southern Austria's gorgeous Styrian region.

Bad Gleichenberg has a long history as a regenerative sanctuary, dating back to the era of the Roman Empire, when its thermal springs were discovered. The area benefits from a mild climate and an idyllic landscape of rolling hills, verdant foliage and grand imperial villas. For a long time, the springs were the exclusive reserve of Austrian nobility, but in the early 19th century, Count Wickenburg – inspired by Enlightenment civic thinking – decided to share his treasure with the public. A 61-acre English park was landscaped in the lush thermal valley, and the oldest spa facility in Austria was built. "So what we're actually doing here is merging a long-existing tradition with a new approach to health care and treatment," explains Köck, who is the CEO of Health Care Company, a holding corporation for health-care investments. It's owned by Austria's Raiffeisen Group and STRABAG, the country's largest construction company. Health Care Company

purchased the property in 2004, together with a group of regional investors.

The resort offers all the traditional wellness services of a central European spa: thermal baths, sauna and a range of indulgent facial and body treatments. But it also provides an impressive array of diagnostic services, including lab testing, allergy profiles, metabolic panels, ultrasounds and pulmonary function analyses. On the basis of the results from these diagnostic tests, a staff of

CHRISTIAN KÖCK

## "FOR US, INTEGRATING THINGS THAT DON'T NORMALLY COME TOGETHER IS IMPORTANT."

medical professionals, nutritionists and physical therapists create personalised wellness programmes for guests. These focus on issues ranging from musculoskeletal improvement to weight loss, from invigorating the immune system to easing arthritis. Each personalised programme uses a specifically chosen combination of on-site treatments – from acupressure therapy, carbonated baths and lymph drainage to Nordic walking, magnetic field therapy and even cryotherapy for rheumatism, administered in a cold chamber cooled to –110 degrees!

Each treatment plan is developed on the basis of a thorough assessment of medical history and current health status followed by an in-depth consultation with a life medicine physician. "We're trying to create an environment where you feel personally cared for," explains Sundfær. "Where doctors and nurses don't see you only as the back ailment in bed number two, but as a person. This is a major step forward."

She should know. A trained political scientist, Sundfær spent years in the health-care industry working as a liaison between patients and hospitals. It was in this context, in fact, that she met her husband. "It was very romantic," she remembers. "We met at the old Hofburg Imperial Palace in Vienna at a medical conference." Köck – who has his first doctorate in medicine and a second in health policy and economics – was giving a talk on quality assessment in a health-care context. "I was arguing that only the patient, not the medical expert, can decide what is or is not good quality. Afterwards, Siv came up to me and said, 'I really liked what you said, but you made one logical error.' We had a coffee, and it turned out she was right." A decade later, the couple lives in Vienna with two sons.

The story is heart-warmingly appropriate for two people who so visibly thrive on conversation and debate. "A good day for us," says Köck, "is having time to communicate." And, Sundfær adds, "to do or talk about something that's interesting." "That," says Köck, "creates challenges. And gives you ..." "Energy," Sundfær breaks in, completing her husband's thought.

The two sit in the lounge area of the life medicine RESORT, wrapped in the warm embrace of two high-backed green armchairs planted before an open fireplace. Although originally from Oslo, Sundfær has an almost »

Parisian air about her. Well-cut grey pants billow around her long legs, and a cream silk shirt hangs loosely from her slender frame. A dash of red lipstick adds a touch of flash to the otherwise understated grace. Her husband wears a classic dark grey suit with a lavender shirt that seems to serve the same purpose as his wife's lipstick.

Köck's urbane appearance makes it easy to forget that he's actually a professor of health politics and management at the Witten/Herdecke University in Germany. But the second he opens his mouth, it's easy to imagine him lecturing to a room full of rapt students. With a riveting voice, he speaks engagingly on everything from ethics to surgery, music to philosophy. He has found his match in Siv Sundfær, who playfully challenges his assertions and could easily teach a few university courses of her own. This is a couple with wide and varied interests and deep knowledge. Together, they harness this shared intellectual capacity in service of a better future, breeding visionary ideas from sustained dialogue. "I have someone whose intellect I admire," says Sundfær. She turns to her husband and puts a hand on his knee, smiling. "You're really good to fight with. And from that fight, something really nice comes up."

The life medicine concept is one of those "nice somethings" borne of conversation. Before they met, Köck and Sundfær had separately come to the conclusion that the traditional health-care system was not working the way it should. "Most people become doctors or nurses because they want to help people," Köck explains, "but they end up creating the most people-unfriendly institutions imaginable." He and Sundfær wanted to change that.

Life medicine was their answer – a hotel environment in which medical diagnosis and treatment can occur in a more cooperative way. "Getting healthy," Sundfær explains, "is a co-creative process between two experts." The doctor is an expert in medicine, and the patient is an expert on himself – his body, his needs and his abilities. The heart of their vision is thus a reformulation of the traditional doctor-patient relationship. Here, guests and medical experts engage in extensive and ongoing consultation to develop a personalised strategy for improving health together. "That way," explains Sundfær, "the doctor treats the person, not the disease."

But health, the couple agrees, is not just about treatment. "We reject this very Christian approach that the body needs to be punished for having had too much fun," says Köck. "Getting healthy also requires something joyful." That's where other factors like design and gastronomy come into play. The life medicine kitchen, for example, strikes an impressive balance between indulgence and health, offering personalised four-course menus consisting of only 700 calories – almost impossible to believe considering how delicious they taste. The key, explains Köck, is using quality ingredients from local producers and including a satisfyingly broad range of flavours.

And this holistic approach to health also encompasses design. "If you ask patients what they most dislike about hospitals," explains Köck, "they'll say, 'that hospitals look like hospitals.' There's no reason why people should be in a setting they don't like." Life medicine, by contrast, is designed to please and soothe. The flowing structure consists of several interconnected terraces, porches and relaxation areas made of natural stone, glass and larch wood, all decorated in browns, greens and reds that mimic the natural beauty of Bad Gleichenberg. The resort consciously integrates the surrounding countryside: a canopy of centuries-old trees hangs over its scattered terraces, and large glass panes in all rooms afford sweeping views of the historical park. "You can look out the window and see something beautiful," explains Sundfær.

To achieve this aesthetic effect, the couple – who personally approved every feature of the resort – travelled to hotels around the world to educate themselves about both the hospitality industry and design. "We became hotel managers by accident," explains Sundfær. "So we had a steep learning curve." In the end, her husband insists, it wasn't all that daunting a transition from the world of medicine to the world of hotels. "I was really surprised that the hospitality business – in the fundamental problem that people have of understanding what the customer needs – is not so different from health care."

This ability to seize upon the hidden connections between things seems to be a particular expertise of both Köck and Sundfær. "For us," explains Köck, "integrating things that don't normally come together is important." This is something he first learned at Harvard, where he earned his second doctorate. "I owe a lot of my intellectual and personal development to my time in America," he explains. "Suddenly, the response to a crazy idea wasn't, 'Well, that's never been done before, so it will never work,' but rather, 'Wow, that's really interesting. I've never thought about that. How can I support you?' This very un-European approach to innovation made me think, 'Well, everything is possible, so why not think things that have never been thought before?'" "Things," adds his wife, "that might look odd to begin with."

"It's about breaking through boundaries and stepping over assumptions," agrees Köck. For the two like-minded thinkers, then, it wasn't so great a leap from health care to hotel – nor is it incongruous to simultaneously run a health-care consulting company, a spa resort and a record label called col legno, which produces contemporary classical music. "Anything's possible," says Köck about the breadth of his and his wife's engagement. "Only if one actually dares to think it." One gets the sense that these two will continue to provide each other with the inspiration and courage to do just that for a long time to come. «

*Jenna Krumminga*

CHRISTIAN KÖCK

# WHY NOT THINK THINGS THAT HAVE NEVER BEEN THOUGHT BEFORE.

# AN EYE FOR
# DETAIL

---

With The Franklin Hotel, entrepreneur Blanche van Berckel combines
the contemporary and traditional to bring back true hospitality to
London's Knightsbridge ... down to the last detail.

07
MADE BY
*ORIGINALS*
---
**BLANCHE VAN BERCKEL**
LONDON

Although her name suggests she might be Dutch and the burgundy hue of her passport confirms it, Blanche van Berckel is far more a citizen of the world than of any one specific country. As the young daughter of a diplomat, van Berckel lived in Japan, Morocco, Belgium, Luxembourg and Israel before spending any serious time in the Netherlands, when she returned as a teenager.

Her international upbringing proved to be a boon to her later career choice. Called upon as a young child to help her parents entertain at diplomatic functions, van Berckel learned valuable lessons that informed the philosophy she has developed as a hotelier. "I gained a love for service and hospitality," she explains.

The values of impeccable service and authentically warm hospitality are the foundations upon which she founded FairQuest Hotels, the hotel management company she runs with a small staff and in partnership with selected investors. A veteran in the hospitality industry, van Berckel began in traineeships in Amsterdam and New York in 1987 before returning to Europe to work for the InterContinental Hotels Group in Belgium, Luxembourg and the Netherlands for more than a decade. She opened and served as general manager of Blakes Amsterdam, the city's first boutique hotel, designed by famed hotelier and London socialite Anouska Hempel.

Now, as one of the few women in the industry heading a hotel group of her own, the 46-year-old entrepreneur has brought her cosmopolitan flair and intrinsic understanding of what a modern traveller requires to London, where FairQuest Hotels has opened an updated and revamped version of The Franklin Hotel in the upscale neighbourhood of Knightsbridge.

Set amongst a row of Victorian houses, The Franklin Hotel has been a Knightsbridge fixture for many years, although its previous incarnation was more traditional than its

present look and feel. A small park in the shape of a half-crescent is down one street of the residential neighbourhood. The bustle of Brompton Road, home to Scandinavian boutiques, a French bakery and the legendary Harrods department store, is just a block away. "This area is very British. It's very upmarket. I like that about it, and I also think it's the London of our clients," explains van Berckel. Indeed, the coffee shop in which she sits for an interview is filled with the moneyed men and women of Britain's (and, increasingly, the Far and Middle East's) upper classes, dining on eggs Florentine and sipping Italian espresso in between business meetings or shopping trips.

BLANCHE
VAN BERCKEL

"WE WOMEN
HAVE AN EYE
FOR DETAIL
AND LOOK
BEHIND THE
GENERAL
PICTURE."

For van Berckel, London has always been one of the cities that embodies the ideal of a modern metropolis. The British capital's successful blend of the edgy with the traditional and elegant is both an attribute special to world capitals and a challenge for its design vision. "It's not easy to create the essence of a city," says van Berckel. "We want it to be felt, but not in a traditional way. But we also don't want it to be cutting-edge and modern. We want to create hotels that people still feel comfortable in, in ten years."

The hotel's façade, composed of four Victorian buildings, maintains the elegant austerity of

its surroundings. But secreted away in the back is the highlight that excites van Berckel the most: a private communal garden. "When we saw the garden, we thought 'Wow,'" she says. London began building public squares in the early 17th century, but it was only two hundred years later that communal gardens, designed by some of the country's best landscapers, became popular. An era known for a new appreciation of privacy hid the gardens behind the majestic estates built in the city's traditionally wealthy western neighbourhoods.

Before closing down the old version of The Franklin (whose rooms likened those found in traditional English country homes) for its comprehensive overhaul, van Berckel and her investors operated the property for six months. It was during her overnight stays that the entrepreneur became convinced that she'd made the right choice: "We'd wake up and hear birds outside," she relates. The garden that The Franklin shares with its neighbours has also informed van Berckel's design philosophy and reminds her of the outdoor space she cherished as a child. "At the end of the day, you just want to sit outside for 10 or 15 minutes."

It is for such reasons that van Berckel, a professed lover of big cities, finds the hotel's location to be the perfect balance of metropolitan life and discreet charm – not only for herself, but also, and more important, for her guests. "We serve the high-end traveller," she says. "The type of clientele that will move around often, and is in London twice a year, or Berlin twice a year."

As a result, the design reflects close attention both to full-service needs as well as to its surroundings' decidedly English influences. A layout that hadn't been tampered with much since the late 1880s has been reconsidered and expanded. The walls separating the ground floor's warren of rooms have been broken down, allowing for space to breathe and views onto the garden's carefully manicured landscape. An intimate »

Illustration: Olaf Hajek
www.olafhajek.com

BLANCHE VAN
BERCKEL

"WE'D WAKE
UP AND
HEAR BIRDS
OUTSIDE."

# "We want to create hotels that people still feel comfortable in, in ten years."

restaurant with only about a dozen tables serves guests and passers-by. Staff members are trained to answer every question and cater to every need. "Our core ethos is that we'd like to go back to the very original idea of hospitality," says van Berckel. "To go back to what it's all about. A lot of times, hotels are designed by people who don't think of the end user."

Visually, The Franklin espouses another ethos of van Berckel and her new company: reflection, on the inside, of the stimulation of the outside world. "What guests see when they look out the window, I want to bring back inside," she says. The idea manifests itself in the choice of colour, from the cream or rust hues of London row houses to the lush green of the city's parks. Rather than hang art in the guestrooms, van Berckel and her partners have decided to recreate the intricate floral patterns found in English country gardens, or crawling up the sides of many of London's red-bricked townhouses, by having them stencilled on the walls by interior designers J2.

The London-based design company is also behind the bespoke furniture in the hotel's public and private spaces, which van Berckel will blend with branded pieces she's encountered on her extensive travels around Europe and beyond. The eclectic approach befits someone with as international an upbringing as hers. "You are confronted with so many different hues, cultures, architectures and so forth, so you automatically have a different approach to life," she says. Seemingly as influential has been the type of environment in which she was raised. A handsome woman who favours well-cut suits, van Berckel has a diplomat's poise and an egalitarian manner suited to an industry in which men dominate leadership positions. "My upbringing is the basis for who I am, and where I am today," she says, the deep orange coat she's wearing the only nod to her Dutch heritage. "It has steered me towards doing what I do well, going for it and achieving the goals and ambitions I've set." Her discreet, professional bearing breaks form only when she talks about the cities she loves or details over which she obsesses.

"We women have an eye for detail and look behind the general picture," she says. "There are a lot of women who work in this industry, but few who run hotel companies, big or small," she observes. "But there are a lot of advantages to being a woman in this industry. We feel and see things differently."

Of all the nuances in her carefully curated concept – from the meticulously handmade wall treatments to the use of light – none do as good a job of representing the hotel's philosophy as the five chandeliers in the lobby and restaurant on the ground floor. A graceful and whimsical design in crystal by Dutch designers Brand van Egmond, the chandeliers resemble upturned leaves and have a Midsummer Night's Dream feel about them. "They are contemporary and elegant, and they have a sense of tradition," she says, perhaps inadvertently describing herself as well. "Those elements, together, speak for who we are." «

*Andreas Tzortzis*

# VENETIAN
## VISION

---

*For hotel developer – and former race-car driver – Emanuele Garosci,*
*Venice is a city filled with mystery, romance, indulgence and fantastically*
*bold statements. His new project slows down just enough to give*
*guests an intimate destination amidst the glamour.*

MADE BY
*ORIGINALS*
---
**EMANUELE GAROSCI**
VENICE

"There's something incredibly daring about working in glass at this level."

EMANUELE GAROSCI

Having spent a considerable portion of his young adult life going at speeds of more than 200 km/h, Emanuele Garosci is finally sitting still for a moment.

Basking in the sunlight pouring in through the huge windows of a Venetian palace on the Grand Canal, the former car and motorcycle racer has stretched out in a crimson velvet armchair, exuding the languidly confident body language of a modern-day Casanova. The sunglasses constantly come on and off, depending more on the intensity of the conversation than on the actual sunlight, and on whether the moment calls for eye contact or cool detachment. Like the famous masks Venetians wear during Carnevale, the sunglasses seem to protect Garosci from the reproachful gaze of Venetian society. And many eyes are on him since he decided to launch an as-yet-unnamed luxury hotel in Venice. Opening in 2009 (ed. note: the property is not yet listed in the hotel section of this book), it will shoulder in along the Grand Canal amid a stable of grand old hotels that have been used to holding sway in La Serenissima for generations. Designed by the famously irreverent maestro Philippe Starck, the hotel offers a glamorous and sometimes cheeky riff on traditionally over-the-top Venetian decorative style. The rooms are clad with huge mirrors (and mirrors on top of mirrors), and a suggestive mask motif peers seductively from a few surprising places.

Specially commissioned pieces of luminous Murano glass by artist Aristide Najean further help, in Garosci's parlance, to "make it Venice." In a city of megahotels, where the average stay is less than 24 hours, the property features just 26 rooms in a clubby private ambience that makes guests feel enough at home to stick around a few days. In a separate palace, there is also a sprawling 800-square-metre maxi-suite, which has been designed for truly grand living – even on the gilded Venetian scale – as well as optimum flexibility as an exclusive event space, given the city's rigorous party schedule.

The hotel building is a 500-year-old "palazzina", which means "little palace,"and was home to the Grassi family before they built the larger palace next door – presently the well-known Palazzo Grassi art museum. Extolling the virtues of the city, its famous art collections and glorious architecture, the festivals for which it is known and the distinct seafood-based gastronomy, Garosci echoes the familiar refrain: "Venice is not part of Italy – Venice belongs to the world."

As would he himself. After several years – and many broken bones – racing cars and motorcycles, Garosci has decided to "get serious." Helming his company, DHD (Design Hotels Development), he travels the globe looking for new markets – from the Swiss Alps to Morocco and beyond – to which to bring his unique brand of hospitality.

## You're often described as the archetype of the passionate Italian – is this how you would describe yourself?

I say that I am 110 percent Italian – my father is from Turin, which was the first capital of Italy, and my mother is from Rome, the present-day capital. I have travelled all over the world, but Italy is still the place that inspires the biggest emotions in me. It does have its problems, but all of Italy should be discovered and explored. And of course I believe that everything we do in life we should do with passion, no? If we're lucky, anyway.

## Why a hotel in Venice?

Because I love Venice! Venice is the city of art, fashion, of romance, of Carnevale and the world's best parties. But it's also a very professional and hardworking city. It's incredibly international, and even after all these centuries it's still one of the most inspiring places in the world. It's beautiful when the sun is shining, and it's even more beautiful when the weather is awful – and it's romantic all the time.

But while respecting all of this, I want to give the city a little kick away from the traditional manner of doing things. To create the most exciting project in Venice today, you need a big vision because there already are lots of famous luxury hotels here. We want something that might help change the cruise-ship mentality that has evolved in the city. Of the more than 20 million visitors who come to Venice, many never spend the night. I want to recuperate the atmosphere that the city had in the 1930s, when it was a long-stay destination.

## At just 26 rooms, the hotel is extremely intimate. Is that part of what attracted you to this property?

A small hotel is easier to manage in terms of service and client comfort. The building, the "hardware" of the hotel, is the designer's responsibility: to make sure it stands out as unique and perfect for the site. The "software" would be the people who work at the hotel and how they react and relate to the guests. I can control this much better at a hotel of this size. It's difficult to succeed at anything if you don't take care of the details, and hotels are nothing but a multiplicity of details. You have to strive for perfection every single day.

Also, a small hotel provides both intimacy and privacy, and can feel a bit like a private club – an aspect that I think distinguishes it from larger luxury hotels. As I've said, to take on Venice, I knew the property had to be something exceptional.

## What drew you to Philippe Starck as the designer for the hotel?

Philippe Starck loves Venice like I do. He owns homes here and has written articles about the city. A few years ago he redesigned the city's logo. He gets the city's rhythm and energy. He understands its soul. He was my only choice to design the hotel, and we had an instant meeting of minds on how the project should be.

Venice opens your mind. Here you have to think differently since you don't do things the same way here as in other cities. There are no cars or nightclubs or discos, for instance. Instead, you walk or take a boat to places and linger in cafés and restaurants – the pace is unique. Starck understands the city and the fact that these palazzi »

# "There are certainly days when I think I must be crazy to try to launch a property like this in Venice."

allow us to create an environment where you can live like a Venetian. You shouldn't come to Venice and feel like you are in Scandinavia.

**With all the masks and mirrors, Starck's design of the rooms seems to play with the city's reputation as a place for indulgence. Does Venice still deliver in this regard?**

Absolutely – during Carnevale, the hormones are through the roof. People will do the wildest things because they think – they think, mind you – that they will not be recognised behind their masks. But there's mystery and romance as well. Just imagine what it's like out there on a gondola, amid the mist rising up off the water.

**Murano glass also seems to be a signature motif of the hotel. Is this material another passion of yours?**

I think there's something incredibly daring about working in glass at this level – if the artist makes even a tiny mistake, the piece is ruined and he has to start over. And here in Venice they have been making the finest glass for centuries, refining new techniques and materials, like "avventurina", a glittery gold glass they say was accidentally invented by alchemists trying to make gold. Whether you know about this history or not, the visual effects of the glass are amazing. Aristide Najean's large sculptural relief just opposite the elevators instantly conveys the splendour and opulence of Venice to guests.

**Why the concept of an 800-square-metre maxi-suite?**

Because Venice is a city for events that cause a stir. Whether it's the Biennale season, the film festival, Carnevale or merely a major fashion designer's last collection and star-studded tribute party, there is always something happening here. Venice is one of few places where people know they can always attract truly international attention. And for that reason, we need amazing spaces, opulent both in their décor and in their scale. In a city of stunning architecture, we need to make a bold statement.

**What makes you original?**

I don't know if I'm original, but there are certainly days when I think I must be crazy to try to launch a property like this in Venice.

**What's next?**

We're working on three very cool projects right now, including hotels in St. Moritz and Marrakesh, and a 93-metre former U.S. military ship being converted into a floating hotel, which can go to any place where the action may be, like St. Barth, for example – or we can take the action with us to wherever we want to go. Between the four, we've covered the mountains, the desert, the sea and Venice. That's all I need. «

*Erik Andersen*

# BLACK
# &
# WHITE

---

*Brilliantly conceived by Portugal's star interior designer Nini Andrade Silva*
*and run by general manager Jorge Cosme, Fontana Park Hotel*
*in Lisbon is a sophisticated game of light and shadow*
*in a refurbished historic building.*

MADE BY
*ORIGINALS*

---

**NINI ANDRADE SILVA
& JORGE COSME**
LISBON

On the one hand, overlooking the verdant gardens from which it takes its name, Lisbon's Fontana Park Hotel is a fitting reflection of both the lush nature found in the nearby Fontana Park and the cosmopolitan, lively atmosphere of one of Europe's long-standing port cities. On the other, it's a beacon of modernity with a striking colour scheme and an avant-garde vibe.

Once an iron foundry, the building stood empty and neglected for a long, long time. But both nature and nurture were lodestars for Portuguese architect Francisco Aires Mateus, who achieved what Fontana Park's general manager, Jorge Cosme, proudly describes as "a combination of the modern and Lisbon's one hundred years of recent history" by preserving the original building's façade and romantic details.

Amongst the latter are distinctive doorframes crafted with curves in the style of Lisbon's beloved 25 de Abril Bridge. But hotel guests who visit the masterpiece that Mateus summoned from the former factory prefer to focus on the hotel's high-end modernist qualities, like the long, dark corridors, as well as its calm and gentle details, like the abundance of plant life and the soft pillows on oversize furnishings. "Fontana Park isn't a hotel for everyone," Cosme explains. "[With the black and white,] it's a full-on concept from A to Z, but the concept is simple. We just want the hotel to be a home for discerning people, modern people, young people and people who are young at heart."

This youthful allure derives from a fresh and friendly atmosphere that delightfully contrasts with the historical details and visual drama. It's a place in which décor and ambience are distilled to their essence, but are not limited by abstract constraints of minimalism. The mind-bending effect is the brainchild of leading Portuguese interior designer and artist Nini Andrade Silva, who decided to look to nature's palette as inspiration for her sharp design concept.

With a colour scheme centred on black and white with touches of rich purple and green,

---

JORGE
COSME

## "THIS IS A COSMO-POLITAN HOTEL. IT COULD BE IN BARCELONA, IN SCANDINAVIA OR IN RUSSIA. PEOPLE WANT TO IDENTIFY WITH A GLOBAL FEELING."

---

Nini fully realises her ambition of bringing the elemental beauty of the real, outdoor Fontana Park inside the hotel building – where guests are invitingly met with glossy and glassy surfaces, smooth contours, peaceful restaurants serving both Japanese and Portuguese fare, and an outdoor garden lined in bamboo. Not to mention the rooms – open-plan, light-filled, ultrasmooth spaces with outsize beds and sweeping views of Lisbon through black-framed windows (a well-placed window even allows a view from the interior bathroom).

"The black and white idea came first," Nini says. One realises she's explaining the starting point of the hotel's chromatic concept as well as connecting her thinking as an interior designer with the creative process central to her work as an abstract artist. Her vibrant personality is an interesting contrast with her consistent love of the colour – or non-colour – black. But as she sits in the light-filled, white-hued restaurant Saldanha Mar, the designer confesses that she loves black less than the other colour that reigns over Fontana Park's overall scheme. "What is my favourite colour?" she asks herself musingly, almost humorously. "Well, it's white. I really like turquoise. I have always loved black. But it is definitely white." (Cosme, on the other hand, says he definitely favours black. Both, by the way, are wearing head-to-toe black.)

What about the green of the nearby parks? As an American art critic who once stayed a few nights in the hotel noted, "The missing colour has been reconcentrated in a thick green stripe of carpet leading from the door, like the mossy tinge of Lisbon's old buildings. It's as though the designers have used novel minimalist strategies to refract Lisbon out into the traditional elements of its own spectrum." The blacks provide warmth and depth, while polished black-and-white floors might remind a few travellers of Lisbon's Moorish tiling. At the same time there's the hotel's generous vegetation, and there's even a wall of water in the outdoor garden. "I wanted green trees and big pictures of trees; and then you have all these trees in the restaurant," explains Nini, offering a raison d'être for century-old bonsai trees adorning the sun-soaked Bonsai restaurant. The swathes of green and dashes of purple manage to brilliantly ground it all. »

JUST WALK IN AND SAY WOW

And grounded it is, a beacon of avant-garde modernity in a historical seaside city. The hotel perhaps represents a logical step in again making Lisbon the international hub and take-off for exploration that it once had been. Right now, the city is one of the world's top destinations, according to travel sections of acclaimed newspapers like "The New York Times." Cosme explains that while most of the overnight clientele is pan-European, the trendy bar and restaurants do attract a local crowd. "This is a cosmopolitan hotel. It could be located in Barcelona, in Scandinavia or in Russia. People want to identify with a global feeling," he says.

A healthy portion of the space's sophistication might just come from Nini's own dynamic, well-travelled personality. Known as an artist, architect and designer for her signature brand of funky minimalism, she injects the Fontana Park Hotel's interior with an irresistible layer of gallery-quality glamour. Portugal's natural splendour is at the core of her creative sensibility. "I'm a painter," she states. "I have a collection called 'The Girl of the Pebble,' because in

Madeira, where I was born, the whole island is surrounded by pebbles. Then I started to paint pebbles and exhibit the paintings around the world, as well as design jewellery. Because I was doing so much work with pebbles, everyone started calling me the girl of the pebble."

Nini earned her degree in interior design from Lisbon's prestigious IADE, or Instituto de Artes Visuais, Design e Marketing, and draws upon experience with internationally celebrated designers David Easton and Starck Designers to perfect a distinctive design aesthetic that she has playfully referred to as "ninimalist," ever since an interviewer coined the term several years ago. "[The interviewer] called me 'ninimalist' because my name is Nini, and instead of being a minimalist, I always like to give warmth to any design concept. I like to do things with a dash of fantasy." Today Nini runs two offices in Portugal that produce comprehensive hotel concepts – from architecture and interior design to furniture design and innovative lighting concepts – for clients around the world. The award-winning

designer is even planning to open a Dubai-based studio in 2009. Last September, she presented a collection of interior and exterior furniture at a Shanghai fair, in partnership with the Asian market.

Although minimalism strips objects down to their barest, most fundamental forms, Nini always ensures that the objects she incorporates in her spaces express not only a spatial clarity but also an energetic and passionate creativity. The soul of her design sensibility lies in its merging of high culture and nature. And the Fontana Park Hotel's appeal is the apex of Nini's artful streamlining, organic and metropolitan influences. "I like when you walk in and go 'wow,'" Nini explains with characteristic passion. "When you walk in and don't say 'wow,' then my work didn't work. The important part of my work is not what you see, but what you feel." Luckily, both the "wow" factor and the level of sublime contentment work just fine here, amidst the black and white. «

*Ana Finel Honigman*

# CASTLES
# IN THE
# SKY

---

*Antonio Pérez Navarro, CEO of Spanish hotel group Hospes Hotels and Moments, is a master at creating contemporary, aesthetically exemplary properties that have their roots in a majestic history. Yes, there's something marvellous about staying in a palace.*

Less than ten years old, the Spanish hotel group Hospes already numbers eight hotels in some of the nation's most storied cities, including Seville, Cordoba, Granada and Madrid. In several locations, Hospes has been the first true high-end brand to arrive in decades, defining a new concept of modern luxury and giving many discriminating visitors a reason to stay the night in towns that have always had so much to offer culturally, but little to recommend them on the hospitality front.

In 2006, Hospes acquired the fabled Lancaster in Paris – with its Michelin-starred restaurant La Table du Lancaster – auguring an expansion beyond Spain. But international dreams have not diminished the passion for Spain; a Hospes will soon open in Malaga, near the city's beloved Picasso Museum, and another will open in Murcia, an up-and-coming international art destination of recent years.

The man behind the magic is Hospes founding CEO Antonio Pérez Navarro. After spending more than a decade working with NH and A.C., two of the hotel chains that first helped bring Spanish hostelry into the 20th century, Navarro set his own course by creating Hospes and defining the market for the 21st century. Blending lovingly restored remnants of Spain's rich architectural heritage – baroque palaces, Neoclassical convents, belle époque mansions – with the most luxe contemporary design and attentive service that is friendly but never informal, Hospes hotels have quickly become reference points on the Spanish landscape. In recent years, Hospes properties have won numerous awards, including the prestigious Wall-paper Design Award. But perhaps there's been no greater testament to the success of the Hospes formula than the fact that Paradores de España, the mighty state-run chain of hotels in historic buildings throughout the country, have begun to redecorate the musty old-world interiors of some of their most emblematic and historic hotels in a slick, modern style.

**Hospes is a relatively new hotel group, yet it has quickly established a strong identity at the top of the luxury market in Spain. How has the company evolved?**

In May of 2000, we opened our first property, Las Cazas del Rey de Baeza, which blends the charm of a traditional Andalusian patio house with contemporary design. Three

years later we revived the famous Maricel in Mallorca, which really generated a lot of buzz. That was followed quickly by hotels in Alicante, Valencia, Granada, Cordoba, Madrid and Villa Paulita in Puigcerda, which is a country estate near the Catalan Pyrenees. Also, in 2006, we acquired the Lancaster in Paris, our first property outside Spain.

**Do you plan to expand further into Europe?**

Oh yes – and beyond Europe. Right now we are building in Budapest and are at work to find properties in London, Chicago, Munich, Hamburg, Vienna and Stockholm. We've also started looking in Istanbul and have discussed plans for Beirut and Syria.

---

## "TO SHOOT YOUR ARROW VERY FAR INTO THE FUTURE, YOU HAVE TO REACH BACK JUST AS FAR INTO THE PAST."

---

**For Hospes, looking for property doesn't mean finding an empty lot on which to build a new hotel. It means locating unique historic palaces or other emblematic buildings, which your architects and designers carefully restore and revitalise with polished modern décor. Is this more or less how you would characterise the Hospes formula?**

The principal ingredient of any Hospes project is authenticity. Historic palaces and other buildings offer a connection to the past in the cities and towns where we're located. They're part of the context of that place and its cultural life. Here in Granada at the Palacio de los Patos, we spent five years working with art historians from the local university to restore this building – the colours, the original materials, the function and flow of the original space.

The palace was built by a family whose fortune came from refining sugar cane; their business had taken them around the world, and they had seen all kinds of architecture. They brought this legacy back to Granada, where they were at the centre of the social and cultural life of the city. Federico García Lorca walked these halls. A new hotel in a modern building can offer many things, but not this patina of history. I think the most magical moments, the ones that linger in the memory, are amplified when they feel authentic.

**Your passion for historic buildings is evident. Did you grow up in one?**

No, but I grew up surrounded by them. Today it's easy to think that new is always better, but I think that without embracing the past, you can't appreciate the modern. A Turkish man recently offered a beautiful metaphor to express this idea by comparing life to archery. To shoot your arrow very far into the future, he said, you have to reach back just as far into the past.

**How do you translate this philosophy to the hotel industry?**

First, by preserving the integrity of our buildings and providing guests with an atmosphere that allows them to feel an authentic connection to the city they are visiting. And there is something about staying in a palace that seems to make people feel marvellous, which is kind of the most we can hope for as hoteliers, no? Our guests should feel marvellous in our properties.

Finally, to continue the Turkish metaphor, today I think we spend too much time worrying about how good the bow is and not enough time taking care of the archer. Somehow it's easier to become obsessed with having the latest gadget, car or cell phone than it is to care about getting a good night's sleep and giving your body the rest it needs. As hoteliers, that is our top priority.

**These days it almost seems like a novelty that a hotel would consider a good night's sleep a top priority. What brought about this return to the basics?**

Restful sleep is the factory of your energy for tomorrow, but it's also the factory of your dreams for the future. In Spanish, there is » one word for both concepts – "soñar" means both to sleep and to dream. Whether you travel for business or tourism, you'll get a better deal if you've had a good night's sleep. As simple as it sounds, life really is better when you sleep better.

Even outside the hotels, Hospes takes the word "soñar" very seriously – putting real money into sleep research as well as other dream-based civic philanthropy. For the past several years, we've given awards to physicians and scientists in the field of sleep research. People say I work in hotels, but really I work so that people can sleep better. Like me, the chambermaid, the waiter, the concierge – we all work so that our guests get everything they need for a good night's rest. So of course we would want to advance this science that aids us in our goals.

Through a different foundation, we also try to aid young people – many of whom have lost a parent and find themselves with limited financial resources – to realise their dreams, or "sueños".

## At Design Hotels™, we see a growing trend towards a holistic health-care approach that hotels can offer. Do you ascribe to this philosophy?

We absolutely believe that it's all connected, and in fact the brand under which all our enterprises – the hotels, restaurants and spas – originated is called Fuenso, which means "source" in Spanish and refers to the restorative nature of what we try to offer. It all fits together – the food that our chefs prepare, the massages our therapists give, the service in the hotels all contribute to the

guest's sense of well-being and relaxation. I love that we have local clients who plan a weekend "Fuenso" in one of our hotels, just because they know that after two days with us, they will feel more balanced and revived when facing their everyday lives after checkout.

---

# "AS SIMPLE AS IT SOUNDS, LIFE REALLY IS BETTER WHEN YOU SLEEP BETTER."

---

## Although the hotels are all very different, Andalusia has the highest concentration of Hospes properties in Spain. Is there a unifying aesthetic or principle to this market presence?

Andalusia has many commonalities, but also many differences. The philosophy of our brand is to showcase the best of wherever we are. In Cordoba we have the 16th-century Palacio del Bailio, replete with references to the city's rich history from the Romans and the Moors, under whom Cordoba was once the largest and most cosmopolitan city in Europe. So one shouldn't miss experiencing the baths of the hotel's luxurious spa. In Seville, it's about the dense urban context of one of Europe's most picturesque cities. In

Granada, if we could ignore the Alhambra and choose gastronomy, I'd recommend our Senzone restaurant for the distinct flavours of the mountainous Alpujarra region that have influenced the city's cuisine for centuries. Granada is the only city in Europe that produces caviar – a local delicacy that's virtually unknown to visitors.

## What makes Hospes original?

For Hospes, I would apply the term original to our concepts of authenticity, sincerity and honesty. I think one of the most authentic things we can accomplish is to help people sleep better – to dream and to rest. It seems easy, but it's hard to do without sincerity. From the reception staff to the people cleaning the rooms and the waiters serving breakfast, if their smiles are sincere and honest, the client knows it. In Spanish, we'd use the verb "seducir", and this kind of seduction is what makes our guests want to be here. Our guests desire – and deserve – to feel fantastic, whether it's because of a massage or staying in a palace or being well looked after during a business trip; that's what we do.

In 2005, President Clinton was staying with his daughter Chelsea at the Maricel in Mallorca, and after a day or two at the hotel, they had a glamorous trip planned to go out on a friend's yacht. At breakfast that day Mr. Clinton told me that he wanted to cancel the boat trip and just lounge at the hotel. To me that meant everything was working right – that a guest wants to give up his plans just to stay with us. «

*Erik Andersen*

# A MEXICAN REVOLUTION

*The ever-evolving vision of three brothers and a good friend, Grupo Habita has revolutionised Mexico's hotel culture. And now the vision is moving beyond the country's borders.*

MADE BY
*ORIGINALS*
---

**CARLOS COUTURIER
& MOISÉS MICHA**
MEXICO CITY

"Sorry I'm late," Carlos Couturier says, extending his hand in greeting and apology. "My pilot was late." As excuses go, it's a pretty good one, and easily forgiven. Couturier has just flown into Mexico City from Veracruz – home of Grupo Habita's laid-back hotel Azúcar, just off the coast – wearing jeans and a black Lacoste polo shirt. Suddenly he's standing in front of a video camera, dressed in a tailored black Jil Sander suit, white shirt and black tie. Transformed, he's ready for a chat on the rooftop terrace of his group's remarkable CONDESAdf hotel. A waiter brings Couturier a Niçoise salad, or a version of it, with thin, dark-red slices of tuna sashimi instead of the usual tinned fish.

Couturier is a hotelier with a certain star quality. It's not just his looks – though at first glance, you might mistake him for Daniel Craig, of the recent James Bond films. He compares the boutique-hotel business to filmmaking. "Except hotels are living, breathing organisms that evolve. Whereas once a film is finished, that's it," he says.

Grupo Habita, a hotel group that boasts trendsetting properties all over Mexico, has consistently broken new ground in the once-conservative country, and is now on the verge of expanding to the United States. Habita's four partners, brothers Rafael, Moisés and Jaime Micha, along with Couturier, have invented a destination sensation.

The group started in 2000, when Moisés Micha and Couturier, friends from university, opened the hotel Habita in Mexico City. At the time, the two knew practically nothing about operating a hotel. Moisés had spent about 15 years in investment banking in New York, and Couturier ran a citrus farm in his native San Rafael, in the Mexican state of Veracruz (he still oversees it, in fact). Couturier's grandparents were winemakers in La Haute-Alsace, France, and came to Mexico seeking adventure after a blight destroyed their vineyards.

Today, Couturier views his family's European-Mexican fusion as a defining influence that informs his choice of the architects, designers and chefs who help create a different atmosphere at each property. "My background not only inspires me, but makes me

original," he says. "I love my roots, and I like meeting new people from all over the world. Yet I've never lost my sense of belonging. Even if I'm travelling a lot, I still appreciate the basic things that life has given me."

If Couturier is the company's visual and emotional force, the Micha brothers are its operational engine. Rafael, the eldest, manages the group's public relations, sales and marketing strategies: tasks he brilliantly augments with such glamorous side duties as liaising with international VIPs and even collecting art for the properties. Jaime, the youngest, takes care of administration and human resources. Moisés oversees the

---

CARLOS
COUTURIER

## "WITH ALL OUR PROPERTIES, IT'S ALMOST LIKE LIVING A FILM."

---

operation of Grupo Habita's seven hotels. Trim in blue jeans, white shirt and blazer, he gives little sign that he runs a high-pressure business. He chuckles at the suggestion: "We have very defined roles," he explains calmly. "We're a total of four partners. I do the operations and new projects."

Yes, new projects. Eight properties, including three in the United States, are now in the planning stage – just in time for the biggest financial crisis in decades. Moisés chuckles again. "We think it's a good moment to be building hotels. By 2010, we think it will be a good time. Yes, our finances are fine. Our construction loan happened before the crisis."

For a relatively new business, Grupo Habita has seen exceedingly rapid expansion, now employing about 600 people. Its destination hotels include the newly opened Habita Monterrey in northern Mexico, Azúcar in Veracruz, CONDESAdf in Mexico City, La Purificadora in nearby Puebla, and

Deseo [Hotel + Lounge] and Básico, both in Playa del Carmen on Mexico's pristine Caribbean coast.

The Habita hotel itself, the company's first property, was once a 1950s-era Mexico City block with 14 apartments. The team converted the structure into a 36-room hotel designed by Mexican architect Enrique Norten. The effect is bright and airy, yet design-intensive. "We saw a niche in the market for something smaller, a hotel that personalises business, but with design a big factor in the overall experience," says Moisés. The hotel's rooftop terrace overlooks a busy city skyline, and features elements that accentuate Mexico City's temperate climate: a swimming pool, and a long fireplace at which guests gather with drinks in the evenings.

Over time, Habita has become something of a landmark, a phenomenon that's helped elevate the hotel into a more public destination, enjoyed by guests and locals alike. Across town, the group's ultrachic CONDESAdf hotel also occupies a reclaimed space, a splendid former apartment block dating to 1928. When Grupo Habita first came across the property, it was abandoned and dilapidating. Architect Javier Sanchez gutted the interior, but kept the original façade – one that would hardly look out of place in Paris or Vienna.

"For the CONDESAdf, we looked for a designer in Mexico and America, and it was very difficult to make them understand what our needs were," Couturier explains. "Condesa [the neighbourhood] has a strong European influence, so we decided to be more ambitious and bring a European designer to Mexico." Paris-based India Mahdavi had done the interior of the famed Townhouse hotel in Miami. "She was sceptical at the beginning, but she loved the property and Mexico City," Couturier says.

Inside the hotel, a courtyard dotted with small white chairs and tables acts as a centrepiece. Adjoining living rooms, painted a refreshing aqua, offer white sofas designed by Mahdavi herself, where guests can enjoy a typically European breakfast, featuring what could be the best homemade granola in the world. At night, the hotel's fourth-floor rooftop terrace pulses with hip patrons »

# "It's not only about creating trends – it's about building a hotel that can outlive a generation."

enjoying the mild evening air with a sake or cocktail. But by day, the partially covered deck is tranquil, offering an atmospheric fourth-storey view of the district's leafy trees and old homes. The intimate feel continues all the way to Conde, the CONDESAdf's resident chocolate Labrador, who is often seen lounging behind the front desk.

What was once nearly a ruin thus became a neighbourhood icon almost overnight, one that attracts both Mexico City's most beautiful young people and savvy travellers. "When our guests get here, they have this sensation that they belong here, somehow. You arrive and you're part of what's going on locally. You're part of the energy. You're not one more person like you are in bigger hotels," says Moisés. "Our hotels are not standard hotels," Couturier jumps in. "We like to break rules. We're influenced by global ideas, and we adapt ideas to our hotels. We could be perceived as trendsetters, but it's a deeper thing. It is not only about creating trends – it's about building a hotel that can outlive a generation."

What strikes visitors to several Grupo Habita hotels is how different each property is from the others. Yet they all have a distinct "Grupo Habita" feel to them. It's not a signature look ("We don't like a property to have the label of a designer, or the owner," says Couturier), but something nearly indefinable. Or rather, simple: "We maximise our surroundings," explains Moisés. Indeed, atmosphere plays an important role in every property that the

company runs and plans. Even the local weather is a consideration. In Tulum, on Mexico's Riviera Maya, the team is planning an eco-chic destination with ten rooms: a hotel with no glass windows. In Acapulco, Habita has two hotels in the works, each playing up different aspects of the beach resort's assets; Boca Chica, the smaller property on a tiny, intimate peninsula, is to play up Acapulco's 1950s flair, while Hotel Hotel at Las Brisas is meant to emphasise hilltop views of the open sea.

Another part of Grupo Habita's success is being able to catch the eye of the international traveller with relatively small properties. Truth be told, Mexico's bountiful natural resources, great weather, beaches, mountains, delectable food and friendly people make it any hotelier's dream. "We were able to bring the charm of Mexico to another level," says Couturier. "We challenged the establishment of what could be done and the way it could be done."

The talkative hotelier is suddenly pensive as Mexico City's late afternoon sun plays a dance of shadows on the CONDESAdf rooftop. There's a long pause. "Here it was easy for us. We're Mexicans with a global mentality. We knew what a visitor to Mexico would like. But now that we're starting to grow outside Mexico, we have to show that we're able to reproduce the formula and yet be original. We have a project in Austin, Texas, which is totally different from our projects in New York City. In every destina-

tion we have to be receptive to what the local community has to say. And what our visitors are expecting from us."

Grupo Habita is planning two hotels in New York – one on the Bowery and the other in Chelsea. Here is where the team will face some of its biggest challenges. "The creativity process starts in world cities like New York, London and Tokyo. That's why you visit these places. So to be original in New York is going to be a big task," Couturier declares. The Chelsea project, in the gallery district on 27th Street between 10th and 11th Avenues, is near the city's Highline Project, with great river views. The Bowery project "complements our property in Chelsea, so visitors get to explore the Lower East Side," says an animated Moisés.

"With all our properties, it's almost like living a film," says Couturier, finishing up his salad. "In Chelsea, if you visit our building site in the morning, it is different than at noon, or at night. And in the morning at the CONDESAdf, you feel like you're waking up in a small town outside Mexico City. But at night, it could almost be a nightclub. The energy of the property changes throughout the day. That's something we really like." «

*Susana Seijas*

1

# *NO TWO SIGNATURES* ARE THE SAME

**RELIABLE STYLE**

Each of our Made by Originals protagonists has taken his, her or their originality and translated it into a many-sided property that reflects a unique set of qualities and experiences. As Reto Gurtner says in his interview (see "On the Rocks," page 50), Design Hotels™ is the opposite of a chain: each property is its own character, and the consortium is a collection of myriad hotel typologies making up a sort of, as he puts it, "community of good people."

Indeed. On top of this, Design Hotels™ sees a few major movements running through its portfolio of properties. It's not about stars or ranking – or even primarily about design – but rather about the experience a guest might have in each kind of hotel. ust as a man might choose to wear a Paul Smith jumper and jeans one day, and then a custom Loro Piana wool suit the next: with Design Hotels™, he can choose an outrageous visual and tactile experience on a wild weekend, a reliably stylish hotel for a two-day business trip during the week, or an indulgent, quiet romantic holiday anytime of year.

The connecting thread cutting the widest swathe through Design Hotels'™collection is a simple philosophy of great aesthetics and a welcoming atmosphere and attitude. Although the hotels' visuals, geographical locations and main concepts vary widely – no two signatures are the same, after all – their reliable sense of style represents the very backbone of a Design Hotels™ experience. Form and function, comfort and attention, an interesting, appealing look that always has a distinctive personality but that never, ever gets too loud: it's all there, and it's what these properties are best at.

02

03

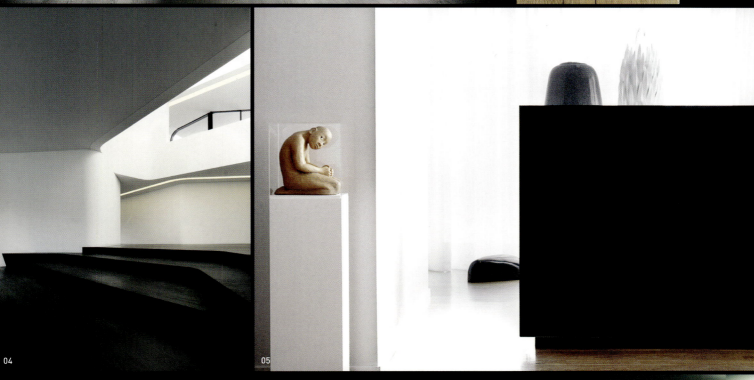

04

05

01

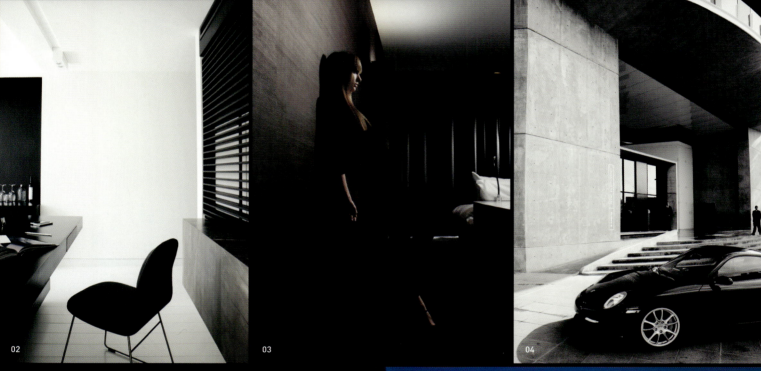

02  03  04

05

# *URBAN RETREAT OR IDYLLIC GETAWAY,* IT'S ALWAYS AESTHETIC

Soothing, dramatic, a trip into minimalist design or mostly about that intangible thing that is true hospitality, the lobby sets the tone for the overall experience. Guestrooms here aren't about major surprises but rather high style and absolute comfort, superb design and up-to-date features. A little bit of eye-popping whimsy, but always with a mind to ease. Like the architecture of German architect Jürgen Mayer H. (see previous page) – these hotels combine innovative concepts, surfaces, curves and lines with old-fashioned comfort.

# FIND UNIQUE SIGNATURES AROUND THE WORLD

In these properties, small revelations and discoveries could be the newest technology, a sweeping view, incredible linens or a commissioned artwork. Your room might be slick and cool, or cuddly and warm. It might be blissfully silent and gadget-free, or super-wired. It might have tons of chic mirrors and vast views, or fascinating, fluctuating light effects. But no worries. Here, nothing is ever exaggerated. Things are as savvy yet as subtle as an iPhone or a Corian countertop, just as they are as consistently "on" as a Hugo Boss suit or Prada dress when confidently facing the world.

In cities, these successful hotels not only supply the peace that business travellers or weekend warriors need, but also attract a local scene to mix with in thriving courtyards, comforting lounges and destination restaurants. Make high-stakes financial deals in high-technology meeting rooms that still manage to offer a design-based atmosphere. Or have power breakfasts in dramatic mezzanines or under the soaring ceilings of a converted industrial building.

It's a kind of signature style that even extends beyond the urban to the smooth beachside lines of exemplary properties in Southeast Asia, to the rarefied high-altitude air of Bhutan, and to the vast sea views of our many members along the Mediterranean. At the end of the day – or even at the beginning – you know you're in just the right place, wherever in the world you are.

# *INDEX 01–B*

# INDEX C–Z

# 101 HOTEL
## *Reykjavik*
---

101 Hotel is undeniably cool. For Iceland's first foray into the realm of chic boutique hotels, owner and designer Ingibjörg S. Pálmadóttir has transformed the Icelandic Social Democratic Party's former home into the quintessence of Nordic style. The former office building, erected in the 1930s, is now Iceland's casual-chic magnet, where guests and locals gather around tree-trunk tables and classic pieces by Eero Saarinen and Philippe Starck, bathed in the warm glow of a communal lounge fireplace. The spare, glossy and masculine bar's style is an innovative mixture of Chinese lacquered tables, wooden blocks and Edwardian chairs. In contrast is the restaurant's ladylike atmosphere, where a white dimpled mural runs alongside the glass roof and guests can perch on iconic Eros chairs. Throughout the public areas, monochromatic design and clear lines showcase the hotel's collection of art by Icelandic artists. But coolness melts away in the guestrooms' rustic warmth. Here is where visitors can bask in Iceland's famous hospitality with heated oak floors, white Italian bed linen, matte and glossy black furnishings, Artemide lamps and a bathroom with a free-standing bathtub waiting to be filled with geothermal waters.

WWW.DESIGNHOTELS.COM / 101HOTEL

ADDRESS
HVERFISGATA 10
101 REYKJAVIK
ICELAND

ROOMS
38

RATES
EUR 145 –
EUR 380

OPEN
03/2003

ICELAND
REYKJAVIK

**ADDRESS**
BAN VATNONG,
SAKKALINE ROAD,
LUANG PRABANG
LAOS

**ROOMS**
15

**RATES**
USD 125 –
USD 360

**OPEN**
04/2003

**LAOS**
LUANG PRABANG

# 3 NAGAS BY ALILA
## *Luang Prabang*

---

Luang Prabang, a UNESCO World Heritage site since 1995, attracts an increasing number of tourists with its gleaming temple roofs, decaying French colonial architecture, beautiful scenery and multiethnic inhabitants. 3 Nagas by Alila, located in the heart of Luang Prabang, offers an elegant blend of Laotian tradition, colonial charm and modern comfort. Visitors can relish the lively surroundings and typical Laotian hospitality in a culturally rich atmosphere. Here, three World Heritage buildings, more than a century old, have been thoughtfully restored using traditional materials and construction techniques. Fifteen spacious rooms and suites boast wooden floors and furnishings and traditional lime washed walls. The spaces are tastefully finished with fine silks and traditional weavings and open onto private verandas to the street or garden – ideal settings to take in Laotian life's languid pace and beauty. Wireless Internet ensures that global nomads can still be connected while they bask in the setting's private serenity; two restaurants offer delightful fusions of Laotian and French cuisine. And for a truly individual experience, the leisure concierge can tailor activities ranging from eco-tours to meditation, as well as interactive learning journeys that provide insight on Laotian rituals and traditions, as well as the fascinating architecture and history of Luang Prabang and its environs.

WWW.DESIGNHOTELS.COM /
AGUASDEIBIZA

ADDRESS
C/ SALVADOR CAMACHO S/N
07840, SANTA EULALIA DEL RIO
IBIZA, SPAIN

ROOMS
112

RATES
EUR 215 –
EUR 1800

OPEN
08/2008

SPAIN
IBIZA

# AGUAS DE IBIZA
# LIFESTYLE & SPA
## *Ibiza*

---

Anchored in Santa Eulalia Bay marina, Aguas de Ibiza Lifestyle & Spa is proof that Ibiza has more to offer than just raves and remixes. With interiors by Barcelona-based Triade Studio, the Torres family-run Aguas blends the charming character of a rural finca with the high-end services and savvy style of a contemporary hotel. The 112 rooms and suites have private terraces and floor-to-ceiling windows, and quirky extras like energy-saving automation systems for personalised ambience. The VIP Cloud 9 Club is a hotel-in-hotel, with separate check-in and services, private outdoor bathtubs and parquet flooring. The sumptuous spa by wellness expert Félix Prado offers rejuvenating water-themed treatments, and biz travellers won't be disappointed by the spacious work centre. Sounds decadent, and it is, but Aguas is also one of Europe's first eco-luxury hotels, with 35 percent lower energy consumption compared to similar properties. At the end of the day, the rooftop Air Ibiza bar and lounge with open-air pool is the perfect place for eco-conscious guests to chill in the glow of an unforgettable Balearic sunset, knowing that what they're doing is low-impact and high-pleasure.

# ALILA CHA-AM
## *Petchaburi*
---

Understated yet unforgettable, the Alila Cha-Am is tranquilly tucked into a charming coastal town on the sunrise side of the Gulf of Thailand. Blending seamlessly into the natural environment of white sand and leafy palms, the beachside resort achieves the perfect balance between privacy and connection. Leading up a grand stairway to a large open-air lobby, arrival at the Alila Cha-Am is designed to give guests an immediate sense of destination. From there, the breathtaking view unfolds across a rooftop reflection pool and a maze of interconnected pathways and private terraces toward the ocean horizon. Seasonal shrubs and ambient lighting create harmony with nature's cycles, while the studied intertwining of paths with open spaces evokes a certain, very private peace. The resort has two restaurants – rooftop and poolside – and a relaxation wellness zone at the Chill Pool and The Red. Guestrooms are intimate hideaways providing both indoor and outdoor seclusion. Private terraces and the ultimate Pool Villa suites serve as full-scale sanctuaries complete with garden, pool and terrace. Spacious rooms offer unobstructed views, with each featuring a unique rain shower that brings the outdoors in and enhances the sense of communion with nature.

WWW.DESIGNHOTELS.COM/
ALILACHAAM

ADDRESS
115 MOO 7, TAMBOL BANGKAO
AMPHUR CHA-AM,
PETCHABURI 76120
THAILAND

ROOMS
79

RATES
THB 13300 –
THB 36050

OPEN
02/2008

THAILAND
PETCHABURI

WWW.DESIGNHOTELS.COM/
ALILAJAKARTA

ADDRESS
JALAN PECENONGAN KAV 7–17
JAKARTA 10120
INDONESIA

ROOMS
245

RATES
USD 100 –
USD 350

OPEN
05/2001

INDONESIA
JAKARTA

# ALILA JAKARTA
## *Jakarta*

---

This hotel in the middle of Jakarta's central business district stays true to its name, a Sanskrit word meaning "surprise." A welcome retreat from the energy of its surrounding streets, Alila Jakarta exemplifies simple elegance and skips all unnecessary ornamentation or excess throughout its 27 floors. Local architecture firm Denton Corker Marshall chose a minimal design aesthetic that offers guests a sanctuary from the outside world. The care and attention lavished on the hotel's clientele is obvious in its generous policies, such as ample meeting space for savvy business travellers. Steel and local stone, such as Indonesian granite, provide the lobby with a gentle grace that is illuminated by large windows overlooking the garden in the peaceful inner courtyard, while an Asian flair is evident in the 215 rooms, decorated in a lush yet soothing palette of dark red tones. Offering a pure and abstract design, Alila Jakarta is an exclusive and surprisingly isolated place to replenish your energy reserves.

# ALILA MANGGIS
## *Bali*

---

With a breathtaking location between the sea and eastern Bali's sacred Mount Agung, Alila Manggis seduces guests with a free-flowing interaction between buildings and surrounding nature. The traditional thatched roof covering the lobby is beautifully offset by floors of polished ivory-coloured concrete. This immediately sets the stage for the quiet luxury that permeates the property. Four two-storey buildings of cool white stone, lit after nightfall in beams of warm orange, contain guestrooms that offer sea views that both soothe and inspire the soul. A golden glow of lights shimmering against the pool's cool turquoise offers a visual alternative. Each guestroom building is both an exercise in contrasting mass and lightness and a skilful study of Balinese architecture. Guests get a taste of local flavour in interiors influenced by the colours of nearby Bali Aga villages: comforting shades of cream, sand and chocolate emphasise the warmth of handwoven textiles and indigenous woods. The resort's leisure concierge can also connect guests with local life by organising private tours of the stunning surroundings or even deep-sea fishing. No matter what visitors choose do, they can always bask in the understated sense of luxury that enhances this Balinese getaway's peace and serenity.

WWW.DESIGNHOTELS.COM /
ALILAUBUD

ADDRESS
DESA MELINGGIH KELOD,
PAYANGAN,
80572 GIANYAR, BALI
INDONESIA

ROOMS
64

RATES
USD 185 –
USD 635

OPEN
04/1996

INDONESIA
BALI

# ALILA UBUD
## *Bali*

---

Exquisitely secluded on a hillside in Bali's picturesque Ayung River Valley and featuring one of the world's finest infinity pools, Alila Ubud is a spectacular retreat where guests can experience the extravagance of profound peace and quiet. It's also a place where architectural details effortlessly mix with natural elements. Straw roofs sit atop smooth plaster walls. Terracotta tiles blend into gravel and crushed rock, clearly delineating where the modern world ends and traditional Balinese building begins. The award-winning pool spreads out to form an elongated rectangle until its edges seem to disappear into the terraced jungle hillside. Here, public spaces resemble the layout of a Balinese village; valley villas are perched on stilts, and the new pool villas offer a sublimely private retreat. Always the centrepiece of the rooms, the beds are made of light wood and covered in subtle hues that draw the guest's attention to the lush views outside. Individual garden terraces and balconies offer expansive views across sculpted rice paddies and the meandering Ayung River Valley. Though located only five kilometres from Ubud, Bali's cultural centre, guests might find it difficult to leave Alila Ubud for even a moment.

**WWW.DESIGNHOTELS.COM /**
**ALILAHADAHAA**

**ADDRESS**
HADAHAA ISLAND, GAAFU ALIFU
(NORTH HUVADHOO) ATOLL
MALDIVES

**ROOMS**
50

**RATES**
USD 1075 –
USD 2250

**OPEN**
04/2009

**MALDIVES**
GAAFU ALIFU
ATOLL

# ALILA
# VILLAS HADAHAA
## *Gaafu Alifu Atoll*
---

Set on an intimate, uninhabited island in the middle of the Indian Ocean, Alila Villas Hadahaa is a floating jewel amidst turquoise waters, white sandy beaches and tropical foliage. "My design evokes a sense of place," explains architect Chan Soo Khian. He does so by obscuring the division between living space and ocean, guest and nature. The resort's 14 aqua villas elevated over the lagoon and 36 island villas – 20 with private pools – feature two sides of private wooden deck where full-size windows enable uninterrupted integration with the outside environment. Contemporary amenities on offer include international and Maldivian restaurants, a poolside cocktail bar, an island spa retreat, a 40-metre swimming pool and fitness, diving and water-sports centres. The innovative new experiential concept "Journeys by Alila" encourages active engagement with the destination and its people. A sensation of space is inevitable due to the expansive views of sky and sea. Built with sustainable materials yet informed by modern design sensibilities, the resort brilliantly fuses modern and traditional. Soo Khian's philosophy of bringing out the best of a location is evident, whether in the villas' sleek, eco-friendly design or in the serene tropical gardens and spa.

WWW.DESIGNHOTELS.COM /
ALILAULUWATU

**ADDRESS**
JL. BELIMBING SARI, BANJAR
TAMBIYAK, DESA PECATU
BALI
INDONESIA

**VILLAS**
61

**RATES**
USD 725 –
USD 3000

**OPEN**
02/2008

**INDONESIA**
BALI

# ALILA VILLAS ULUWATU
## *Bali*

---

The Alila Villas Uluwatu is the first resort in Bali designed from the ground up to achieve Green Globe certification, the highest level of Environmentally Sustainable Design (ESD) certification. And its leitmotif is harmony with nature, expressed in everything from the locally sourced building materials to the seamless transitions between indoor and out. The dramatic tropical landscape of Bali's Bukit Peninsula served as both foundation and inspiration: "We are not starting from scratch," explains landscaper Lim Swe Ting, "but helping the soul of the place come alive." Atop a 100-metre cliff, the luxuriously spacious villas are thus open to the outdoors, offering Indian Ocean views from bed to bathtub. Each villa is equipped with private pool, cabana, garden and pavilion, and is executed in a contemporary design softened by traditional Balinese touches. Thanks to the resort's attention to water conservation, recycling and energy-saving, guests can relax in guiltless bliss in the knowledge that their ecological footprint is being kept at a minimum. At the same time, they can enjoy all the services and amenities inherent to a five-star resort. The Alila Villas Uluwatu proves that celebrating nature doesn't mean forsaking comfort.

WWW.DESIGNHOTELS.COM /
ALMYRA

ADDRESS
POSEIDONOS AVENUE
8042 PAFOS
CYPRUS

ROOMS
190

RATES
EUR 100 –
EUR 875

OPEN
1972

CYPRUS
PAFOS

# ALMYRA
## *Pafos*

---

The timelessly impeccable craftsmanship of Cyprus's Almyra resists decorative trends in favour of clean architectural lines and Thanos Michaelides's ultra-chic interior elegance. Inspired by Aphrodite, the island's patron goddess, Almyra is an overall sensual and tactile experience. The sleek modern furniture in the monochromatic interior was selected by Joelle Pleot, designer of Karl Lagerfeld's private home. She vamped up hand-assembled Byzantine chandeliers for the lobby and the Mosaics restaurant, and added energizing splashes of 1970s-style flair, such as white leather sofas and ottomans, to enhance the blend of natural and manufactured lighting. Because the hotel also places high emphasis on a successful family experience, the concept focuses on practicality. Banquette sofas and low oakwood tables in the public spaces face windows with breathtaking ocean views – as do the new Aethon Sea View rooms and Kyma ("wave") suites. Natural materials as well as glass and Carrera marble come together to create a calming ambience; this atmosphere continues in the brand-new Almyra Spa, which offers organic products and a range of innovative treatments. Generously sized guestrooms can house families or provide ample play space for couples intending to worship the goddess of love in private.

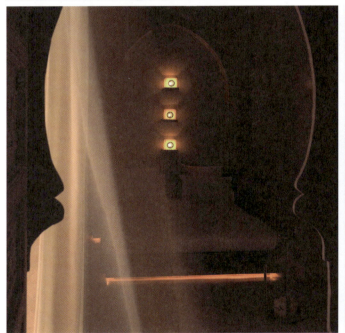

WWW.DESIGNHOTELS.COM/
ANAYELA

ADDRESS
28 DERB ZERWAL
40000 MARRAKECH MEDINA
MOROCCO

ROOMS
5

RATES
EUR 290 –
EUR 490

OPEN
01/2008

MOROCCO
MARRAKECH
MEDINA

# ANAYELA
## *Marrakesh*

---

AnaYela, a gorgeous 300-year-old palace transformed into an opulent boutique hotel, is the newest jewel of Marrakesh's *medina*, or ancient quarter. Like a passionate affair, the luminous three-room and two-suite city palace will leave lucky guests breathlessly drunk with the thrill of new discovery. More exciting than its mesmerising appearance, however, is the love story that took place behind AnaYela's closed doors: that of a 16-year-old girl and her future beau, and their clandestine night meetings in the palace's *tapis volant*, or Flying Carpet tower, still standing today. We know this because a handwritten manuscript was discovered in a hidden room behind a wall during a full-scale restoration in 2007 – it had not been seen for centuries. Luckily for us, the tale has now been engraved, in Arabic calligraphy, onto every door on the property. The silver characters can be viewed chronologically by guests as they amble through the roofless indoor courtyard, which features a heated limestone pool, up to the beguiling rooftop terrace with its extraordinary panoramic views of Marrakesh. Enveloped as AnaYela is in so much mystique, it's no wonder guests report feeling as if they've stepped into a mirage.

# ARTUS HOTEL
## *Paris*
---

Fine-art lovers and style mavens alike flock to the newly renovated Artus Hotel in Paris's beloved Saint Germain des Près because it typifies the city's focus on simplicity, fluidity and chic. An airy, open entrance invites guests into a luxurious yet understated universe, where traditional decorative style has displaced faddish décor. On the wall of the grand staircase leading to the breakfast room hangs a stunning enlargement of a detail from a painting by Delacroix, who once lived mere steps from the hotel's site. The guestrooms were conceived as miniature versions of traditional loft spaces, and, like an artist's loft, each room contains unique works of art. The light, minimalist design of the rooms is warmed by a mixture of such exquisite natural materials as fired clay walls, carved wood, Murano glass, stucco and the Arabescato marble which anchors the design of the bright, open bathrooms. In short, the Artus is not merely a place to sleep. Instead, it's an opportunity to be alive in the true heart and soul of *la rive gauche*.

WWW.DESIGNHOTELS.COM / ARTUSHOTEL

**ADDRESS**
34 RUE DE BUCI
75006 PARIS
FRANCE

**ROOMS**
27

**RATES**
EUR 255 –
EUR 415

**OPEN**
03/2005

**FRANCE**
PARIS

WWW.DESIGNHOTELS.COM /
AUGARTEN

ADDRESS
SCHOENAUGASSE 53
8010 GRAZ
AUSTRIA

ROOMS
56

RATES
EUR 115 –
EUR 240

OPEN
09/2001

AUSTRIA
GRAZ

# AUGARTEN HOTEL
## *Graz*

---

In this eclectically designed glass and metal structure, open communication between the universe within and the environment without is the name of the game – literally. Architect Günther Domenig's creation makes a unique statement for modernity in Graz – an Austrian city dominated by Gothic, Renaissance and baroque architecture. To Domenig, good architecture is all about capacity, economy and stature. At the same time, the hotel calls Domenig the "architect of the game," meaning that at Augarten Hotel, guests are also invited to play. In the guestrooms, contemporary pieces by Cappellini and Ligne Roset are juxtaposed with classics such as Verner Panton's cantilevered chair, perhaps even moving guests to enjoy the stylish fun in utter privacy. No space is overlooked as a creative and potentially inspiring venue: take, for example, the 24-hour bar and indoor pool ringed by rainbow-coloured "Supra sofas" made from high-density, high-tech foam. Vibrant works by 80 different contemporary painters and sculptors are displayed like museum pieces in surprising places such as the courtyard, next to stairwells and even on the rooftop terrace, which offers magnificent views of the old city below.

**WWW.DESIGNHOTELS.COM / AVALONHOTEL**

**ADDRESS** KUNGSTORGET 9 411 17 GOTHENBURG SWEDEN

**ROOMS** 101

**RATES** SEK 1890 – SEK 18500

**OPEN** 07/2007

**SWEDEN** GOTHENBURG

# AVALON HOTEL
## *Gothenburg*
---

At Gothenburg's Avalon Hotel, fragrances and sounds as well as lighting, furnishings, colours and lines are deployed to compose a harmony so powerful that the hotel is Sweden's first to earn a genuine Feng Shui certification. Guests seeking such a supreme sanctuary will admire how otherwise sharp corners are rounded, classic Arne Jacobsen chairs are combined with clean Nordic design, and the functional architecture offers a comfortable and uncomplicated stay. Almost one-third of the rooms are completed by private mini-spas and bathtubs, and suites offer commanding views over the city. But guests can design their own level of personal comfort from the spaces' many soothing options. They can separate work from rest with foldaway workplaces that disappear into walls and instead focus on the Egyptian cotton linens and tailor-made duvets, Bang & Olufsen entertainment systems and hand-tufted Kasthall rugs. And to fully unwind, they can decide to dip into the rooftop pool, read before the large open fireplace in the lobby, or share relaxation tips with other guests at the lovely hotel bar where pumpkin-orange seating shoots energy into the otherwise calm and serene setting.

WWW.DESIGNHOTELS.COM/
BECKERS

ADDRESS
OLEWIGER STRASSE 206
54295 TRIER
GERMANY

ROOMS
32

RATES
EUR 110 –
EUR 240

OPEN
04/2007

GERMANY
TRIER

# BECKER'S
# HOTEL & RESTAURANT
## *Trier*
---

Nestled amidst the vineyards and rolling hills of the ancient German city of Trier, Becker's Hotel & Restaurant is a family tradition that proudly dates back five generations, but remains a tribute to modern style despite its historic status. From the outside, the lobby glows through large-paned windows, greeting guests with an inviting warmth. Still, Becker's self-professed heart is its kitchen, which prepares true German comfort cuisine. Done in black and white, the restaurant it serves suggests a sophistication befitting a black-tie event or a white wedding, while the wine bar's deeper, darker tones evoke a cosmopolitan night out. The serene stone floors of the lobby and restaurant give way to the guestrooms' finely patterned dark wood combined with the mellow mood of low spot lighting. A simple pane of glass separates the dark tiled shower from the sleeping area, adding a hint of airiness to the otherwise earthy elements embodied in the hotel's design. At Becker's, German wine-country hospitality is writ large, though it is certainly characterised by its own brand of modern sophistication.

WWW.DESIGNHOTELS.COM / BELAMI

ADDRESS
7–11 RUE SAINT-BENOÎT
75006 PARIS
FRANCE

ROOMS
115

RATES
EUR 360 –
EUR 1050

OPEN
02/2000

# BEL-AMI
*Paris*

---

Originally an 18th-century abbey on Rue Saint-Benoît in Paris, the Bel-Ami has been transformed by a new generation of French designers into a modern masterpiece of pared-down luxury. Working under architect Christian Lalande, French design duo Nathalie Battesti and Véronique Terreaux – known for their invigorating interiors scattered around Paris and Tokyo – accomplish a pristine simplicity that offers warmth and character, style and comfort. In 2003, Parisian interior designer Michel Jouannet, inspired in part by Stanley Kubrick's *A Clockwork Orange*, created 23 new rooms with lively colour schemes such as orange and olive green, each with white marble bathrooms. And in 2007 and 2008, French designer Pascal Allaman created new rooms and suites with pure, simple lines enhanced by contemporary tones. Now, guests can bask in the spaces' calm, informal sophistication. Natural materials such as Wenge wood give the rooms an earthy touch, while a rich, subtle palette of chocolate, pistachio, coffee and caramel tones produces an understated and artistic refinement that gently intertwines the themes of nature and urbanism. The Bel-Ami dares to be fun and exerts an unpretentious appeal on global fashionistas, all the while providing a soothing backdrop to the urban bustle of the Left Bank outside.

**WWW.DESIGNHOTELS.COM / BENTLEYHOTEL**

**ADDRESS** HALASKARGAZI CAD. NO:75 34367 HARBIYE ISTANBUL TURKEY

**ROOMS** 50

**RATES** EUR 200 – EUR 800

**OPEN** 01/2003

**TURKEY** ISTANBUL

# BENTLEY HOTEL
## *Istanbul*
---

Befitting its location in Istanbul, the city that straddles Europe and Asia, the Bentley is a careful balance of Orient and Occident, of colourful tradition and contemporary cool. The work of Milanese architects Piero Lissoni and Nicoletta Canesi, it's a temple of radiance and light in the pulsating heart of the city's European section, and a meeting point for the young, international elite. Oversized windows usher in visual stimulation from the streets outside, enhancing an interior filled with the formal purity and colourful shades typical of Italian design. In the lounge, guests can taste a blend of Eastern and Western influences, as Ottoman-turquoise velvets provide a voluptuous juxtaposition to the sleek table by Finnish architect Eero Saarinen. The light-flooded interiors of 40 guestrooms and 10 suites bask in pale hues of blue and beige, green and grey, with a hint of the traditional in parquet flooring and furniture of olive-stained oak. Guests can step onto private terraces with evocative views of the ancient skyline, or mingle with local trendsetters in the chilled-out lobby bar. Amid all the clamour and jumble of Istanbul, the Bentley is a haven of harmony and calm.

WWW.DESIGNHOTELS.COM/
CAPISANI

ADDRESS
DORSODURO 979/A
30123 VENICE
ITALY

ROOMS
29

RATES
EUR 192 –
EUR 594

OPEN
12/2000

ITALY
VENICE

# CA' PISANI HOTEL
## *Venice*

---

A revived merchant's townhouse owned by the Serandrei family, Venice's noble Ca' Pisani hotel is more than 500 years old, but has been brilliantly modernised by architects Roberto Luigi Canovaro and Gianluigi Pescolderung into an experience that's nothing less than inspiring. The pair blended elements of the Italian Futurist movement with original architectural features such as exposed wooden beams. Each of the 29 guestrooms also boasts original furniture from the 1930s and 1940s collected from across Italy by the Serandrei family. Guests first encounter their room's individuality in uniquely decorated doors, which are inspired by posters of that era. And bathrooms feature a special masonry technique that gives the effect of sparkling stars. The hotel's restaurant, La Rivista, where traditional food with a modern twist is served, offers another variation on the Futurist theme, with glistening blue tables that underscore a dreamy and unreservedly romantic atmosphere. Canovaro and Pescolderung's clean, sharp lines only enhances Ca' Pisani's status as an exclusive Venetian spot, where guests enjoy the successful melding of two very contrasting design eras in a quiet, picturesque part of the city.

ADDRESS
EUROPALAAN 38
3600 GENK
BELGIUM

ROOMS
60

RATES
EUR 130 –
EUR 200

OPEN
04/2008

BELGIUM
GENK

# CARBON HOTEL
## *Genk*

---

The Carbon Hotel is part of the vibrant rejuvenation of the commercial centre of Genk, the heart of the 19th-century Limburg coal-mining industry. The retreat dedicates itself to life's vital elements in both name and design, and is built from materials that are based on carbon and the five basic elements – wood, fire, earth, metal and water. The shimmery façade and the interior's attention to texture help to enhance the atmosphere with subtle luxury without becoming distracting. The hotel's clean and minimal aesthetic aims to give guests a stylish escape from the everyday. The lobby and restaurant are dotted with mellow, calming accents, like Swedish-designed floors that radiate warmth and absorb sound to soothe even the most agitated urbanite. And in each of the 60 rooms, the use of indirect, coloured light allows for easy adjustments to suit one's mood. On top of it all is a vast (608-square-metre) spa that gives guests the ultimate space to pamper both mind and body. Here, a spacious hammam, sauna cabins, chromotherapy and even a 204-square-metre terrace with southern exposure keep all the elements in balance.

**WWW.DESIGNHOTELS.COM/**
**CASADELMAR**

**ADDRESS**
ROUTE DE PALOMBAGGIA BP 93
20538 PORTO – VECCHIO CEDEX
SOUTH CORSICA
FRANCE

**ROOMS**
34

**RATES**
EUR 360 –
EUR 4000

**OPEN**
05/2004

**FRANCE**
SOUTH CORSICA

# CASADELMAR
## *South Corsica*
---

Situated on Corsica's south-eastern coast, Casadelmar takes advantage of the brilliant blues, soothing sounds and salty aroma that envelop its breezy seaside location. Designed by French architect Jean François Bodin with the deliberate intent to harmonise the property with nature, Casadelmar successfully amplifies its already beautiful surroundings with subtle luxury. The hotel's 34 guestrooms are washed in mellow shades of honey, caramel and ivory and splashed with vibrant accents for a tranquil ambience that serenely complements Bodin's use of local materials like red cedarwood and grey stone. Canopied king-size beds and classical design accents like Le Corbusier's 1930s chaise lounge provide ample stylish outlets for guests to kick back. But despite the sumptuous refinement of its furnishings, Casadelmar's real attraction is its surroundings, which guests can enjoy from their private terraces or by simply staring at unobstructed ocean views from the hotel's enormous windows. Lighting by iGuzzini illuminates relaxed evening strolls across the grounds, revamped by renowned landscape designer Jean Mus, to wind down for the night in style. The overall effect is sleek and simple – a luxurious reflection of Corsica's pure beauty.

# CERÊS AM MEER
## *Binz*
---

Located an the German island of Rügen, CERÊS AM MEER is a cosmopolitan highlight of the sea resort Binz, and complements the lively beach promenade's beauty. Through his use of smoked oakwood parquet flooring and natural black Chinese stone, architect and interior designer Moritz Lau-Engehausen has infused this idyllic haven with clear, sensual and modern sensibility. A soft, neutral mood is found in all the elegant, spacious rooms. Tall French windows lead to each room's balcony or terrace, offering a panoramic view of the island's velvety white sand beaches and glistening blue water. The impression that the Caribbean has been transplanted to north-eastern Germany is central to the hotel's design concept. Luxurious treatments focus on water in all of its forms and temperatures in the Senso Spa. The restaurant, Negro, extends the aquatic theme even as its roof terrace location offers a spectacular glass cupola for nighttime stargazing. From that perch, guests can perhaps spy the small black planet that gives this dreamy hotel its name. With immaculate charm and classical lines, the Baltic's new star – already the winner of multiple awards – is a veritable love letter to purity, and Germany's ultimate seaside experience.

WWW.DESIGNHOTELS.COM /
CHOUPANAHILLS

ADDRESS
TRAVESSA DO LARGO DA
CHOUPANA
9060-348 FUNCHAL
PORTUGAL

ROOMS
64

RATES
EUR 270 –
EUR 830

OPEN
03/2002

PORTUGAL
MADEIRA

# CHOUPANA HILLS
# RESORT & SPA
## *Madeira*

---

Perched 500 metres above the Atlantic, this serene, subtropical retreat combines Asian and African accents with local materials like volcanic stone for a safari-inspired experience. On a south-facing slope, looking down on the Madeiran capital of Funchal, individual bungalows stand on stilts, their interiors decorated with coconut mats and custom-made furniture: canopied four-poster beds both offer a sublime night's sleep and recall the island's old-fashioned ox-drawn carts. French architect Michel de Camaret and designer Didier Lefort brought together clean, eco-friendly aesthetics without sacrificing style, like the larger communal building, whose post and beam construction attractively marks the resort's open spaces with massive Tali wood pillars. A bar suspended above the Asian-styled Xôpana Restaurant references local geology, while the lounge's modern sofas are Lefort's version of the famous sleds that provide rides from Monte to Funchal. Despite the exquisite attention to detail indoors, including imported antiques such as 17th-century Italian and Spanish dressers adorned with ivory, gold leaf and tortoiseshell, it's the spectacle of city rooftops and endless ocean that is truly breathtaking, especially when savoured from the comfort of a jacuzzi on the suite terraces or the tranquillity of the outdoor infinity-edge pool.

WWW.DESIGNHOTELS.COM/
CONDESADF

ADDRESS
AV. VERACRUZ 102
MEXICO CITY 06700
MEXICO

ROOMS
40

RATES
USD 175 –
USD 495

OPEN
01/2005

MEXICO
MEXICO CITY

# CONDESA*df*
## *Mexico City*
---

Tucked between historic façades on a tree-lined road in Mexico City's trendy Condesa neighbourhood, the Condesa*df* fuses the spirit of its bohemian surroundings with a playfully simple design aesthetic. Housed in a 1928 building in the French Neoclassical style, the hotel is filled from head to toe with custom furniture, stone tiles and an abundance of local colour. The feel is modern yet warm, hip but not haughty. The 40 rooms and suites reflects the tranquillity of monastic bedrooms – without a lack of amenities, of course. The result is 40 calming, airy spaces, some of which open onto wooden terraces. But the most prominent interior feature is the flora-filled inner courtyard, El Patio, where a destination restaurant serves delicious fare in a series of scattered privacy-optional rooms both indoors and out. Downstairs, a basement bar offers a whimsically modern cocktail spot, while further aloft, the rooftop bar La Terraza affords stunning castle views. At the charmingly titled Myself area, a hammam, therme, wet area and gym invite guests to indulge in relaxation. Meanwhile, an overarching floral theme – visible on everything from cushion covers to chopstick wrappers – serves to enhance the relaxed warm-weather vibe.

WWW.DESIGNHOTELS.COM /
CONTINENTALE

ADDRESS
VICOLO DELL'ORO, 6R
50123 FLORENCE
ITALY

ROOMS
43

RATES
EUR 310 –
EUR 1550

OPEN
01/2003

ITALY
FLORENCE

# CONTINENTALE
## *Florence*

---

Considered by many to be the crown jewel of the fashion-designer Ferragamo family's small chain of hotels, Continentale in Florence pays tribute to the spirit of the 1950s and 1960s with a candy-coloured mix of both vintage and contemporary style, offset by just the right amount of playful kitsch. Billowy drapes in light pink, lemon and pistachio tones greet guests in the reception, a mellow space second only to Ferragamo's favourite "relaxation room" on the second floor. The cocktail lounge's bar glows in more pink, and the cosy breakfast room's pink-upholstered furnishings continue the theme, but without crossing into camp. Nods to glamorous vintage design are scattered throughout the hotel, but evenly balanced out by the colour composition's happy-go-lucky charm, as intended by interior designer Michele Bönan. The hotel's 43 guestrooms are appointed with sheer-draped beds and flowing curtains that catch the Tuscan light, yet the rooms also manage to evoke the noir feeling of a 19th-century steamer, thanks to well-placed steel and leather accents. Reassuringly retro black-and-white photo-montages complete the glorious modern look that goes hand in hand with a positive, mid-century feel in the heart of this romantic Italian city.

WWW.DESIGNHOTELS.COM /
COPPERHILL

**ADDRESS**
ÅRE BJÖRNEN
83013 ÅRE
SWEDEN

**ROOMS**
112

**RATES**
EUR 199 –
EUR 837

**OPEN**
12/2008

**SWEDEN**
ÅRE

# COPPERHILL
# MOUNTAIN LODGE
## *Åre*

---

On the very top of Sweden's picturesque Mount Förberget, more than 730 metres above sea level, rests a new idyllic ski getaway. With the exclusivity of a five-star hotel, the warmth of a mom-and-pop operation and the thrilling design of master architect Peter Bohlin, the Copperhill Mountain Lodge is a gem in Sweden's snowy mountains. Known for his work on the iconic Apple stores, Bohlin has succeeded in making the hotel's 112 earth-toned guestrooms feel lustrous and comfortable as well as invitingly private. Guests can take in 360-degree views of the Jämtland mountains through large bay windows. Åre's renowned Alpine ski area, the largest in Scandinavia, is right beyond the doorstep, and ski-in/ski-out access makes exploring everything as simple as strapping on a pair of skis. The comprehensive Ski Club offers lessons, mountain guides, ski rentals, and heli-skiing for the very adventurous, while the gourmet restaurant Niesti and the boîte-spot Coppermine Co nourish ruddy-cheeked guests with hearty European delicacies. The luxurious Level spa, as well as a pair of top-shelf watering holes, are on hand to help guests kick back after a long day on the slopes. Here's a ski lodge that's just as inviting inside as out.

WWW.DESIGNHOTELS.COM /
DAS TRIEST

ADDRESS
WIEDNER HAUPTSTRASSE 12
1040 VIENNA
AUSTRIA

ROOMS
72

RATES
EUR 169 –
EUR 572

OPEN
12/1995

AUSTRIA
VIENNA

# DAS TRIEST
## *Vienna*

---

One of Vienna's first design hotels was born in 1995 in an old coach station used by travellers en route to the spas of Trieste, then part of the Austro-Hungarian Empire. Austrian architect Peter Lorenz and British interior designer Sir Terence Conran preserved parts of the original structure, combining elements of imperial elegance with sober lines, and providing well-heeled guests with a haven of elegance and warm colour amongst the city's 19th-century buildings and Art Nouveau façades. While cross-vaulted ceilings give the rooms a distinctive Viennese flair, carpeting and armchairs in solid planes of reds, yellows and royal blues lend a contemporary fell. Guests can enjoy the subtle luxury of handcrafted upholstered pieces by the Austrian firm Wittmann; Conran's choice of instantly recognisable modern classics also includes Artemide light fixtures. The bathrooms have porthole windows, which, along with railings and flag motifs in the rest of the hotel, offer an emotional link to the Adriatic port of Trieste. Specially commissioned black-and-white photographs of Trieste and Vienna further celebrate a connection to the building's historic role in international travel. Today's travellers yearning for a certain reserved nostalgia mixed with modern comforts have found what they're looking for.

WWW.DESIGNHOTELS.COM / DELASLETRAS

ADDRESS
GRAN VIA, 11
28013 MADRID
SPAIN

ROOMS
102

RATES
EUR 125 –
EUR 345

OPEN
07/2005

SPAIN
MADRID

# DE LAS LETRAS
# HOTEL & RESTAURANTE
## *Madrid*

---

Guests enter this iconic belle époque building to be immediately immersed into the warm, intimate atmosphere of Madrid's ultramodern De Las Letras Hotel & Restaurante. Here, on the legendary Gran Vìa, history and contemporary cool live in perfect harmony. Many of the building's historic details remain intact, including vintage woodwork, tile mosaics, an antique elevator and a noble staircase. The hotel also features a spacious library, reading room and a state-of-the-art spa. Ochre, burgundy or orange walls are adorned with quotations of Dylan Thomas, Friedrich Nietzsche and many of history's other great intellects. But the modern world is also more than welcome inside, where high ceilings and wide windows create a sensational showcase for the hotel's generous use of space. Each of the 102 coolly modern guestrooms is individualised with its own colour scheme and layout, with the suites allowing stunning views of the city from the three domes crowning the property. Local revellers who queue up to enter DL's Lounge are lured by its chic ambience, discretion, impeccable service and bohemian aesthetics. Far more than the sum of its many intriguing parts, De Las Letras is a perfectly poetic sun-drenched getaway in the very heart of Madrid.

A nada.

Valente (1929-2000)

**WWW.DESIGNHOTELS.COM /**
**DISTRITOCAPITAL**

**ADDRESS**
JUAN SALVADOR AGRAZ 37
MEXICO CITY 5300
MEXICO

**ROOMS**
30

**RATES**
USD 205 –
USD 975

**OPEN**
01/2009

**MEXICO**
MEXICO CITY

# DISTRITO CAPITAL
## *Mexico City*

---

Surprising interiors, dazzling panoramic views and double-height ceilings are a few of the eye-catching highlights of Distrito Capital. Located in the highest area of Mexico City – the skyscraper district of Santa Fe – this hotel is a testament to how cool Mexico's capital has become in recent years. Designed around the idea of creative minimalism, the 30 well-appointed guestrooms and suites look more like chic art spaces than hotel rooms. Any visitor will be simultaneously awed by impeccable design touches and excited by personal service flourishes. Fashionable without being *zeitgeist*-y, the inviting décor allows visitors to truly kick back and relax. The hotel is punctuated by vintage furnishings by Charlotte Perriand and other famous mid-century designers. And Parisian interior designer Joseph Dirand has also successfully created thought-provoking social spaces within the property, such as a lounge-friendly pool area, several spectacular terraces and a film projection room. In fact, the Enrique Olvera-curated restaurant on the fifth floor is one of Mexico City's newest hot spots. Guests will feel as if they've stepped into their dream apartment.

ADDRESS
STEPHANSPLATZ 12
1010 VIENNA
AUSTRIA

ROOMS
43

RATES
EUR 225 –
EUR 1550

OPEN
04/2006

AUSTRIA
VIENNA

# DO & CO HOTEL
## *Vienna*

---

DO & CO already enjoyed global notoriety as gastronomic genius Attila Dogudan's exclusive catering company. Now, with the brilliant renovation of its flagship property in Vienna's Haas Haus, it has firmly established itself as a purveyor of elite hospitality. Pritzker prize-winning architect Hans Hollein upgraded his iconic building with the additional design expertise of FJ Stijl, creating a futuristic interior that seamlessly blends both high- and low-tech accents. Four floors of the sparkling glass and metal structure have been transformed into 43 unique cone-shaped, spacious guestrooms and suites that offer luxurious comfort as well as unparalleled views of the city's most majestic square. In the rooms, high-quality natural materials underline the hotel's more tech-savvy furnishings, such as generous two-square-metre showers, Bang & Olufsen mega flat-screens and even Nintendo Wiis. Sophistication is also reflected in the property's culinary offerings, which are given an equally sparkling setting in the hotel's restaurants, the roof garden, the chic sixth-storey Onyx Bar and the Temple, a 12-seat private dining pavilion. Adjacent to St. Stephen's Cathedral, Hollein's cantilevered structure, despite its sci-fi style, remains reassuringly anchored in Viennese tradition, giving guests an unrivalled taste of past and future in the Austrian capital.

WWW.DESIGNHOTELS.COM /
DOURO41

ADDRESS
EN 222, KM 41
4550-631 RAIVA
PORTUGAL

ROOMS
42

RATES
EUR 139 –
EUR 467

OPEN
01/2009

PORTUGAL
RAIVA

# DOURO 41
## *Raiva*

---

Hidden amongst the winding roads, rugged hills and steep, vine-covered terraces of the Douro River Valley and located precisely 41 kilometres upstream from the Portuguese city of Porto is a highly unique river hotel: Douro 41. A surprising retreat in the heart of Portugal's port-wine region, the 42-room boutique hotel with restaurant, spa and private marina is masterfully embedded in the hillside, with contemporary terraced architecture echoing the region's famous vineyards. Here, lucky guests can enjoy the beautifully calm river view from sunrise to sunset. Or move to the indoor pool and wellness centre, where they can indulge in water-themed spa treatments, a sauna and more. The hotel's riverside restaurant offers fine dining with Portuguese flair. For a closer connection to the environs, explore the 2,000-year-old World Heritage wine region with a boat ride along the Douro or fishing excursions in the neighbouring Paiva and Arda rivers. Sport-hungry guests can make use of the hotel's private marina which offers waterskiing, jet-skiing, canoeing and white-water rafting on the Paiva River, considered Europe's purest water stream.

WWW.DESIGNHOTELS.COM/
EAST

ADDRESS
SIMON-VON-UTRECHT
STRASSE 31
20359 HAMBURG
GERMANY

ROOMS
128

RATES
EUR 155 –
EUR 850

OPEN
10/2004

GERMANY
HAMBURG

# EAST
## *Hamburg*

---

Located in a former iron foundry near Hamburg's notorious red-light district, East blends gastronomy, hospitality and nightlife in one of the city's most daring structures. Chicago-based star architect Jordan Mozer calls his design "a surreal mixture of East and West, old and new," which sums up the building as well as its interior, an eclectic mix of Gothic glamour, aromatic oriental accents and contemporary aesthetics. The hotel's first impression is one of impressive scale and dramatic lighting; resplendent floor-to-ceiling velvet curtains illuminated by candlelight create a unique sensory experience for it exclusive clientele. Various floors are refreshingly scented in ginger, lotus, jasmine or cinnamon, enhancing the sensuality of the surroundings even further. The 128 rooms, lofts and suites are outfitted in futuristic, curving forms and bright tones with extravagant details such as curvy headboards and original contemporary art, while the top floor's low-key spa and roof terrace offers an urban retreat for rest and rejuvenation. The hotel's restaurant doubles as a party zone, and in warmer months, guests can dine out on the terrace before sampling the diverse entertainment offerings of the lively city below.

WWW.DESIGNHOTELS.COM / ELITEPLAZA

ADDRESS
VÄSTRA HAMNGATAN 3
SE-404 22 GÖTEBORG
SWEDEN

ROOMS
130

RATES
SEK 850 –
SEK 18000

OPEN
01/2000

SWEDEN
GOTHENBURG

# ELITE PLAZA HOTEL
## *Gothenburg*

---

A remarkable entrance of fine-cut, partially polished granite welcomes guests into the embrace of this meticulously restored neo-Renaissance building. The home of the Svea Fire & Life Insurance Company in the 1880s, and the work of top architects of that era, today it has been transformed into a masterpiece of elegantly refined tradition by designers Christer Svensson and Lars Helling. An English mosaic floor in the lobby and pillared halls with arches of Italian marble stucco and wrought-iron detailing invite guests to stroll in the ornate splendour of an earlier age. Neoclassical highlights are scattered throughout the 130-room hotel; dark wood panelling surrounds clusters of deep, comfortable armchairs in the cosy bar. The same material is integrated to great effect into the design of spacious bedrooms. On the fifth floor, a dozen new suites and doubles in an updated mood featuring shades of beige, cherry and lime contrast a modern penthouse lifestyle with prime views of medieval Gothenburg. Wonderfully located at the heart of Sweden's second city, the Elite Plaza is a carefully understated melding of past and present, and a perfect place for business and leisure travellers alike.

**ADDRESS**
AN DER GERMANIA BRAUEREI 5
48159 MÜNSTER
GERMANY

**WWW.DESIGNHOTELS.COM /
FACTORYHOTEL**

**ROOMS**
144

**RATES**
EUR 100 –
EUR 230

**OPEN**
11/2008

**GERMANY**
MÜNSTER

# FACTORY HOTEL
## *Münster*
---

The old Germania Brewery in Münster has found a second life as The Factory, a surprising and successful combination of old and new buildings that fuses urban buzz with quiet haven. The landmarked brewery building at the complex's centre looks out over a relaxing fountain lake and is surrounded by a lively combination of shops, restaurants and clubs. The modern wing created by architect Andreas Deilmann houses the Factory Hotel with 128 airy rooms and 16 luxury suites designed with materials such as wood, concrete and felt, which reflect the original site's industrial flair at the same time as fostering a comfy sophistication. Guests can get some personal training or simply relax at the amazing and expansive 3,500-square-metre fitness centre with swimming pool, spa and roof terrace before they re-emerge into Factory life. It's a life that serves up traditional German and Austrian cuisine in the main restaurant, Mediterranean snacks and tapas at the Spanish restaurant and casual French fare at the bistro. Things heat up at night with poetry slams and jazz at the Live Club in the brewery basin, or dancing till dawn Grey, in the brewery basement nightclub.

WWW.DESIGNHOTELS.COM /
FALCONARA

ADDRESS
SS 115 KM 243 C.DA FAINO
93011 MARINA DI BUTERA (CL)
ITALY

ROOMS
65

RATES
EUR 125 –
EUR 670

OPEN
07/2007

ITALY
MARINA
DI BUTERA

# FALCONARA
# CHARMING HOUSE & RESORT
## *Butera*

---

Overlooking the clear blues of the Mediterranean Sea and Africa beyond, the Falconara Charming House & Resort is neighbour to a Norman castle – an unusual atmosphere in which traditions, history and even decadence meld with utter beauty. Yet its fine lines and contemporary aura make this southern Sicilian property a classic of understated chic: medieval, yet refreshingly modern. Guests can't help but to feel at ease amongst the original wood-beam ceilings, sweeping archways, rugged floors in local stone and Caltagirone ceramics decorating stairs and windows. The resort dedicates its updated design and impeccable amenities to its guests in two remarkable buildings. La Fattoria was once an annex to the nearby medieval Castle of Falconara and now boasts part of the accommodation just steps from the resort's private beach, while the sleek, newly built Club House boasts a modern restaurant, bar, 39 rooms and spa facilities and the nearby outdoor swimming pool. Baron Roberto and Antonella Chiaramonte Bordonaro, the owners of both the adjacent castle and the resort, personally oversaw the interior design to ensure that the Club House's aesthetic is up-to-the-minute, yet La Fattoria's rooms are embellished with timeless traditional elements. The Sicilian and Moorish design influences invite guests to marvel at La Fattoria's eclectic collection of art objects and curiosities, offering rare insight into inspiring local culture and Mediterranean beauty.

**ADDRESS**
AV. REI HUMBERTO II DE ITÀLIA, FAROL
NO. 7
2750-461 CASCAIS
PORTUGAL

**WWW.DESIGNHOTELS.COM/
FAROL**

**ROOMS**
33

**RATES**
EUR 110 –
EUR 480

**OPEN**
05/2002

**PORTUGAL**
CASCAIS

# FAROL
# DESIGN HOTEL
## *Cascais*
### ---

Mounted on the rocky shoreline of Portugal's Estoril Coast, Farol Design Hotel overlooks the sparkling waters and delightful fishing boats of the local marina. The hotel is set in the Count of Cabral's 19th-century mansion, with a daring architectural extension in 2002 by CM Dias Arquitectos. Fully renovated in 2008, the interior surroundings are now in ever-so-cool black and white, with sumptuous accents hinting at the building's regal history. Nine of the 33 guestrooms have been "dressed for bliss" by acclaimed Portuguese fashion designers in the revamp. Endless ocean views also amaze; the entire structure has been designed to blur the boundaries between the building and its stunning natural surroundings. Aquatic retreats are integrated throughout the property, including hydro-massage bathtubs in each of the rooms. Guests will find it hard to leave the terrace garden, complete with saltwater pool and exquisite deckchairs that evoke the distinct impression of floating on water. Visitors can relax with a creative house cocktail at the On the Rocks bar. Or head to The Mix restaurant, which comprises three distinct dining areas that flow gracefully into one another and extend towards the sandy beach. Bliss is guaranteed.

# FIRST HOTEL
# GRIMS GRENKA
## *Oslo*

---

Devotees of an organic kind of chic will appreciate the traditionally Norwegian touches artfully woven into the luxurious and sensual atmosphere of Oslo's Grims Grenka hotel. Here, tactile stone, wood and leather are paired with folk art, lamps made from reindeer antlers and a moss garden embedded in the reception desk. Ancient Norwegian wooden stave churches are the inspiration for the long, continuous walnut panelling running throughout the space. But an ultramodern twist comes from integrated lighting, which varies according to the time of day and season, and privat niches into which guests can tuck themselves at the bars. This fascinating sensitivity to season extends to the 42 rooms and 24 suites, where guests can choose their own time of year: Summer rooms are done in green and black tones with natural oak, and Winter rooms are blue, white and grey in combination with a darker, warmer oak. Throughout, one finds the joyful sense of organic harmony, which appeals to fashion-forward travellers seeking timeless Norwegian elan.

WWW.DESIGNHOTELS.COM /
GRIMSGRENKA

ADDRESS
KONGENS GATE 5
0153 OSLO
NORWAY

ROOMS
66

RATES
NOK 1900 –
NOK 7000

OPEN
03/2008

NORWAY
OSLO

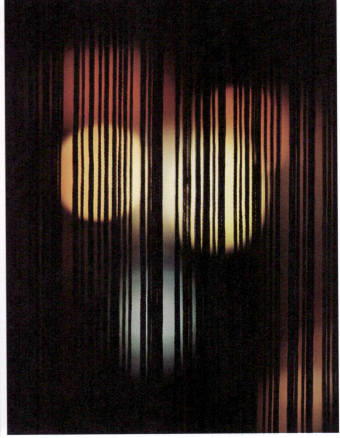

WWW.DESIGNHOTELS.COM /
SKTPETRI

ADDRESS
KRYSTALGADE 22
DK 1172 COPENHAGEN
DENMARK

ROOMS
268

RATES
DKK 1195 –
DKK 21000

OPEN
07/2003

DENMARK
COPENHAGEN

# FIRST HOTEL
# SKT. PETRI
## *Copenhagen*

---

Situated on a beautiful street in Copenhagen's quaint, trendy Latin Quarter, the First Hotel Skt. Petri is a fine example of minimalist Scandinavian design – with a warm welcoming glow. Escalators that glide up to the sexy, light-filled lobby offer the first of many quirky experiences created by Danish design studio Erik Møllers Tegnestue at the Skt. Petri – a renovated 1930s department store named after the famous church nearby. The mezzanine lobby is filled with clean lines and curves, and the glamourous large rings of light hanging overhead crown the soaring space. The lobby restaurant is open in summer to a soothing courtyard garden; the lobby also showcases the elegant nightspot Bar Rouge, one of Copenhagen's most exclusive lounges. One of Denmark's leading visual artists, Per Arnoldi, selected a tricolour scheme for both public and private spaces: bright whites contrasting with his signature cool blues and vivid reds adorn the hotel's interiors down to the smallest accessory. This kind of attention to detail is also evident in impeccable, personal service that makes the 268-room hotel feel much smaller. The First Hotel Skt. Petri is all about modern comfort and magnificent to-the-point functionality.

NETHERLANDS
ANTILLES
CURAÇAO

OPEN
08/2001

RATES
USD 150 –
USD 450

ROOMS
72

ADDRESS
PISCADERA BAY
CURAÇAO
NETHERLANDS ANTILLES

WWW.DESIGNHOTELS.COM /
FLORISSUITE

# FLORIS SUITE HOTEL
## *Curaçao*

---

This all-suite hotel is a reflection of Curaçao's unique cultural heritage: its mix of Dutch colonial design and traditional West Indian elements magnificently befits the location's history as the most important of the Dutch Antilles islands. The property's 72 Junior Suites, Royal Suites, Lofts and Imperials represent a modern translation of classic Caribbean comfort, featuring cool, subtle tones and custom-made neocolonial furniture. Each comes equipped with a private patio, where guests can enjoy al fresco breakfasts in the shade of elegantly arched roofs. The compound is enveloped by a splendid tropical garden full of meandering pathways that eventually lead to the hotel's focal point, the swimming pool and lounge area. Arranged like a Caribbean version of a Roman bath, the pool is comprised of several interconnecting squares of Bisazza glass mosaics in various colours. Guests feel like they've landed in an ambrosial playground, the perfect place to relax, tan, swim or enjoy the offerings of the poolside bar and open-air restaurant. Those in search of the kind of refreshing experience that only the open sea can provide can head to the hotel's on-site dive headquarters and private beach – which, incidentally, is one of the most sought-after on Curaçao.

ADDRESS
RUA ENGENHEIRO
VIEIRA DA SILVA, 2
1050-105 LISBON
PORTUGAL

ROOMS
139

RATES
EUR 100 –
EUR 535

OPEN
12/2007

PORTUGAL
LISBON

# FONTANA
# PARK HOTEL
## *Lisbon*

---

Constructed as part of a project focused on refashioning old buildings, the Fontana Park Hotel gives a modern makeover to a century-old iron factory, marvellously perched on a hill overlooking Lisbon's old city. But while the building may be historical, the interior is as contemporary as can be. This thrilling contrast comes thanks to award-winning designer Nini Andrade Silva, who injected her soulful personality and signature brand of funky minimalism (which she terms "ninimalist") into Portuguese architect Francisco Aires Mateus's strong modernist space. Guests can curl up in their simple and unfussy rooms and feel comforted by the clarity of a black and white design palette but also invigorated by the occasional flashes of green. Even the bathrooms emanate haute design. Here, guests can relax in an illuminated bathtub after dining at the hotel's upscale all-white seafood restaurant Saldanha Mar or lounge with Japanese fare in the chic boîte spot Bonsai, where imperial purple rugs and inset lighting highlight the century-old tree on view. With black bar stools, a black lacquer counter and enormous lit images of natural elements by Dutch photographer Alma Mollemans, guests will surely agree that "ninimalism" is evergreen.

WWW.DESIGNHOTELS.COM/
FRESHHOTEL

ADDRESS
26 SOFOKLEOUS &
KLISTHENOUS ST.
105 52 ATHENS
GREECE

ROOMS
133

RATES
EUR 140 –
EUR 390

OPEN
04/2004

GREECE
ATHENS

# FRESH HOTEL
*Athens*

---

The aptly named Fresh Hotel adds a candy-box kaleidoscope
of colour to an emerging industrial quarter in the Greek capital.
Deliciously designed by Tassos Zeppos, Eleni Georgiadi and ther
associates, the nine-storey property provides a cool sanctuary from
the flurry of downtown Athens just outside. The flagship of state-of-
the-art design boldly mixes splashes of bright pink and orange with
rich natural materials like oak and walnut. The reception is housed in
an attractive pink glass box in a soaring lobby, giving visitors a taste
of the funky feel to come upstairs. The 133 guestrooms, six with private
gardens, are sleek, modernist temples to purity of form; wild bathrooms feature brightly coloured light boxes, translucent screens and
mosaic flooring. Visuals aside, even the most demanding guests have
ample opportunity to tend to wellness of both body and soul with
exquisite fitness and spa areas. And the very fresh breakfast buffet
has earned its own reputation. At the end of the day, the Air Lounge
Roof Bar invites you to chill out next to the pool with the Acropolis
directly in view. The brand-new Imperia Ice Club, with live DJs and
30 tons of ice, definitely cools things off when Athens gets hot.

WWW.DESIGNHOTELS.COM /
GASTWERK

ADDRESS
BEIM ALTEN GASWERK 3
22761 HAMBURG
GERMANY

ROOMS
141

RATES
EUR 136 –
EUR 340

OPEN
01/2005

GERMANY
HAMBURG

# GASTWERK HOTEL HAMBURG
## *Hamburg*

---

Seasoned hotelier Kai Hollmann makes turning Hamburg's 19th-century municipal gasworks (or *Gaswerk*) into Europe's first loft-style hotel look as easy as dropping a "t" into its name, instantly transforming the red-brick complex into a "guest works." Natural light floods the atrium lobby's heights through two enormous arched windows, and a gigantic green industrial machine and old tower clock serve as reminders of the building's days as a power station. Suspended overhead is a bridge leading to the white modern elements housing the guestrooms, where interior designers Regine Schwethelm and Sybille von Heyden have created an ambience combining modern functionality with original features and materials like carved stone and Asian wood. Oversized chairs, light neutrals and soothing textures soften the rough industrial structure, giving its once purely functional form new life. Guests can kick back in comfy rooms with exposed brick walls and arched multipane windows; then head down to business meetings in ultramodern conference rooms (five of them!) or the buzz of the low-lit bar, which is just as popular with locals as with visitors.

**WWW.DESIGNHOTELS.COM / GERBERMÜHLE**

**ADDRESS** GERBERMÜHLSTRASSE 105 60594 FRANKFURT AM MAIN GERMANY

**ROOMS** 18

**RATES** EUR 140 – EUR 600

**OPEN** 07/2007

**GERMANY** FRANKFURT AM MAIN

# GERBERMÜHLE
## *Frankfurt am Main*
---

Here, on the banks of the Main River, is where German author Johann Wolfgang von Goethe met Marianne von Willemer, the love of his life. Interspersing cosy architecture with sleek modernity, the Gerbermühle is also a kind of amorous alliance between medieval and contemporary Frankfurt. Originally a flour mill built in the 1520s, the property contrasts masculine elements, like exposed beams and mezzanines, with ultramodern feminine magenta lighting in charmingly rustic stairwells. Then there are the dashes of trendy design, like the full-size horse lamp in the lobby. The café's lodge-like atmosphere, complete with antlers on the wall and old-fashioned light fixtures, makes it the ultimate place to sip regional apple wine, while the modern guestrooms and bedroom suites evoke the best of European hospitality with handsome leather furniture and glossy parquet floors. The old-world-meets-new atmosphere continues outdoors: along the River Main is a lovely 500-seat summer garden that's long been a favourite place for locals. Yes, it was near this embankment that Goethe met Willemer in 1814. This elegant 18-room hotel carries on the literary legacy on the outskirts of what is now Germany's financial capital.

WWW.DESIGNHOTELS.COM / GRANADOS83

ADDRESS
ENRIC GRANADOS, 83
08008 BARCELONA
SPAIN

ROOMS
77

RATES
EUR 215 –
EUR 560

OPEN
03/2006

SPAIN
BARCELONA

# GRANADOS 83
*Barcelona*

———

A unique experience in remixed neoclassicism, built on the site of Barcelona's venerable Pujol i Brull clinic, Granados 83 brings an entirely modern concept of luxury to a notable old-city location. Constructed around a luminous central courtyard crowned by a glass ceiling, it's a building that looks just as good in real life as it does in pictures. Original colonnades are enhanced by steel, red marble, glass and iron, but the lobby's also dotted with antiques and art objects. The soothing atmosphere and low, social buzz give guests a sense of constant, languid movement; friendly, generous service ensures they're absolutely comfortable not only in public spaces but also in the 77 loft-style guestrooms. Here, Asian pieces of art soften the high-tech facilities and ultramodern materials, while there's a literal Asian flavour in the restaurant "3." Extensive use of white Thassos marble and zebrawood as well as phosphorescent iron pieces adds chic throughout; raw leather inserts on headboards and chairs lend a wonderful warmth. It's a textural mix that's as inspiring and soothing as everything else in this smart urban getaway.

**SPAIN**
BARCELONA

**OPEN**
01/2008

**RATES**
EUR 190 –
EUR 450

**ROOMS**
147

**ADDRESS**
VIA LAIETANA, 30
08003 BARCELONA
SPAIN

WWW.DESIGNHOTELS.COM /
GRANDCENTRAL

# GRAND HOTEL CENTRAL
## *Barcelona*

---

The elegant façade and stylish architecture of Grand Hotel Central offer guests a flavour of those times when the needs and pleasures of travel and trade saw the appearance of "grand hotels" in cities around world. But today, the property is a minimalist-meets-historical, savvy-meets-sexy retreat near Barcelona's Born district. Carrying the signature of two architects who worked 85 years apart (Adolph Forensa designed the original 1924 building; Oriol Tintoré created its contemporary look), the hotel is built around a diaphanous central patio, with a lobby laid out largely in its original format – a kind of blast from the past to remind guests of the hotel's former function as an office building. A library and living rooms provide common space and break up the typical hegemony of rooms and corridors. The interior design stresses urban modernity with cool, natural materials, while all guestrooms have large windows offering street views of Europe's best-preserved medieval quarter. Bedroom and bath merge, creating a flowing sense of space enhanced by subtle sconce lighting. To crown it all, guests can stretch out beside the fabulous rooftop infinity pool, one of the most spectacular in the Catalan capital.

WWW.DESIGNHOTELS.COM / HILLSIDESU

ADDRESS
KONYAALTI
07050 ANTALYA
TURKEY

ROOMS
294

RATES
EUR 200 –
EUR 900

OPEN
05/2003

TURKEY
ANTALYA

# HILLSIDE SU HOTEL
*Antalya*

---

On a green bank overlooking the Mediterranean, Hillside Su Hotel is a clean white stage on which guests are invited to play out Turkish designer Eren Talu's seductive disco dream – at a breezy pace and to the soft beats of ambient music. White is the colour of choice, but Talu breaks up its monotony with a dazzling light display that begins the moment guests enter the reception area. Six huge disco balls hang in the six-floor atrium lobby. At dusk, they start to spin, launching a mesmerising and playful light show that sets the tone for exploration and inner freedom. On this stage neither designer furniture nor fixed settings play the leading roles but rather funky details that never cease to surprise. The catwalk-like lobby and the Iroko-wood deck of the expansive pool area both act as a socialising magnet, while the 294 guestrooms are sleek white cubes of calm. With a name derived from the Turkish word for water and providing endless surprises to the eyes, Hillside Su Hotel is a destination in its own right.

# HOPE STREET HOTEL
*Liverpool*

---

As confident and down-to-earth as the historic port city in which it is located, Hope Street Hotel brings a clean new style to one of Liverpool's most handsome quarters. It's also a perfect home base for culture vultures who love cosy indulgence. The landmark 1860 building, built in the style of a Venetian palazzo, was originally home to the London Carriage Works. Interior designer Basia Chlebik dramatically reinterpreted the space, using woods, stone and glass to complement original exposed brickwork, pitch pine beams and cast iron columns. This openness and transparency is also reflected in the warm, welcoming, yet always discreet hospitality of this proprietor-managed hotel. Guestrooms are individually decorated with bespoke furniture in maple, cherry and American black walnut, with floors in oak and beech. Guests can indulge in king-size beds covered in Egyptian linens and underfloor heating. A sculptural installation of triangular glass slices a vertical cut through the highly celebrated restaurant on the ground floor, The London Carriage Works, while expansive glazing affords guests a ringside seat for people-watching onto one of the city's most vibrant streets.

WWW.DESIGNHOTELS.COM /
HOTELCLARIS

ADDRESS
C/ PAU CLARIS, 150
08009 BARCELONA
SPAIN

ROOMS
120

RATES
EUR 235 –
EUR 1500

OPEN
02/1992

SPAIN
BARCELONA

# HOTEL CLARIS
## *Barcelona*

---

Part of Barcelona's renaissance as a centre for commerce and the arts, the Claris has been a beacon of outstanding design and luxury since 1992. Built 100 years earlier as the exterior of the Neoclassical Vedruna Palace, the façade was reworked by MBM Architects and incorporated into the hotel space. The lobby's alcove lighting and copper accents segue into elegant stair-rails that lead to a retro-cool rooftop pool with a view. The 120 guestrooms' modern, elegant lines soothe, while detailing in steel and copper subtly stimulates. No two rooms are alike: from furniture construction to the choice of marble and wood, everything has been traditionally handcrafted, and combinations of old and new come in to their own. More than 400 *objets d'art* are scattered throughout the building and rooms, and include a group of Indian and Burmese sculptures from the 5th to 13th centuries, more than 100 engravings commissioned by Napoleon in 1812, Turkish kilims, Roman and Carthaginian mosaics, and engravings by the Catalan artist Guinovart. It's all a feast for the eyes as well as food for the soul at one of the Catalan city's best addresses.

# HOTEL CRAM
## *Barcelona*

---

With its creative take on tradition and modernity, light and water, Hotel Cram is a soothing reflection of the vibrant seaside city that it inhabits. The 67-room hotel elegantly fuses a stately, historical exterior with a stylishly modern reconstruction, which wraps around a central cylinder. The public spaces make extensive use of light and water as elements of movement in an environment of sultry contrasting colours and black ceilings. Stepping in from the downtown bustle of Barcelona's Eixample district, guests can settle down into a dark modernist aesthetic with floor-to-ceiling curtains and sleek black couches. The Mareva lobby bar is a tranquil spot for a cocktail, while the Michelin-starred restaurant Gaig is a meeting ground for gastronomy and surprise, featuring Catalan cuisine from chef Carles Gaig. Each guestroom is different, but all are smoothly efficient, offering contrasts of dark and light, a cool, chromatically harmonious feel and adjustable lighting that allows guests to create their own individual atmospheres. In a new aesthetic play on light, the hotel even illuminates its revamped 1892 façade with the "prevailing emotion" of its guests as night falls.

**ADDRESS**
PIAZZA WALTHER
39100 BOLZANO
ITALY

**ROOMS**
33

**RATES**
EUR 180 –
EUR 360

**OPEN**
01/2000

**ITALY**
BOLZANO

# HOTEL GREIF
*Bolzano*

---

*Greif* is the German word for "griffin," the mythical creature with lion's body and eagle's wings, beak and talons. Just as the griffin combines diverse strengths, Hotel Greif fuses tradition with modernity, offering an exclusive setting from which to view and explore northern Italy's Dolomites. The main entrance expresses this marriage of historic and contemporary, with its sophisticated mix of original antique wooden features and transparent steel and glass. The 33 extraordinary guestrooms were individually designed by Viennese architect Boris Podrecca in collaboration with owner Franz Staffler, whose family has owned this property since 1816. Some are split-level lofts; some feature terraces and bay windows, others steam saunas or whirlpool baths; one even has a grand piano. All offer a feast for the senses, featuring the luxury of raw silk, walls covered in silver leaf, and fine examples of antique Biedermeier furniture. Each room also displays a specially commissioned artwork by a different artist, and even the bathrooms are lined with their own individual marble. The often-lauded warmhearted service is just as unique. To really get to know Hotel Greif, you'll need at least 33 nights … one for each room.

MEXICO
MEXICO CITY

OPEN
10/2000

RATES
USD 175 –
USD 425

ROOMS
36

ADDRESS
AV. PRESIDENTE MASARYK 201,
COL. POLANCO
MEXICO CITY 11560
MEXICO

WWW.DESIGNHOTELS.COM/
HABITA

# HOTEL HABITA
## *Mexico City*
---

Like an ice cube on a hot street corner, Mexico City's Habita exudes a paradoxically austere luxury at the heart of one of the world's most populous cities. In a complete makeover of the 1950s building, Mexican group TEN Arquitectos has encapsulated the 36-room hotel in frosted glass panels. The result is a sensational floating glass box suspended from the five-storey structure's facade, which mediates the views and provides a stylish privacy for the cosmopolitan jet set. Sandwiched between new and old façades are original balconies and newly designed corridors. Contemporary art is served by the inclusion of the metal Jan Hendrix mural hanging in the reception area. Guestroom space contains only a bed, Eames chairs and a cantilevered plane of glass serving as both desk and table; everything else is concealed behind a polished panelled wall – a spatial clarity that gives travellers peace of mind. Meanwhile the daylight from floor-to-ceiling glass windows and doors onto balconies is aesthetically matched by Artemide and Flos lamps. The ground-floor Mexican bistro and rooftop pool and bar offer radical refuelling and spectacular views after a day spent exploring the chic boutiques and tree-lined boulevards of the fashionable Polanco district.

WWW.DESIGNHOTELS.COM /
HABITAMONTERREY

ADDRESS
VASCONCELOS 150 OTE
SAN PEDRO
GARZA GARCIA 66220, MEXICO

ROOMS
39

RATES
USD 195 –
USD 975

OPEN
09/2008

MEXICO
MONTERREY

# HOTEL HABITA
# MONTERREY
## *Monterrey*

---

Why would a world traveller, a global nomad, an itinerant business person or just an aesthete want to check into the Habita Monterrey? Because it's the seventh property by Mexican hoteliers extraordinaire Grupo Habita – a group known for its style, energy, innovation and even intuition. Because the 39-room building is a curvilinear vision in clean, clear black and white – a true oasis in the desert and an homage to classic mid-century design. Because it's already a hopping nightlife and social hub in the northern Mexican city of Monterrey, the crossroads between the United States, Mexico and the world. Because the rooftop terrace, with two pools and a bar, has jaw-dropping 360-degree views of the mountainous surroundings and rests under a cool concrete canopy. Because guests here to get work done find not just wireless Internet, but also a computer, and even the peace and quiet to concentrate as they make deals and move mountains. Because service is five-star – and always cordial, never cold. Because chef Enrique Olvera's restaurant Lobby and a musical concept by Parisian DJ Monsieur X make eating and lounging here unforgettable. That's why.

WWW.DESIGNHOTELS.COM / HEALDSBURG

ADDRESS
25 MATHESON STREET
HEALDSBURG, CA 95448
UNITED STATES

ROOMS
55

RATES
USD 295 –
USD 820

OPEN
11/2001

UNITED STATES
HEALDSBURG

# HOTEL
# HEALDSBURG
*Healdsburg*

---

Located in the heart of California's North Sonoma wine country, Hotel Healdsburg stands on a historic town square, minutes away from some of the world's best vineyards. The three-storey stucco building's warm ambience invites guests to embrace the healthy local lifestyle. Light floods through French doors leading onto private balconies, and artfully landscaped garden paths cut across the well-kept grounds. A garden pool and spa offer everything in the way of serenity and relaxation, while an extensive bar provides a menu of inventive cocktails. The real highlight, though, is star chef Charlie Palmer's Dry Creek Kitchen restaurant, a celebration of fresh seasonal ingredients straight from the Healdsburg Farmer's Market, served either indoors or on a garden patio overlooking the historic plaza – usually with a bottle of exclusive local wine. Twice a week, the restaurant hosts complimentary tastings featuring local wineries, while live jazz plays in the hotel lobby, completing the picture of tranquil sophistication. Guestrooms display a bountiful mix of elements including teak furniture, hickory-pecan wood floors, Tibetan rugs, goose-down duvets and six-foot soaking tubs.

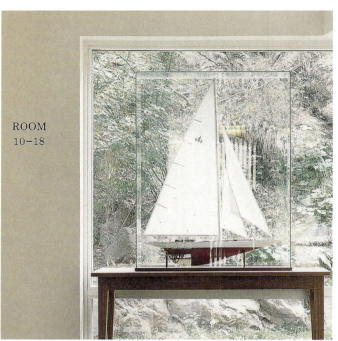

ROOM
10–18

ADDRESS
ELLENSVIKSVÄGEN 1
131 28 NACKA STRAND
STOCKHOLM
SWEDEN

ROOMS
45

RATES
SEK 1995 –
SEK 3495

OPEN
05/2000

SWEDEN
STOCKHOLM

# HOTEL J
## *Stockholm*

---

On the water's edge at Nacka Strand, Hotel J has its own 25-berth guest harbour and offers sweeping views of the Royal Djurgården park, the island of Lidingöand, and the boats on Saltsjön. The architects at Millimeter and designers at R.O.O.M. have transformed the 1912 brick building into a stylish shrine to seafaring – and an American one at that. The concept draws on the nautical design of historic America's Cup J–class boats and the distinct feel of the New England coast. The evocative red, white and blue of the Stars and Stripes invite visitors from across the Atlantic to feel completely at home. But guests from anywhere will appreciate the homey feel of white wood, cotton textiles and solid oak furniture. In the lobby, fireside seats afford wide-angle views of the islands near Stockholm, just 15 minutes' sailing time away. The 45 guestrooms, on the other hand, revel in natural materials and fine linens that evoke an authentic feeling of comfort and ease, just like on a private boat. The Restaurant J, perched out on the pier, satisfies the palate and rounds off the experience with modern international seafood.

CZECH REPUBLIC
PRAGUE

OPEN
06/2002

RATES
EUR 142 –
EUR 339

ROOMS
109

ADDRESS
RYBNA 20
110 00 PRAGUE 1
CZECH REPUBLIC

WWW.DESIGNHOTELS.COM/
JOSEF

# HOTEL JOSEF
## *Prague*

---

At the very heart of one of Europe's most beautiful medieval cities, Hotel Josef is a masterpiece of contemporary cool, with Eva Jiricna's award-winning design building on a great 20th-century tradition of modern Czech design. The 109-room hotel is formed of two buildings – the Pink and the Orange – centred around a peaceful landscaped courtyard that gives the hotel a chilled-out counterpoint to the active, urban lifestyle of Prague's Old Town. The reception and bar area is a stark, white modernist utopia, featuring clean lines, glossy surfaces and the high-tech steel and glass staircases for which Jiricna is famous. The restaurant's understated elegance has an instantly calming effect, with its floor-to-ceiling windows leading out to the Zen of the courtyard. Guestrooms are designed with a well-proportioned mix of efficiency and luxury that pervades the rest of the hotel, and are fully equipped with the latest communication technology. A business centre and gymnasium, along with a new sauna and massage room, complete the sophisticated environment of Hotel Josef, which has already become a major feature in Prague's growing business and tourist economy.

WWW.DESIGNHOTELS.COM/
LACOLUCCIA

ADDRESS
LOCALITÀ CONCA VERDE
07028 SANTA TERESA
GALLURA (SS), SARDINIA
ITALY

ROOMS
45

RATES
EUR 174 –
EUR 662

OPEN
06/2003

ITALY
SARDINIA

# HOTEL
# LA COLUCCIA
## *Sardinia*

---

In a spectacular coastal setting of pines, cypresses and craggy rock formations, Hotel La Coluccia's red wave-crested façade cuts a distinctive presence against the blazingly blue Sardinian skies. Just 50 metres from the beach, the dazzling complex takes advantage of its sea-sloping location to maximise exposure to the Mediterranean. A sail-shaped wall borders part of an open square in the hotel's centre, paved with local Orosei marble. A lattice-roofed walkway links the main services to some of the ground-floor rooms, while a romantic path leads to the sea through pines that shade the beachfront lawn – a stunning sea view can be enjoyed from the comfort of the sculpted swimming pool. Interiors fashionably mix modern and traditional materials ranging from polished cement and soft leather to rich, dark woods. Serious relaxation is to be had at the stylishly monochrome Space Comfort Zone, with its two massage rooms, Turkish bath, gym and relaxation area, but for guests who feel more active, Hotel La Coluccia also offers all the fun of the beach, with pedalos, rubber boats and excursions to the nearby Maddalena archipelago or Corsica. This is a place whose beauty offers a casual yet elegant respite from anything everyday.

# HOTEL OMM
## *Barcelona*

---

In Barcelona's posh Passeig de Gràcia district, Hotel Omm at first looks like the ultimate hot spot for international movers and shakers. But behind the sexy appearance is also a kind of smooth, effortless usability. Sections of the unusual limestone façade teasingly peel back like pages of a book, about to reveal the rooms inside. Yet what seems like decorative fantasy is actually functional: the angled windows shield guests from outside views and street noise, but allow direct sunlight to flood in. The spacious lobby cleverly flows into a sleek bar, then the restaurant Moo, with furnishings kept at a low, uniform height to allow guests to glide through just as freely; a full-service spa in an adjacent wing echoes the hotel's jet-set elegance. Interior designers Sandra Tarruella and Isabel López based their concept on simple lines, a balance of colours and volumes, and the use of natural materials, but chic surprises abound. Yes, the black rubber-lined corridors absorb sound, but with two tubes of light spanning their length, they also create a fantastically futuristic atmosphere. Guests pass through, enter their wide-open, light-filled rooms, and immediately feel the perfect marriage of form and function.

WWW.DESIGNHOTELS.COM/ HOTELOMM

ADDRESS ROSSELLÓ 265 08008 BARCELONA SPAIN

ROOMS 91

RATES EUR 215 – EUR 1300

OPEN 12/2003

SPAIN BARCELONA

ADDRESS
PODMANICZKY STREET 45.
1064 BUDAPEST
HUNGARY

ROOMS
70

RATES
EUR 150 –
EUR 300

OPEN
2009

HUNGARY
BUDAPEST

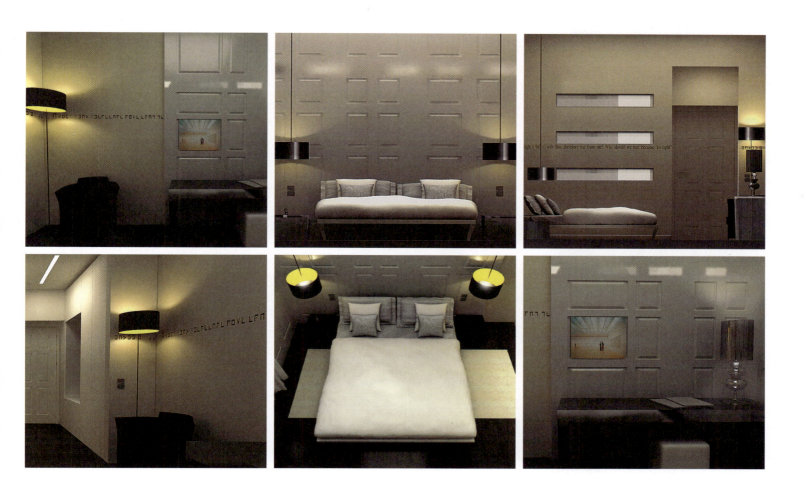

# HOTEL ROSSLYN
## *Budapest*
---

On the border between Budapest's historic centre and emerging business district stands an 18th-century stone building with an elaborately decorated façade. Once a Freemasons Grand Lodge, this turn-of-the-century edifice is now Hotel Rosslyn. Although the historic building was completely refurbished, many of its original features remain – from intricate ornamentation on the exterior to frescoes, arches and *seminato veneziano* flooring on the interior. Hotel Rosslyn thus exudes an antique look and feel, despite the revamp and high-tech creature comforts and amenities. Circulating the clean-lined yet cosy, trendy rooms is like stepping back in time to an old Masonic world of intimate camaraderie and esoteric ritual. The 70 guestrooms and suites also feature a pared-down design, and a single line of black writing wraps around each one, spelling out poetry in both English and Freemason symbols. This detail serves to enhance the hotel's intriguing historical atmosphere, which co-exists with the air of contemporary sophistication generated by modern spaces and minimalist fixtures. It's a perfect place for those travellers seeking just a little adventure, mystery and depth with a serving of modern elegance.

WWW.DESIGNHOTELS.COM/
HOTELSEZZ

ADDRESS
6 AVENUE FREMIET
75016 PARIS
FRANCE

ROOMS
27

RATES
EUR 285 –
EUR 720

OPEN
04/2005

FRANCE
PARIS

# HOTEL SEZZ
## *Paris*

---

Paris is known as a city for romance. But few locations typify Parisian charm as assuredly as the Hotel Sezz in the 16th arondissement. Away from the city's hustle and bustle, each guest in this striking, unconventional hotel enjoys the service of an unobtrusive but meticulously attentive personal butler, and is welcomed to taste Oriental delicacies in a breakfast room under a glorious glass dome. Designer Christophe Pillet, a protégé of celebrated stone and chrome devotee Philippe Starck, crafted the Sezz's minimalist aesthetic, with its defining virtues being spaciousness and privacy. Instead of an intimidating concierge desk looming in the hotel's entrance, two salons in muted colours greet guests as they arrive. Even the smallest room is vast for a city as cramped as Paris. This rare luxury only highlights the hotel's other delicate design treasures, such as austere khaki-grey stones from the Portuguese town of Cascais and a Parisian palette of slate, blue-grey and red leather, which Pillet uses generously throughout. With its quiet French chic and refinement, the Sezz will win even the most worldly guest's heart.

# HOTEL SKEPPSHOLMEN
## *Stockholm*

---

On the small, vibrant island of Skeppsholmen, attached by bridge to Stockholm's city center, Hotel Skeppsholmen resides in two long buildings that date back to 1699, when the "Long Row" was built to house Sweden's Royal Marines. Casually luxurious, ultramodern and historically protected, this pared-down property gives visitors to Stockholm a taste of the old, a twist of the new and a whole lot of charm. Ideal for both the active and culturally curious guest, the quaint yellow building is next door to the renowned Museum of Modern Art, the fascinating Swedish Museum of Architecture and the extensive Museum of Far Eastern Antiquities, as well as within walking distance of the area's gorgeous antique ships and waterfront restaurants. Fittingly, the artistic theme chosen by designer/architect trio Claesson Koivisto Rune for the hotel and its facilities is fog. The word aptly describes the hotel's soft color scheme, enchanting maritime surroundings and peaceful atmosphere which naturally lends itself to contemplation. Surrounded by white light and solid colors, many guests report Skeppsholmen's calming effects upon their senses, while Swedish natives view the islet itself as an urban oasis in the middle of their capital.

WWW.DESIGNHOTELS.COM /
HOTELSTPAUL

**ADDRESS**
355 RUE MCGILL
MONTREAL, QC H2Y 2E8
CANADA

**ROOMS**
120

**RATES**
CAD 199 –
CAD 299

**OPEN**
06/2001

**CANADA**
MONTREAL

# HOTEL ST. PAUL
## *Montreal*

---

Given that this ten-storey high-rise is often stylistically described as "muscular Beaux Arts," it comes as a surprise that the Hotel St. Paul's interior is so soft and ethereal. Located in one of Montreal's hippest quarters and housed in what was one of the city's first high-rises when it was built in 1900, the hotel artfully blends old and new. Several majestic details, such as a massive lobby fireplace now covered in a layer of translucent alabaster, reveal the property's rich history. But the rest has been charged with a contemporary flair that's long attracted the attention of design aficionados as well as travellers looking for urban elegance. Drawing inspiration from the Canadian landscape, guestrooms feature fire, ice, earth and sky as abstract metaphorical design themes that comfort and soothe guests in different ways: earth rooms are solid, grounded and tactile in their colours and textures, while sky rooms are atmospheric spaces imbued with light and air. Furnishings and accents in silk, stone and metal are consistently understated, while windows on each of the hotel's nine floors of guestrooms afford beautiful views of the skyline and Montreal's historic Old Port.

WWW.DESIGNHOTELS.COM /
URBAN

ADDRESS
CARRERA
DE SAN JERÓNIMO, 34
28014 MADRID
SPAIN

ROOMS
96

RATES
EUR 275 –
EUR 1500

OPEN
11/2004

SPAIN
MADRID

# HOTEL URBAN
## *Madrid*

---

In the cultural centre of Madrid on the Carrera de San Jerónimo, the Hotel Urban invites guests into a fusion of avant-garde design, art and technology behind a steel and glass facade. The very "urban" vision begins the second guests set foot in the property's door: they pass through a tubular atrium crafted in stainless steel and alabaster to a majestic reception area, panelled in black Zimbabwe stone with metallic seam finishes. But an alternative entrance – through the crystal floors, silver sofas and transparent tables of the popular Glass Bar – is inspiring in another way. In the Europa Decó restaurant, glass mosaics and walls covered in Brazilian rusted stone are a cosmopolitan backdrop for intelligent, convivial dining. Two transparent elevators whisk guests to 96 elegant rooms and suites. Each features a piece of ancient art – such as a 2,000-year-old Buddhist figure – as well as leather headboards, antique furniture and bathrooms separated by glass screens that can be moved at the touch of a button. Up on the roof, the pool and restaurant offer both spectacle and exclusivity, with views of the city and the sheltering Spanish sky.

WWW.DESIGNHOTELS.COM /
JERONIMOS8

ADDRESS
RUA DOS JERÓNIMOS, 8
1400-211 LISBON
PORTUGAL

ROOMS
65

RATES
EUR 150 –
EUR 300

OPEN
08/2007

PORTUGAL
LISBON

# JERÓNIMOS 8
## *Lisbon*
---

Just steps from the Tagus waterfront, Jerónimos 8 is a brilliant merging of the best of Portugal's past and present. Located in Lisbon's historic Belém district, the 1940s building has been reinvigorated by locally based architects Capinha Lopes and Associates. The revamp allows guests to experience the ornate gables, statues and reliefs of the nearby 16th-century Jerónimos Monastery while basking in a clean, urban-contemporary vibe. Windows in the wine bar peer out at the monastery and other historical buildings, so guests sipping from bottles of coveted Bussaco wines produced for generations by the hotel owners' family can reflect on the city's heritage while admiring the bar's rich savoury palette of red, white and brown. The Wenge wood reception desk stands before a crimson wall, and guests pass to their rooms through brightly lit corridors carpeted in alternating stripes of browns and reds. But despite the rooms' proximity to the monastery, they are anything but ascetic. Rather, they are snugly appointed in shades of chestnut, burnt sienna and cream. Each room has a pale marble bathroom generously bathed in natural light. Lustrous, dark chocolate hues can be sound everywhere throughout the artfully crafted public and private spaces.

WWW.DESIGNHOTELS.COM /
KEMANGICON

ADDRESS
JALAN KEMANG RAYA 1
JAKARTA 12730
INDONESIA

ROOMS
12

RATES
USD 225 –
USD 350

OPEN
01/2006

INDONESIA
JAKARTA

# KEMANG
# ICON BY ALILA
## *Jakarta*

---

Kemang is one of Jakarta's chicest neighbourhoods, bursting with art galleries, boutiques and upscale restaurants. At its heart is the Kemang Icon by Alila, an all-suite hotel that combines high-tech functionality with innovative design. This urban retreat, located in one of the world's busiest cities, contains eight Courtyard and four Edge suites, each individually designed to reflect the hotel's primary focus: personalisation. At the Icon, everyone knows your name before you even set foot through the door. In advance of arrival, guests choose everything from the type of pillow they would like to sleep on to the aromatherapy scents in their rooms. Bathrooms are equipped with personally chosen accessories and meals prepared to specific culinary tastes. High ceilings, wide-open spaces and large windows provide a peaceful backdrop for both leisure and business, work and play. Cultural sophistication is the name of the game in the hotel's public areas, which range from sunlit yoga studio to rooftop restaurant and infinity pool. Indeed, the hotel lobby is more art gallery than reception area, complete with a 1,000-year-old stone sculpture of Ganesh, two French mirrors from the sultan's palace at Surakarta and a painting by Indonesian master Srihadi Soedarsono.

WWW.DESIGNHOTELS.COM / KIRIMAYA

ADDRESS
1/3 MOO 6, THANARAT RD.
MOO-SI, PAKCHONG
NAKORN RATCHASIMA 30130, THAILAND

ROOMS
120

RATES
THB 9000 –
THB 33000

OPEN
12/2004

THAILAND
KHAO YAI

# KIRIMAYA
## GOLF RESORT SPA
### *Khao Yai*

---

Nestled on the edge of lush Khao Yai National Park, Kirimaya was designed by Februar Image Company, a Bangkok-based collective of architects, interior and landscape designers. More urban chic than tropical rustic, the two-storey property and spa, which extends across several outdoor and indoor pavilions, merges the local with the exotic. Organic gardens provide all the ingredients for the Acala Restaurant, modelled on a traditional northern Thai rice barn. Open on three sides, it seems to float on the on-site lake and boasts a panoramic view across the resort's challenging 18-hole golf course. Guests are gently led to the hotel's main residence through a romantic thatch-covered walkway and an exquisite antique carved door. Bamboo daybeds in the guestrooms are another example of the hotel's successful combination of Asian touches and innovative design, but it's the retreat's four Tented Villas that offer the epitome of luxury. With rugs created from water hyacinths and spaces sweetly separated by flowing curtains, these Tented Villas are utterly intimate. Even more romantic are the newly expanded Muthi Mayo Pool Villas, located nearby along a contour of cascading hills. Here, thoughtfully landscaped private infinity edge pools offer the utmost in tranquility.

**ADDRESS**
BULEVARDI 2-4
00120 HELSINKI
FINLAND

**ROOMS**
137

**RATES**
EUR 185 –
EUR 550

**OPEN**
11/2005

**FINLAND**
HELSINKI

# KLAUS K
*Helsinki*

———

Inspired by emotional contrasts and drama, Helsinki's Klaus K bears the stamp of Finland's finest architectural and literary traditions. A long-time landmark located in the late-19th century Rake building, the Klaus Kurki Hotel was transformed into the Klaus K, an intriguing property that brings Finland's national epic, the *Kalevala*, down to an intimate human scale. Each of the 137 guestrooms expresses a theme illustrating the *Kalevala*'s primary emotional elements – desire, passion, mystical and envy – in sumptuous details and rich textures. Likewise, an array of upscale food and drink opportunities range in style from modern and chic to comfortably casual, to suit guests' specific moods. Toscanini serves delicious flavors from Italy, and the restaurant Ilmatar, named after the "goddess of air", celebrates hyper-pure Finnish ingredients from around the country. Guests can have quick drink at the bar looking onto the street, settle into the champagne bar for a leisurely aperitif or get their nightlife fix at the in-house club. There's even a state-of-the-art event centre with a *fin-de-siècle* ballroom. Creating an ultra designed lifestyle experience where contrasts abound, the Klaus K takes the "hotel out of the hotel" and delivers a luxurious experience of tradition and cutting-edge Nordic modernity.

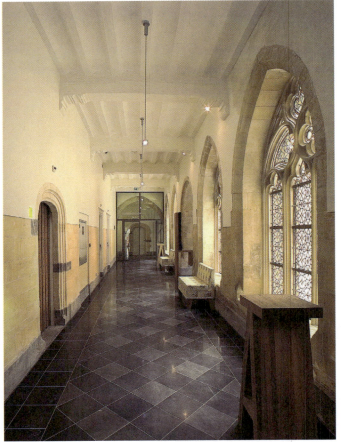
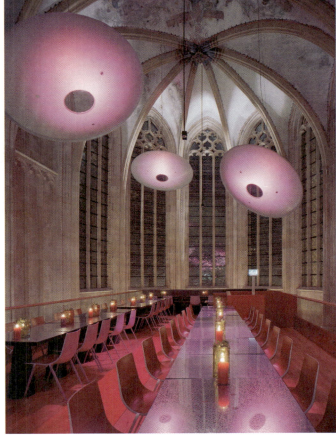

**WWW.DESIGNHOTELS.COM/ KRUISHEREN**

**ADDRESS**
KRUISHERENGANG 19-23
6211 NW MAASTRICHT
NETHERLANDS

**ROOMS**
60

**RATES**
EUR 380 –
EUR 470

**OPEN**
09/2005

**NETHERLANDS**
MAASTRICHT

# KRUISHERENHOTEL
# MAASTRICHT
## *Maastricht*

---

Located in the picturesque Kommelplein square in central Maastricht, the Kruisherenhotel is a remarkable renovation of a Gothic church and monastery, a tour de force synthesising original 15th-century architecture and dressed-down modernism. The church, dating from 1438, now houses the integrated reception area, conference rooms, a library, boutique and coffee bar. In the newly installed mezzanine restaurant, guests are served breakfast while taking in views of Maastricht through the chancel windows. It's also open every day for light lunches or dinner, when the chef presents a variety of culinary surprises. The monastery, once home to the Order of Crutched friars, now hosts most of the guestrooms; these feature original architectural elements and daring modern interventions by interior designer Henk Vos. The intimate wine bar, or "espace vinicole," is no less stunning both for its impressive offerings of wines and for the strikingly large glass vault that houses them. Surrounded by peaceful cloistered corridors, the monastery gardens are a sanctuary of etheral beauty, landscaped with dramatic modern forms. The overall result is a bold exercise in architectural juxtapositions, paying tribute to contemporary design while honouring age-old constructions and detailing.

WWW.DESIGNHOTELS.COM/
LAPURIFICADORA

ADDRESS
CALLEJÓN DE LA 10 NORTE 802
PASEO SAN FRANCISCO
BARRIO EL ALTO
PUEBLA 72000
MEXICO

ROOMS
26

RATES
USD 155 –
USD 399

OPEN
05/2007

MEXICO
PUEBLA

# LA PURIFICADORA
## *Puebla*

---

Located in the historic centre of Puebla, a colonial city on the road between Mexico City and Veracruz, La Purificadora is
the new incarnation of a late 19th-century factory long used to purify water for the production of ice. The tradition of purity
is still the guiding leitmotif at the minimalist yet modern and edgy hotel, the sixth by Mexico's trendsetting Grupo Habita.
The retention of many of the building's original elements – crumbling walls, stone aqueducts – lends an air of authenticity, while
modern additions like a glass-walled swimming pool and sleek purple lounge chairs create a clean, sophisticated ambience.
The resulting mix of new and old is truly stunning, nowhere more so than in the hotel's public spaces, which include a roof
terrace with lively bar, ground-floor patio, restaurant, library and wine cellar. Most of the hotel's 26 guestrooms – including
three suites with private whirlpools – offer spectacular views of the hotel gardens and the city centre beyond, a UNESCO World
Heritage Site. As would be expected of the innovative hoteliers at the Grupo Habita, La Purificadora offers travellers and locals
alike a comforting yet always stimulating experience, a melange of tradition and contemporary flavour in its purest form.

ADDRESS
PO BOX 1500
MORNE ROUGE
GRENADA

ROOMS
16

RATES
USD 415 –
USD 1550

OPEN
12/2000

GRENADA
WEST INDIES

# LALUNA
*West Indies*

---

Festooning a picturesque hillside of Grenada, Laluna stirs a tasty mélange of Caribbean, Balinese and Italian design elements to create a smart and utterly tropical hotel overlooking Portici Beach. Designed by Gabriella Giuntoli, who has built villas for Giorgio Armani and Sting, Laluna is a masterpiece on ten acres of untouched land in the West Indies. Surrounded by emerald hills, crystal waters and leafy bougainvillea-filled grounds, the hotel paints a perfect picture of Caribbean island getaway. Guests can relax at a secluded private beach, cool off in an idyllic pool or chill out at an open-air lounge – that is, if they want to leave their rooms. The 16 traditional, thatched-roof cottages feature a West Indian take on "concrete chic": local details round out a stunning aesthetic based on warm colours and breathtaking views. Each spacious cottage offers an open-air bathroom, an exquisite line of bath products made exclusively in a monastery in the Italian Alps and a king-size Balinese bed that opens onto an expansive bamboo-framed veranda with a plunge pool. As the sun sets, guests can lie on the silk-covered daybeds of these private decks and watch the silver moon, Laluna's namesake, rising in the cobalt sky.

WWW.DESIGNHOTELS.COM /
LANCHID

ADDRESS
LÁNCHÍD UTCA 19
1013 BUDAPEST
HUNGARY

ROOMS
48

RATES
EUR 83 –
EUR 377

OPEN
08/2007

HUNGARY
BUDAPEST

# LÁNCHÍD 19
## *Budapest*
---

Named after Budapest's famed Chain Bridge, which spans the Danube, and situated near both it and the Buda Royal Castle, the Lánchíd 19 has become a contemporary architectural landmark that attracts a new kind of cosmopolitan crowd. A remarkable moving glass façade glows with subtly changing light effects, and the lobby is equally dramatic; its ultra modern Bloomy chairs seem to float on a glass floor revealing ancient Medieval ruins below. Principles of flowing space and light dominate the experience of this stylish urban getaway, from the glass atrium towering above the foyer to the rooms' and suites' open-plan design. The feeling of openness and transparency is enhanced by the clear views from the lounge to the restaurant to the intimate garden beyond. The hotel's team of Hungarian architects also took every opportunity to exploit the potential for fantastic views over the city, which can be enjoyed from the suites' terraces or even from their deep bathtubs. The Lánchíd 19 is a beacon of innovation while still paying homage to its historical settings. A perfect point of departure for discovering Budapest's wonders.

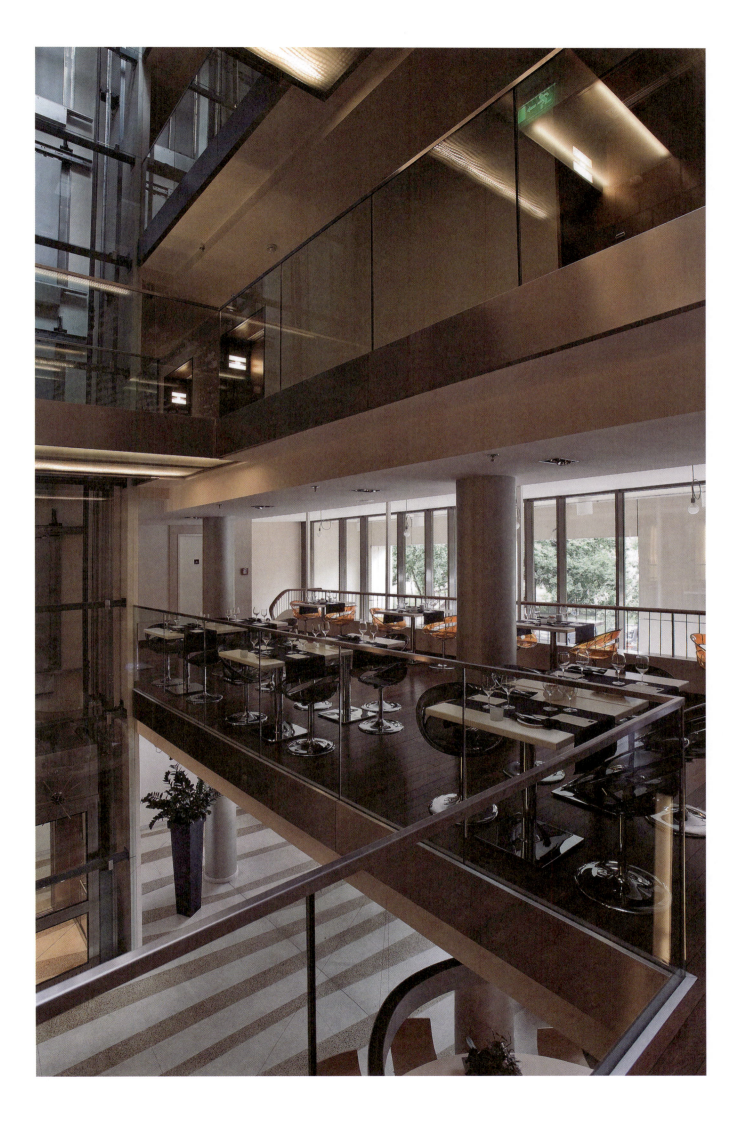

WWW.DESIGNHOTELS.COM/
LEONSPLACE

ADDRESS
VIA XX SETTEMBRE 90/94
00187 ROME
ITALY

ROOMS
56

RATES
EUR 190 –
EUR 515

OPEN
08/2008

ITALY
ROME

# LEON'S PLACE HOTEL
# IN ROME
## *Rome*

---

A short walk away from such famous Roman sights as the Via Veneto, Spanish Steps and Trevi Fountain, Leon's Place is the perfect home base from which to explore the Italian capital. Designed by Hotelphilosophy's creative director Alvin Grassi, this brand-new hotel has 56 guestrooms and spacious suites with luxurious French beds, marble bathrooms and tons of natural light. The rooms are elegantly thought-through and rather than distract guests with extra fluff, aim to provide them with a cool, clear enviroment in which they can fully unwind. Public areas are clean and contemporary as well, offering a respite from the wealth of visual information outside. Speaking of respite, wellness is a priority at Leon's Place, whose Wellness Centre features a sauna, steam bath and fitness centre staffed by specialists eager to pamper guests with facial treatments, body therapies and a range of massages. Both leisure and business travellers feel perfectly at home here, and might find themselves staying in to sample the international and Italian fine dining at Leon's Place Cocktail Bar & Restaurant, a culinary destination in itself.

WWW.DESIGNHOTELS.COM /
LIFEGALLERY

ADDRESS
103, THISSEOS AVENUE
14578 EKALI ATHENS
GREECE

ROOMS
29

RATES
EUR 200 –
EUR 1040

OPEN
03/2004

GREECE
ATHENS

# LIFE GALLERY ATHENS
## *Athens*
___

Gently tucked into lush grounds on the northern outskirts of Athens, the Life Gallery's elegant sea-green glass façade hints at an interior infused with Eastern influences and suburban Zen. The complex rambles across 3,200 square metres in Ekali, one of Athens's most sophisticated suburbs, with interior design that takes a slick and poppy slant on modernism. True to the hotel's name, public areas double as a refined gallery setting for local artists. The property's expansive landscaped gardens are dotted with mature pines and cedar trees, whose Mediterranean fragrances transport guests to a sensual paradise. The 29 spacious, open-plan guestrooms feature stone floors and bamboo details in a relaxing, muted colour scheme, providing a tranquillity that continues on the sundecks and in the transparent swimming pools outside. The impressive views of Mount Parnes and Mount Penteli offer a finishing touch of natural grandeur to complete the picture. Life Gallery Athens provides a mix of culture, nature and nurture that gives weekend and business travellers a new, relaxed take on the Greek capital, or even a new lease on life.

WWW.DESIGNHOTELS.COM /
LIFEMEDICINERESORT

ADDRESS
BRUNNENSTRASSE 31
8344 BAD GLEICHENBERG
AUSTRIA

ROOMS
110

RATES
EUR 111 –
EUR 149

OPEN
05/2008

AUSTRIA
BAD
GLEICHENBERG

# LIFE MEDICINE RESORT
## *Bad Gleichenberg*

———

In the rolling hills of the Styrian countryside near the Austrian city of Graz, a medical spa resort offers its guests a unique proposition that unites top preventive and therapeutic medicine, 170 years of spa tradition, and the full luxuries of a 21st-century architecturally discerning hotel. The innovative life medicine RESORT focuses not only on style, but also on *life* at its most vital. Along with an extensive thermal bath and a spa with healing waters, the resort's 110 well-appointed guestrooms and suites reflect a holistic philosophy implemented in natural stone, glass and wood by renowned Norwegian architectural team Jensen & Skodvin. In the lush 50-acre, 170-year-old heritage park, large terraces and relaxation areas connect guests with their surroundings and unify interior and exterior spaces. Health-conscious guests are in the best of hands at the medical facilities, with diagnostics, individual health programs and therapy treatments offered by more than 60 medical therapists and doctors. Here, clean Scandinavian architectural sophistication meets Austrian hospitality. The aesthetic is complemented by the regional and organic life medicine CUISINE: calorie-conscious, tasty gourmet meals in perfect synch with the property's healthful concept. Life medicine RESORT is a luxurious place to heal – or simply soothe – both body and soul.

WWW.DESIGNHOTELS.COM /
LUNA2

ADDRESS
JALAN SARINANDE 22
SEMINYAK, BALI, 80361
INDONESIA

ROOMS
5

RATES
USD 3000 –
USD 4000

OPEN
02/2007

INDONESIA
BALI

# LUNA2
# PRIVATE HOTEL
## *Bali*

---

Luna2 Private Hotel has touched down on the prime beachfront of Seminyak in Bali, making waves of its own with a retro-modernist design – which stands in stark contrast to the ubiquitous "modern Bali" style seen elsewhere. Named after the first spacecraft to reach the moon in the late 1950s, the Richard Neutra-inspired architecture is the launch pad for owner and interior designer Melanie Hall's James Bond-esque interiors – a feast of funky sixties inspired custom designed furnishings, paired with nostalgic design classics and 21st-century innovation. Extravagant to the last detail, Bisazza mosaics are featured throughout, even at the base of the 20-metre pool where Marilyn Monroe lies forever young in her renowned white dress. With just five bedrooms, Luna2 boasts supernaturally good service within the privacy of a home. Inherent to the property's success and at its helm is General Manager and Executive Chef Danny Drinkwater, with no less than 23 staff members to cater to each guest's every whim. It's quite simply a dining and quaffing pleasure dome with "lunafood" that's out of this world. The ultimate destination for culturally savvy, discerning singles, couples or groups, with or without kids, Luna2 defines new heights of playing, dining, sleeping and relaxing.

**WWW.DESIGNHOTELS.COM/**
**MAURITZHOF**

**ADDRESS**
EISENBAHNSTRASSE 17
48143 MÜNSTER
GERMANY

**ROOMS**
39

**RATES**
EUR 103 –
EUR 242

**OPEN**
10/2003

**GERMANY**
MÜNSTER

# MAURITZHOF
# HOTEL MÜNSTER
## *Münster*

---

Just a few steps from the historic town centre in the heart of Münster is an inviting red-brick building with a four-metre-high ultramodern, glass-and-steel construction at its base. Bathed in natural light, Mauritzhof Hotel Münster's revamped entrance serves as a transparent channel to a cool lobby and bar and creates an arena for conversation and interaction among guests and even locals. The design is stylishly practical down to the last detail; the service promises to never say no. A library and garden terrace offer guests a sheltered work environment, a small meeting place or simply an attractive location to unwind in style. Spacious, individually designed rooms and suites feature not only star-designer furniture but also high-grade natural woods and a palette of harmonious colours to calm and soothe. With its distinctly urban brand of chic in a small northwestern German city known for its university lifestyle, bicycle culture and beautiful parks, the Mauritzhof provides a cheerful, friendly ambience with all the advantages of a world-class business travel hotel.

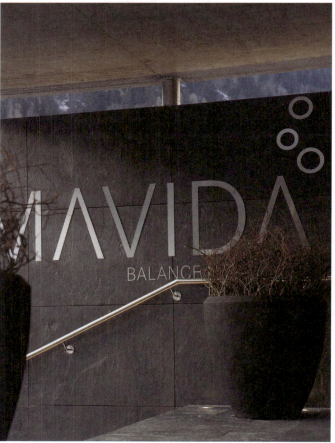

WWW.DESIGNHOTELS.COM/
MAVIDA

ADDRESS
KIRCHENWEG 11
5700 ZELL AM SEE
AUSTRIA

ROOMS
47

RATES
EUR 105 –
EUR 740

OPEN
2009

AUSTRIA
ZELL AM SEE

# MAVIDA
# BALANCE HOTEL & SPA
## *Zell am See*
---

With its holistic concept of "flowing privacy," the MAVIDA Balance Hotel & Spa offers guests a soothing and homogenous space that always places the individual at the centre. Located in the splendid mountain landscape near Austria's Lake Zell and affording views of snow-capped Alpine peaks, the MAVIDA is *the* destination for wellness and recuperation. Its inviting, understated modern design not only generates an atmosphere of relaxing elegance, but is sensitively implemented to promote inner balance. The 47 unusually large guestrooms are in soothing natural wood and stone, but the real peace can be found in the stunning state-of-the-art spa. Here massive blocks of slate create a dramatic backdrop for ultimate relaxation in a wide array of treatments and services: recharge in one of many saunas, relax in the floatarium, rejuvenate in a "blue box" with special light and sound techniques, or refresh near the new 25-metre outdoor pool. If you're feeling particularly invigorated and energised, the surrounding mountains, reaching altitudes of 2,700 metres, eagerly await you. Then walk to the resort's private lakeside beach, watch the sun set over the glassy water, and experience a sublime natural calm. Time, space and peace are today's truest luxuries, after all.

# MEMMO
# BALEEIRA HOTEL
## *Algarve*
---

Flanked by the pristine beaches and ragged red sandstone cliffs of the Algarve peninsula, Memmo Baleeira Hotel rests on the south-western-most tip of Portugal – and Europe – in the Costa Vicentina Natural Park in Sagres (a place known to the ancient Romans as "the end of the world where the waters of the ocean boil at sunset"). First opened in 1962, the hotel's recent make-over preserves the original architecture's clean lines while outfitting the interior with a comfortable minimalist décor that includes furnishings by Ron Arad as well as select vintage pieces that decorated the Baleeira in the 1960s. A Moorish colour palette of warm earth tones and brilliant whites complements relaxing views of lush greenery or sparkling ocean from the spacious balconies of the 144 rooms, suites and duplexes. Guests can take in the legendary Algarve light from the outdoor swimming pool and sunset massage beds, or unwind at the extensive spa with sauna, Turkish bath, heated indoor pool and gym. Children aren't left out of the equation either: professional caregivers lead educational, creative and outdoor activities at the kids club. Meanwhile, adult guests can confer with guides on windsurfing, scuba-diving and boat trips in the area's spectacular waters.

WWW.DESIGNHOTELS.COM/
MEMMOBALEEIRA

ADDRESS
SITIO DA BALEEIRA
8650-357 VILA DE SAGRES
PORTUGAL

ROOMS
144

RATES
EUR 75 –
EUR 380

OPEN
08/2007

PORTUGAL
ALGARVE

WWW.DESIGNHOTELS.COM/
METROPOLITANLONDON

ADDRESS
19 OLD PARK LANE
LONDON W1K 1LB
UNITED KINGDOM

ROOMS
150

RATES
GBP 375 –
GBP 3200

OPEN
02/1997

UNITED KINGDOM
LONDON

# METROPOLITAN LONDON
## *London*

---

The Metropolitan's unassumingly inviting glass-front entrance belies the simple, bright elegance that interior designers Keith Hobbs and Linzi Coppick created on hotelier Christina Ong's mandate 11 years ago. Now, with Coppick's recent "soft refurbishment" solo update, the chocolate leather desks, polished concrete surfaces, voluptuously curved sofas and the lobby's strong lines convey a subtly sexy elegance, offering the perfect nudge toward informal business meetings or leisurely lounging. Flower-filled guestrooms in coffee and cream colours with a signature shade of rich plum tie together cosmopolitan multicultural influences, like a Japanese rock garden, Finnish blinds, Italian-made sofas and the employees' Emporio Armani uniforms. The newly flexible Lobby Lounge invites guests to nestle behind screens that Coppick designed for additional privacy. The Metropolitan's warmth might surprise those familiar with the exclusive aura surrounding the hotel's internationally acclaimed Nobu restaurant, members-only Met Bar and the spa, COMO Shambhala Urban Escape, where visitors can indulge in exquisite Eastern-inspired treatments. But the hotel's whimsical *objets d'art* and playful modernism are made to be appealingly accessible and friendly. It's a perfectly soothing haven amidst London's buzz.

WWW.DESIGNHOTELS.COM /
METROPOLITANBKK

ADDRESS
27 SOUTH SATHORN ROAD
TUNGMAHAMEK
SATHORN
10120 BANGKOK
THAILAND

ROOMS
171

RATES
USD 260 –
USD 2000

OPEN
10/2003

THAILAND
BANGKOK

# METROPOLITAN BANGKOK
## *Bangkok*
---

The Metropolitan Bangkok is located in the heart of the city's central business district, minutes away from the main shopping and nightlife areas. Tucked on a side street, it is set at a remove from the hustle and bustle of the busy Asian metropolis: an urban oasis, a peaceful retreat in a glittering city. It is the pinnacle of cosmopolitan sophistication, with a staff bedecked in Comme des Garçons, and impressive Asian antiques scattered throughout the premises. Like its sister hotel in London, The Metropolitan Bangkok features a Met Bar open only to guests and members that attracts a dynamic crowd of urbanites. And like London's Nobu, the hotel's main restaurant Cy'an is not just a place for guests to dine in fashionable privacy, but a gourmet destination in its own right. The 171 spacious guestrooms feature a mix of both Thai and European elements that create an international look with a comfortable local feel. The hotel's 1,200 square-metre spa, COMO Shambhala Urban Escape, completes the picture of Bangkok luxury; equipped with ten treatment rooms, hydro pools, steam rooms, a yoga studio and a gym, it meets every wellness and rejuvenation need. The organic restaurant Glow serves fresh foods in a healthy, feel-good environment.

**WWW.DESIGNHOTELS.COM/ MIRO**

**ADDRESS** ALAMEDA MAZARREDO 77 BILBAO 48009 SPAIN

**ROOMS** 50

**RATES** EUR 89 – EUR 270

**OPEN** 10/2002

**SPAIN** BILBAO

# MIRÓ HOTEL
## *Bilbao*

---

Antonio Miró, Spain's answer to Donna Karan and Calvin Klein, transfers his elegantly understated mens- and womenswear aesthetic to an interior in which international sophisticates can meet and be mellow. In an area known for its artistic attractions, architect Carmen Abad Ibáñez de Matauco's dignified design holds court with the nearby spectacles of Bilbao's Guggenheim Museum and the Museum of Fine Arts. In addition to making its own strong style statement, the light-soaked, ten-storey white structure doubles as an inviting showcase space for the Miró Hotel's striking in-house contemporary art collection. At the popular Bar Miró, artistically discerning locals and guests can lounge in chrome metal chairs while admiring images by artists such as famed Spanish photographers Concha Prada and Marc Viaplana. It's a plethora of visual stimulation, but the hotel's real rewards are its 50 cleanly designed rooms, where the sleek décor is done largely in the palest beige, and flowing draperies, not walls, separate living from work areas. From inside their wall-size windows, guests can view the city's enticements, or simply retreat into their private cocoons by drawing the curtain.

WWW.DESIGNHOTELS.COM /
THEOXENIA

ADDRESS
84600 KATO MILI
MYKONOS
GREECE

ROOMS
52

RATES
EUR 158 –
EUR 705

OPEN
05/2009

GREECE
MYKONOS

# MYKONOS
# THEOXENIA
## *Mykonos*

---

A legendary classic of 1960s hotel architecture, the Mykonos Theoxenia has made a glamorous comeback: revamped in 2004, the 52-room property manages to harmoniously meld with Mykonos's radiant seascape as well as perfectly suit the Greek island's dynamic local nightlife culture. During the day, sun-worshippers can soak up golden rays on white Moroso beach chairs or luxuriate within curtained four-poster beds overlooking the Aegean Sea. Later, they can chill out amongst the cool stone details and crisp turquoise, lime, orange and bright white décor emblazoned in the interior of Aris Konstantinidis' iconic structure by designers Yiannis Tsimas and Angelos Angelopoulos. Their novel use of energetic colours renders the design experience as exciting and joyful as a bowl of ripe fruit; the rest of any guest's experience is in the expert hands of the relaxed spa, restaurant and service staff. The voluptuous curves of Patricia Urquiola's deep-blue Fjord barstools, the organic sensibility of stone pillars, and clean feel of beech period furniture evoke the relaxed elegance of mod-era jet-setter luxury. It's something the Mykonos Theoxenia exemplified in its first heyday and embodies once again.

WWW.DESIGNHOTELS.COM/
HOTELNERI

ADDRESS
SANT SEVER, 5
08002 BARCELONA
SPAIN

ROOMS
22

RATES
EUR 265 –
EUR 485

OPEN
07/2003

SPAIN
BARCELONA

# NERI HOTEL & RESTAURANTE
## *Barcelona*

---

Tucked into a narrow street in Barcelona's winding Gothic Quarter, between the Cathedral and Sant Jaume Square, the Neri H&R breathes romance the moment guests walk through the door. The 18th-century palace has been transformed into an airy and spacious three-storey property that offers a uniquely enveloping sensual experience. The lobby gently nudges the olfactory with fragrant candles and essential oils; the aromas of jasmine and orange blossom drift across a secluded roof terrace. Indirect light and soft music make for a soothing experience in the plush public spaces, and a generous central atrium leads guests to 22 rooms and suites that shimmer in tranquil tones dotted with subtle splashes of colour. Throughout the entire hotel, original artworks add dramatic visual diversions to the building's historical elements, rich velvet contrasts with rough-hewn wood, and antiques pair off with avant-garde accents. Even the restaurant's spicy Mediterranean offerings are inspired by the age-old ethnic diversity in this neighbourhood. Here is a place where time can delightfully and soothingly stand still, letting the senses take over.

# NORDIC LIGHT HOTEL
## *Stockholm*
---

Passing by Stockholm's Nordic Light Hotel at night, one can't help but observe the subtle, warm colours glowing from the understated façade's windows and wonder about the activities inside. Those who enter won't be disappointed by the welcoming world they encounter, enriched by hundreds of different light sources that vary in tone and intensity. Architect Rolf Löfvenberg and interior designers Lars Pihl and Jan Söder transformed the 1970s building into a modern design statement. With a black-and-white colour scheme dominating both the exterior and the sober cubist furniture within, these classical touches heighten the tapestry of light provided by lighting architect Kai Piippo and play off against Sweden's naturally radical transformative seasonal sunlight. In the lobby area, guests are treated to an atmosphere that expertly mixes the stimulating with the subdued: stalactite lights hanging from a recessed circle in the ceiling create ever-changing patterns of blue, orange and pink that splash onto the hotel's walls. These organic light shows continue throughout the Nordic Light's 175 rooms, where guests can play with the lighting to suit their own changing and certainly uplifted moods.

**WWW.DESIGNHOTELS.COM / NORDICLIGHT**

**ADDRESS**
VASAPLAN 7
101 37 STOCKHOLM
SWEDEN

**ROOMS**
175

**RATES**
SEK 1530 –
SEK 4300

**OPEN**
01/2001

**SWEDEN**
STOCKHOLM

WWW.DESIGNHOTELS.COM/
ONEHOTEL

ADDRESS
VIA DIODORO SICULO, 4
96100 SIRACUSA
ITALY

ROOMS
44

RATES
EUR 129 –
EUR 249

OPEN
05/2007

ITALY
SYRACUSE

# ONE HOTEL
*Syracuse*

---

Dramatically situated on the side of a cliff in Sicily and not far from the archaeological site of Syracuse, One Hotel may be set in ancient surroundings, but its design defines the urbane contemporary. Architect Mario Rizza managed to give the three-storey building an impression of both power and grace through a sculptural steel façade, which vaguely resembles a gilded cage. The guestrooms are all rigorously composed in black, white and grey for a sleek and ultramodern atmosphere. The executive room includes a balcony complete with its own mini Kyoto garden, and a large roof terrace provides space for public sun worshipping. Carved directly into the natural rock beneath the hotel is a hammam, sauna and hydrotherapy area for those in search of total serenity. The lobby's wave-like Aspen sofa is merely a prelude to the sushi bar and restaurant, where walls and benches are covered with jet-black crocodile leather. Black-on-black floral pattern wallpaper highlighted by mellow tinted lighting also endows One Hotel with a certain calm reflecting the retreat's appealing contrast of energising activity and peaceful reflection.

WWW.DESIGNHOTELS.COM /
BARBARIGO

ADDRESS
SAN POLO 2765
30125 VENICE
ITALY

ROOMS
18

RATES
EUR 160 –
EUR 520

OPEN
09/2007

ITALY
VENICE

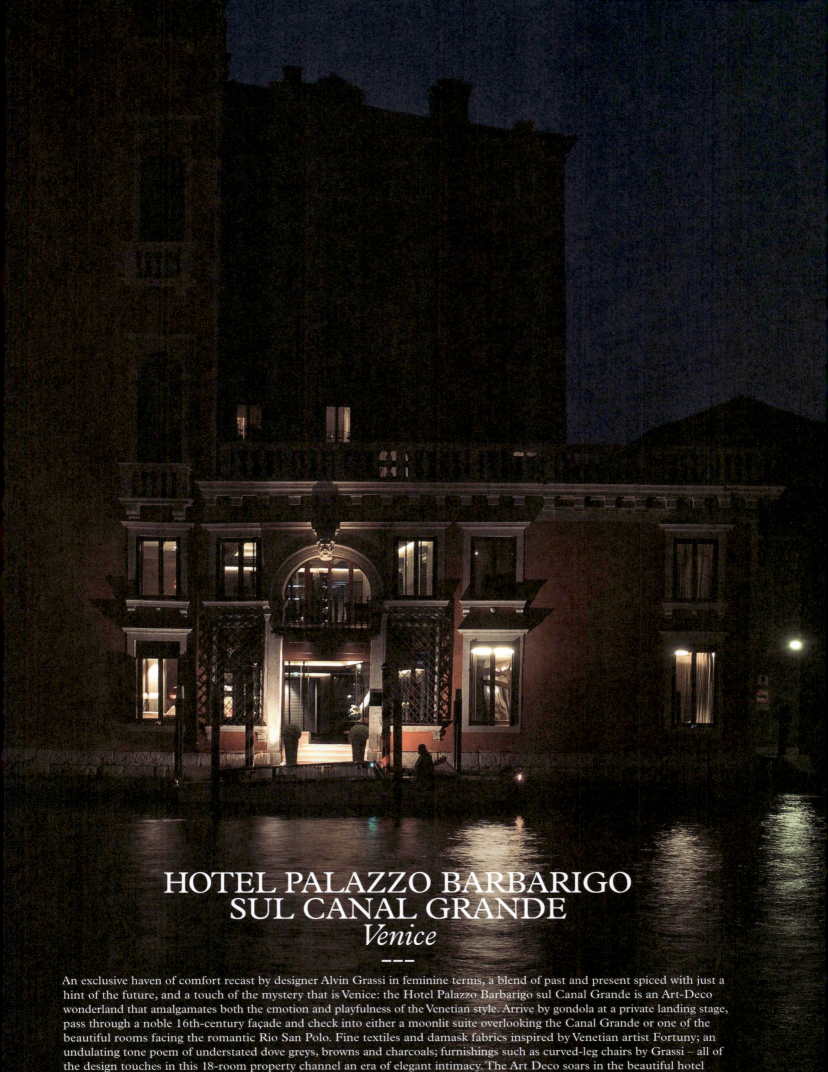

# HOTEL PALAZZO BARBARIGO
## SUL CANAL GRANDE
### *Venice*

---

An exclusive haven of comfort recast by designer Alvin Grassi in feminine terms, a blend of past and present spiced with just a hint of the future, and a touch of the mystery that is Venice: the Hotel Palazzo Barbarigo sul Canal Grande is an Art-Deco wonderland that amalgamates both the emotion and playfulness of the Venetian style. Arrive by gondola at a private landing stage, pass through a noble 16th-century façade and check into either a moonlit suite overlooking the Canal Grande or one of the beautiful rooms facing the romantic Rio San Polo. Fine textiles and damask fabrics inspired by Venetian artist Fortuny; an undulating tone poem of understated dove greys, browns and charcoals; furnishings such as curved-leg chairs by Grassi – all of the design touches in this 18-room property channel an era of elegant intimacy. The Art Deco soars in the beautiful hotel glass bar back-painted black, a space recalling this unique city's Golden Twenties. Like a 1940s film set, the hotel's luminous *mise en scène* is alluring, vibrant, and disarmingly regal.

JAPAN
TOKYO

OPEN
09/2003

RATES
JPY 21000 –
JPY 105000

ROOMS
273

ADDRESS
SHIODOME MEDIA TOWER
1-7-1 HIGASHI SHIMBASHI, MINATO-KU
TOKYO 105-7227, JAPAN

WWW.DESIGNHOTELS.COM/
PARKTOKYO

# PARK HOTEL TOKYO
## *Tokyo*

---

The sleek triangular skyscraper that French interior designer Frederic Thomas created for the Park Hotel Tokyo embraces downtown Tokyo's lively milieu without succumbing to its fast pace. Located in the Shiodome Media Tower, Park Hotel Tokyo is home to leading international media organizations and television companies. But the tower also offers an oasis of elegant living amidst the area's bustle and flow. While all of the guestrooms face outside, the curvaceous lines of the furniture, cloth-covered walls and soft, off-white colour scheme cushion guests from the city's distractions – just as custom-fitted pillows cushion necks, assuring a good night's sleep. Those who want to explore the city have a smooth transition from the hotel's sanctuary into the Waterfront Transit Station by way of low-level exits that lead directly to the heart of Tokyo. Inside the hotel, natural light that enters via a ten-storey atrium to illuminate the space is one of the business district's wonders. Equally as attractive is the soothing haven of sunlit trees and greenery trees planted on the obsidian and teak lobby floor to embody Japan's cultural tradition of incorporating nature into even the most forward thinking man-made marvels.

WWW.DESIGNHOTELS.COM /
ROCKSRESORT

ADDRESS
C/O WEISSE ARENA GASTRO AG
7032 LAAX
SWITZERLAND

ROOMS
85

RATES
CHF 90 –
CHF 517

OPEN
12/2008

SWITZERLAN
LAAX

# ROCKSRESORT
## *Laax*

---

The Swiss canton of Grisons contains some of the country's (and the world's) best skiing and freestyling. And now it's host to a resort to attract design aficionados as well: rocksresort. As the name implies, the property's façade is rough stone that refers to the surrounding landscape and rock formations. The complex's eight buildings are disarmingly simple cube forms: some are arranged around a central square at the bottom of a ski slope, while others cuddle up to the edge of a nearby forest. Domenig Architects, authors of outstanding projects in the area, have thus created a multi-use complex that defies categorisation and standardisation: the outbuildings contain different guestroom and apartment styles, the latter in two- to four-bedroom layouts. Within cubic interiors, bedrooms feature untreated wood, limestone and light-finished wood along with complementary textiles, creating an elegant, intimate ambience. The use of regional natural materials reflects the developers' vision of a resort that is as sustainable as possible – all construction meets current Swiss minimum energy standards. Built on a town-square model, restaurants and shops give the complex a life of its own. Here, guests can feel both earthy and progressive in a ski-land getaway that calms the mind and spirit.

GERMANY
FRANKFURT
AM MAIN

OPEN
2009

RATES
EUR 170 –
EUR 700

ROOMS
117

ADDRESS
GUTLEUTSTRASSE 85
60329 FRANKFURT AM MAIN
GERMANY

WWW.DESIGNHOTELS.COM/
ROOMERS

# ROOMERS
## *Frankfurt am Main*

---

Classic curves meet progressive design at Roomers, an ambitious new venture in Germany's business capital. With its gleaming glass façade set in specially glazed white concrete, Roomers offers a glossy snapshot into the city it inhabits: all timeless charm and modern architecture. Conceptualised by architectural firm Grübel and designer Oana Rosen (known for her work at The Pure and Gerbermühle), Roomers is an elegantly futuristic five-storey hotel full of electrifying design flourishes, such as an illuminated bubble-domed wellness centre on the rooftop designed by 3deluxe-biorhythm. Once an office building, Roomers has morphed into a cosy space full of swirling dark colours. Guests enter the lobby and are transported into a world of posh luxury – the bar will be Frankfurt's first members-only establishment. The 117 guestrooms' interior design is both indulgent and minimalist, two seemingly contradictory concepts that meet to superb effect. Three conference areas in Roomers' illuminated top level are kitted out with the chicest accoutrements, making them the ultimate business experience for up to 80 people. Just minutes away from the river Main, visitors are hard pressed to find a better backdrop to relax and indulge in Frankfurt.

WWW.DESIGNHOTELS.COM / ROSASANDXOCOLATE

ADDRESS
CALLE 56-A #480 X 41,
COL. CENTRO
MERIDA, 97000 YUCATÁN
MEXICO

ROOMS
17

RATES
USD 255 –
USD 875

OPEN
03/2009

MEXICO
MERIDA

# ROSAS & XOCOLATE
## *Merida*

---

Rosas & Xocolate, named after the two most popular lovers' gift items, is designed for guests who take romance seriously. Located in Merida, the capital of the state of Yucatán in Mexico, the all-natural boutique hotel lies in the resource-rich area where long ago, the Mayan civilisation first discovered cocoa and offered it up to their gods. Once made up of two colonial mansions, the haute-pueblo building was designed and restored by architect Salvador Reyes Rios and his partner Josefina Larrain. The duo perfectly melded the rustic elegance of the historic mansions with modern accoutrements like state-of-the-art entertainment systems and dazzling open-sky bathtubs for guests who desire the utmost in under-the-stars indulgence. Upping the romance factor, fresh-cut roses have been placed liberally throughout the 17 rooms and suites, and chocolate-based spa treatments and sweet-smelling amenities have been lovingly engineered by master chocolatier Mathieu Brees, who runs an in-hotel Belgian-Mexican fine chocolates boutique. With its prime location on the prestigious Avenue Paseo de Montejo and stylish use of local materials such as hand-fabricated cement tiles and chucum stucco, Rosas & Xocolate offers guests all the old-world charm of the Yucatán Peninsula – but infused with irresistable contemporary romance.

WWW.DESIGNHOTELS.COM /
PALMBEACH

ADDRESS
AVENIDA DEL OASIS S/N
35100 MASPALOMAS
GRAN CANARIA

ROOMS
328

RATES
EUR 98 –
EUR 344

OPEN
10/2002

SPAIN
GRAN CANARIA

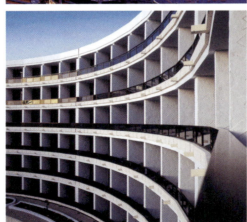

# SEASIDE HOTEL
# PALM BEACH
## *Gran Canaria*

—

Alberto Pinto's redesign of the classic 1970s Palm Beach is much more than the usual superimposition of a new identity onto an old structure. Pinto clarified original design elements, resulting in an award-winning late-modernist statement that appeals to savvy world travellers and design aficionados alike. Located in an ancient palm grove, the Miami Beach-inspired façade curves into a flowing interior and exterior space. Turquoise mosaic pools and public spaces in a muted palette enhance the primal experience of sun and shade. Bold Pucci-style patterns are reinterpreted in an array of textures, and materials such as chrome, mirrored glass, travertine and marble add a touch of old-school elegance throughout. The 328 rooms offer guests a deliciously decadent slice of seaside glamour. Walls are bathed in warm tones, floors come alive in cool colours. The overall effect is less retro than contemporary, something that shows just how forward-looking the original design was. Guests can dive into full indulgent modernity in an extensive, state-of-the-art wellness and spa area, where Thalasso saltwater treatments are just one of the many options.

WWW.DESIGNHOTELS.COM / SIDE

ADDRESS
DREHBAHN 49
20354 HAMBURG
GERMANY

ROOMS
178

RATES
EUR 170 –
EUR 725

OPEN
04/2001

GERMANY
HAMBURG

# SIDE HOTEL HAMBURG
## *Hamburg*

--- 

Architect Jan Störmer's glass and steel façade emerges from Hamburg's staid residential area as a potent urban chic style statement. Though only twelve stories high, Side evokes visions of luminescent skyscrapers. A spectacular light show designed by iconic theatre director Robert Wilson pulses through the hotel's soaring atrium with an ever-changing intensity that mimics the course of daylight. Complementing Wilson's work is star designer Matteo Thun's eighth-floor lounge, whose suggested weight-lessness is achieved by curved furniture and floating disk lighting along with 360-degree views of the harbour city. Guests and non-guests alike are welcomed into the lounge to rest on orange and blue voluptuously round Rossi di Albizzate furnishings and drink in Thun's natural touches. But only guests can enjoy the buttery creams and sumptuous soothing canvas decorating the rooms. While public spaces are full of strong colour such as bright red leather seating and lush velvets, journeys deeper into the hotel reveal energetic oranges and the warmth of mellow yellow walls in the restorative spa treatment rooms. Here, private spaces feel like sanctuaries and public areas pop with fun and possibility.

WWW.DESIGNHOTELS.COM /
TENBOMPAS

ADDRESS
10 BOMPAS ROAD
DUNKELD WEST 2196
JOHANNESBURG, SOUTH AFRICA

ROOMS
10

RATE
ZAR 3100

OPEN
10/1996

SOUTH AFRICA
JOHANNESBURG

# TEN BOMPAS
## *Johannesburg*
---

At the heart of Johannesburg's business district, this small, suite-only establishment offers visitors a retreat of warmth and tranquility, a pool and peaceful gardens, and a diversity of African experiences. A different designer created each of the ten unique suites, following proprietor Christoff van Staden's directive to provide natural light and outdoor access as well as a fireplace and steam bath. The assurance of an earlier era is radiated by Gill Butler's Edwardian suite, where sand-hued walls and robustly coloured leather-embossed furnishings combine with modern tile and steel. Other suites blur cultures with military-style canvas and splashes of colour typical of the South African landscape. The ethno-African highlights in couturier André Croucamp's silk-enhanced suite remind visitors that business isn't everything, while a contemporary confidence is reflected by the "ethnic turned high-tech" approach in the suite designed by the project architects, Luc Zeghers & Associates. Originally a private dwelling, Ten Bompas has been reimagined as a "home away from home in Africa," combining calm and reassurance with adventure and a sense of discovery.

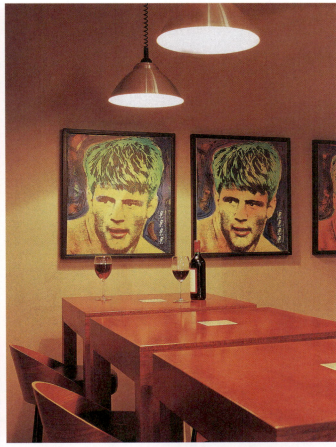

WWW.DESIGNHOTELS.COM /
CHEDIMILAN

ADDRESS
VIA VILLAPIZZONE 24
20156 MILAN
ITALY

ROOMS
250

RATES
EUR 248 –
EUR 538

OPEN
03/2007

ITALY
MILAN

# THE
# CHEDI MILAN
## *Milan*

---

Many designers seek inspiration from Indonesia's paradise of sensual buildings and attention-grabbing textiles; others look to Italy's revolutionary industrial design and transcendental sculptural forms. But few have the vision of renowned hotelier Adrian Zecha and designer Jaya Ibrahim, who spiced up Milan's Bovisa district by combining alluring Eastern décor with Italian style, hospitality and a gleaming Neoclassical pedigree. Jet-setters will recognize Ibrahim's signature autumnal palette from his work on the stunning Setai in Miami and the luminous Chedi Muscat in Oman. Earth tones, red accents, dark woods and Balinese art make The Chedi Milan a supremely sensual experience. Ibrahim even adds innovative textiles to the world-class restaurant, glass-walled bar, spa and swimming pools. The delights to the senses extend to the olfactory as well: the hotel's signature fragrance – a mix of mandarin and green tea – gently permeates each space. Guests can bathe in this exemplary marriage of East and West, enhanced by Nathan Thompson's warm lighting design within and Mario Botta's virtuoso restoration of the Teatro alla Scala, located nearby. The Chedi, which means "spiritual monument" in Thai, emerges as the proud synthesis of two design traditions that expertly manage to both surprise and utterly soothe.

WWW.DESIGNHOTELS.COM /
CHEDIPHUKET

ADDRESS
118 MOO 3,
CHOENG TALAY TALANG,
PHUKET 83110, THAILAND

ROOMS
108

RATES
EUR 150 –
EUR 800

OPEN
11/1982

THAILAND
PHUKET

# THE CHEDI PHUKET
*Phuket*

---

Amidst coconut palms and gently rolling slopes, The Chedi Phuket elegantly sashays down a varied landscape to rest along the island's finest white sandy beach at Pansea Bay. Paris-based architect and designer Edward Tuttle, known for his work in tropical locales, teamed up with Bangkok-based designer Jon Vorapot Somton to create a resort that beautifully combines local materials and traditional Thai designs with modern functionality. Elevated walkways link pavilions and public buildings, offering guests unobstructed views of the ocean, while the private thatched-roof cottages literally invite the surrounding nature inside through their shuttered doors. A private veranda and secluded sun deck ensconce each cottage beautifully in its own patch of paradise; here, guests can breathe easy amidst custom-made designs and the earthy colours that reflect the organic aesthetic of Tuttle's tropical vision, or take advantage of discreet, yet always attentive service. It all stands in contrast to the restaurant's dramatic lighting and the hotel library's graphic elegance. Lustrous black anthracite makes up the hexagonal pool's tiling and creates dramatic reflections at night, enhancing the already other-worldly wonder of this tropical retreat – the ultimate in Southeast Asian seaside serenity.

BELGIUM
BRUSSELS

OPEN
11/2007

RATES
EUR 150 –
EUR 1450

ROOMS
150

ADDRESS
LEOPOLDSTRAAT 9
1000 BRUSSELS
BELGIUM

WWW.DESIGNHOTELS.COM /
THEDOMINICAN

# THE
# DOMINICAN
## *Brussels*

---

Tucked behind Brussels' famous theatre and opera house la Monnaie, The Dominican makes impressive use of its historical status, but with the added flavour of forward-thinking, eclectic design. Designed by the renowned Dutch duo FG stijl along with architect Bart Lens, the hotel's sweeping archways channel the spirit of the Dominican abbey that once stood on its site in the 15th century, while the original façade has also been integrated into the hotel's new construction. A stroll through the Monastery Corridor evokes an almost medieval feeling of elegance with original Belgian stone flooring, and the Grand Lounge, considered the heart of the hotel, calls to mind the extravagance of old European decadence with soaring windows and exquisite metalwork. The 150 guestrooms and suites – each with an individual look – are situated around a quiet inner courtyard and feature a rich combination of contemporary design and luxurious textiles, offering peaceful comfort in a cloister-like setting. It's a wonderful respite from the Continent's new governmental hub, and a space in which old and new Europe effortlessly meld.

# THE ELYSIAN
# BOUTIQUE VILLA HOTEL
## *Bali*

---

Each of The Elysian's 26 private villas comes equipped with its own pool and walled-in garden, making this retreat both a traditional luxury resort and an exclusive community of individual hideaways designed with a refined blend of Balinese architecture and modern lines. Both short- and long-term guests can alter their villas to match their moods by sliding a door panel or unfolding an oversize window, creating a sense of openness and bringing the living area into the garden. From bedrooms with three-metre-high ceilings, guests look out through sliding glass doors onto a private patio, a modern version of the traditional Balinese "bale," hugged by an L-shaped pool and surrounded by frangipani trees. At the centre of the resort, designed by Kuala Lumpur-based firm Quirk & Associates, are the lush yet refined public areas, including the bar and restaurant, a gym and spa, and a library for private dining. Guest can dip into a 25-metre pool and its trellis-covered waterfall, above which sits a Balinese shrine. Even here they can enjoy privacy by pulling the linens down around one of the four-poster cabanas and forgetting the outside world.

WWW.DESIGNHOTELS.COM/
THEGEORGE

ADDRESS
BARCASTRASSE 3
22087 HAMBURG
GERMANY

ROOMS
125

RATES
EUR 159 –
EUR 376

OPEN
10/2008

GERMANY
HAMBURG

# THE GEORGE
## *Hamburg*
---

No membership is required at this smart interpretation of an English-style club, which light-heartedly evokes the old while lending a touch of timeless glamour to the new. Offering 125 impeccably dressed guestrooms and suites, The George is ideal for savvy travellers seeking the utmost in privacy. Designer Sibylle von Heyden of SynergyHamburg has also created regally appointed common spaces for discreet deal-making, after-dinner reflection and civilised conversation – notably the handsome meeting club rooms with dark timber flooring, a light-flooded rooftop spa, a sophisticated restaurant-bar, and a cosy, beautifully wallpapered library. Each offers its own made-to-measure take on the privileged surroundings of an exclusive club. And each can be privately hired for any event a guest or visitor would like to host. Nothing's too much trouble in this unhurried haven of refined seclusion. It's also an endlessly enjoyable contrast to the bright and bustling neighbourhood outside. St. Georg is one of worldly Hamburg's most inclusive multicultural districts, where hip boutiques, cosmopolitan restaurants and bohemian cafés jostle against the evocative remnants of the area's intriguingly disreputable past.

ADDRESS
VIA SAN RAFFAELE, 6
20121 MILAN
ITALY

ROOMS
21

RATES
EUR 300 –
EUR 2000

OPEN
05/2008

ITALY
MILAN

# THE GRAY
## *Milan*

---

Designed with Milan's most exclusive fashionista set in mind, the simply named Gray treads a careful line between elegance and opulence. Unashamedly elitist and purely residential, The Gray grants only the most established names access to its private club-like atmosphere. Housed in what were once residential buildings, the hotel is hidden away in a narrow street running between the cathedral and the glass-domed Galleria; guests are welcomed into a sumptuous lobby featuring a swinging red velvet divan and bathed in an ever-changing myriad of coloured light. Here, in a scene cloaked in style and scent of eminence, the murmur of barely spoken conversations is interspersed with the musical clink of glasses from the bar. Each of the 21 guestrooms offers a completely unique interior and finely handcrafted details. Two rooms feature their own gyms; other are spread out over two storeys connected by a filigree steel staircase. The open-air lounge, Aria, offers guests an exotic ambience under the stars. A model of gracious living, The Gray is select, intimate and mysterious – a modern classic.

# THE HOTEL
## *Lucerne*
---

Any guest yearning for surprise, sensuality and an elegant, even cinematic experience should simply check into, well, The Hotel. This small corner property built in 1907 has been transformed by none other than French "starchitect" Jean Nouvel, a Pritzker Prize winner whose celebrated Culture and Convention Centre Lucerne is just a few steps away. Owner and hotelier Urs Karli wanted to transcend the usual hotel experience by offering not a home away from home, but a place to be surprised and truly inspired. The strategy obviously works. Nouvel's restrained yet clever interplay of mirrors makes the tangible barrier between the pavement outside and the Gault Millau-awarded restaurant Bam Bou inside vanish in the eyes of the beholder: people outside feel as if they're inside and vice versa. Furnishings bear Nouvel's hallmark as well (they should, he designed every piece himself): horizontal lines are drawn in wood, vertical ones in stainless steel. Perfecting the element of surprise, Nouvel selected film stills from his favourite directors, including Buñuel, Almodóvar and Greenaway, to project onto all the rooms' ceilings, bringing iconic scenes like one taken from *Fellini's Casanova* to life when you lie in bed.

WWW.DESIGNHOTELS.COM/
THEHOTEL

ADDRESS
SEMPACHERSTRASSE 14
6002 LUCERNE
SWITZERLAND

ROOMS
25

RATES
CHF 370 –
CHF 570

OPEN
04/2000

SWITZERLAN
LUCERNE

WWW.DESIGNHOTELS.COM /
THELALU

ADDRESS
142 JUNGSHING ROAD
555 YUCHR SHIANG, NANTOU
TAIWAN

ROOMS
96

RATES
NT 15500 –
NT 72800

OPEN
03/2002

TAIWAN
NANTOU

# THE LALU
## *Nantou*

---

An idyllic 26,000-square-metre resort located near the aquamarine waters of Taiwan's enchanting Sun Moon Lake, The Lalu exemplifies cultural design, inspired by the Zen principles of serenity and purity. Drawing inspiration from both Taiwanese and Japanese tropical building, acclaimed Australian architect Kerry Hill has endowed the former summer retreat of Chinese president Chiang Kai Shek with an abstract yet timeless allure. Gorgeous blue-stone villas and elegantly austere wooden terraces channel the calm of nearby Lalu Island, once a holy place for the indigenous Thao people. Another soothing element is The Lalu's lighting design, which changes depending on the sunshine's intensity and subtly combines the locale's natural lighting with the hotel's indoor illumination. Created by shadow specialist Nathan Thompson, this concept provides magnificent mood lighting in the 98 rooms, suites and lakeside villas. True to the Zen aesthetic, the gentle buildings are nestled modestly into the wild hillside and its lush evergreen broadleaf trees and white frangipanis. And all attention is drawn to the misty lake – a fitting centrepiece for this resort and its emphasis on reflection, both literal and spiritual.

WWW.DESIGNHOTELS.COM / LEVANTE

ADDRESS
AUERSPERGSTRASSE 9
1080 VIENNA
AUSTRIA

ROOMS
70

RATES
EUR 150 –
EUR 380

OPEN
05/2006

AUSTRIA
VIENNA

# THE LEVANTE
# PARLIAMENT
## *Vienna*

---

Just behind Austria's parliament building in central Vienna, The Levante Parliament surrounds an elegant 400 square metre courtyard. Here, separated from the bustling city, guests find a relaxing lounge ambience; an oasis of tranquillity detached from summer heat and winter frost. Like the rest of the property, the courtyard reflects a concept based on the four natural elements. In this airy space, water features are complemented by fire-orange details and contemporary sculpture, all set against a background of earthy natural materials. Guests are also privy to high culture and a little history. Modern design influences infuse an original Bauhaus building dating from 1908, and then it functions also as an art gallery. Black-and-white portraits of dancers from the State Opera by noted Viennese photographer Curt Themessl grace the hotel walls, and glass objects by artist Ioan Nemtoi are on display in the prominent exhibition area. Nemtoi was also instrumental in the hotel's design – a restaurant-bar bearing his name pays homage to his vision with both eye-catching works of glass art and seasonally changing multicultural fusion cuisine. A lovely urban getaway, The Levante Parliament is a successful marriage of art and design, of both historical and contemporary Viennese culture.

**WWW.DESIGNHOTELS.COM/ MANDALA**

**ADDRESS** POTSDAMER STRASSE 3 10785 BERLIN GERMANY

**ROOMS** 163

**RATES** EUR 270 – EUR 3800

**OPEN** 05/1999

**GERMANY** BERLIN

# THE MANDALA HOTEL
## *Berlin*

---

Potsdamer Platz is Berlin's epicentre of modern architecture, which puts the Mandala Hotel in good company. With an unassuming entrance and small lobby, the all-suites residence provides long-term and business guests discreet relief from the area's bustle: most rooms face the inner courtyard and service is impeccably professional but never obtrusive. Interiors pare luxury down to its serene and subtle essence, but spare no expense with furnishings by Donghia and Chinese antiques handpicked by proprietor Lutz Hesse. Windows of the second floor QIU lounge hideaway offer glimpses of the rush outside, but the mohair sofas and water cascading down a Bisazza glass mosaic wall are welcome distractions. The restaurant FACIL is hidden on the fifth-floor courtyard, which is almost entirely open-air in summer. In the spacious guestrooms, handcrafted tables and ornaments provide solid dark accents amongst the soft colours of raw silk curtains and cherry wood floors. The 600 square-metre, top-floor ONO Spa is a world of holistic well-being high above Berlin. Lucky guests enjoy panoramic city views during indulgent treatments tailor-made for those who value individualism and privacy and want maximum relaxation and fitness in the shortest time possible. Black-and-white photographs by Ellen Auerbach complete the serenely style-savvy picture.

WWW.DESIGNHOTELS.COM /
MORGAN

ADDRESS
10 FLEET STREET
TEMPLE BAR, DUBLIN 2
IRELAND

ROOMS
121

RATES
EUR 140 –
EUR 290

OPEN
11/1997

IRELAND
DUBLIN

# THE MORGAN HOTEL
## *Dublin*

---

With The Morgan, architect Niall D. Brennan and designer Brian Mc Donald of Design Farm in collaboration with owner Paul Fitzpatrick have created a haven of understatement in Dublin's vibrant Temple Bar district, the city's cultural quarter on the south bank of the River Liffey. The design brief was to create a Hotel that was full of surprises and fun yet had all the comforts and facilities of an internationally recognised Design Hotel. The inspiration for the space draws on the connection to the natural environment and artist Robert Shaw specially commissioned some of the art pieces for the bedrooms. Bedroom pieces include etched mirrored wardrobes, Philippe Starck chaise and chairs, counter lit writing tables, glass encased bathrooms, white ash floors and walls, white quartz finishes, relaxing balconies and baths in the middle of some suites. The reception area features a hand-carved snow flake wall, hanging egg chair and black leather couches with crystal chandeliers whilst the reception desk juts from a support column like a mere afterthought. The Morgan is the perfect place for businesses travellers and savvy weekenders who yearn for an experience that is as pure and timeless as it is classic and elegant.

**WWW.DESIGNHOTELS.COM /**
**PARKBANGALORE**

**ADDRESS**
14/7, MAHATMA GANDHI ROAD
BANGALORE 560 042
INDIA

**ROOMS**
109

**RATES**
INR 15000 –
INR 28000

**OPEN**
02/2001

**INDIA**
BANGALORE

# THE
# PARK BANGALORE
## *Bangalore*

---

When the design team surrounding British icon Sir Terence Conran first encountered The Park Bangalore, it was a squat, low-budget hotel located in the heart of Bangalore's business district. But by balancing a pristine white exterior with an interior popping with transcontinental internationalism and modern amenities like a hip 24-hour restaurant, they turned it into India's first, and certainly one of its foremost, boutique hotels. The glass façade and polished marble floors of the spacious lobby are complemented by black columns of carved Indian designs; black leather lines the lifts. Guests are soon in for even more visual surprises: each floor has its own colour scheme, such as lush aqua and oranges on the first floor. Lime dominates the next two storeys, evoking an abstract, jungle-like feel highlighted by burnt amber and deep purple. Guestrooms on the top floor, The Residence, are similarly resplendent in luxurious silks, leathers and woods that add a pinch of Eastern opulence through grace notes of hot pink, jade and gold. With their sumptuous palette and sensual use of fabrics, Conran & Partners have successfully fused modern European chic with toned-down Indian design, creating a one-of-a-kind style and introducing lifestyle culture to the subcontinent.

WWW.DESIGNHOTELS.COM/
PARKCHENNAI

ADDRESS
601 ANNA SALAI
CHENNAI 600 006
INDIA

ROOMS
215

RATES
INR 13000 –
INR 40000

OPEN
05/2002

INDIA
CHENNAI

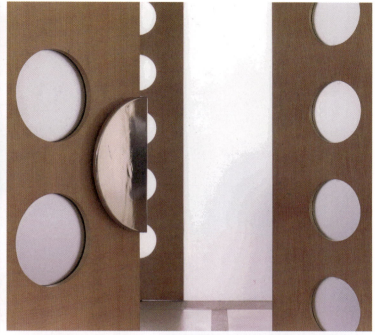

# THE
# PARK CHENNAI
*Chennai*

---

Located on the historic premises of the erstwhile Gemini film studios, The Park Chennai offers a glamorous film-star-style haven in the heart of Tamil Nadu's vibrant capital. Without lapsing into Bollywood kitsch, Los Angeles architectural firm Hirsch Bedner Associates pays homage to the site's glittering cinematic past. Offering a traditional welcome to guests are giant lotuses arranged by the artist Hemi Bawa, while a screen in the multilayered lobby displays an ever-changing line-up of projected films. Luring guests across an atrium area adorned in pale cream limestone, aqua-coloured leather and cocoa velvet, the lounge emanates calm during the day. At night, the lobby is transformed into one of Chennai's hottest spots, where locals mingle with the international clientele. Guests who want to retreat from the fun will appreciate the guestrooms' light and breezy atmosphere, where understated décor is enlivened by subtle ornamental extravagances such as the coconut-shell inlaid tables and parchment lamps. Although vintage film posters adorn the hotel hallways, it is really the hotel's consistently cool, contemporary design that emerges as the star of the show.

WWW.DESIGNHOTELS.COM /
PARKKOLKATA

ADDRESS
17 PARK STREET
KOLKATA 700 016
INDIA

ROOMS
149

RATES
INR 12000 –
INR 20000

OPEN
08/1967

INDIA
KOLKATA

# THE
# PARK KOLKATA
## *Kolkata*

---

The Park Hotel group's Kolkata space might be nearing 40 years of age, but this business-district landmark has all the energy and verve of the hot young things on the international hotel scene. Thanks to architects Prakash Mankar & Associates, Made Wijaya and Carl Ettensperger, its current incarnation gracefully merges innovation with traditional aspects of Bengal's regional aesthetic. Under their guidance, a distinct modern-colonial style blends seamlessly with polished marble and lightwood alongside Bengali features such as the Kantha embroidery panels, whose intricate patterns also decorate guestroom bedspreads and cushions. The team pays further homage to the region's rich visual culture by converting public spaces into exhibition areas, which fizz with the hip, creative energy of a fashionable downtown art gallery. On The Park Kolkata's walls, works by top Indian artists such as M.F. Husain, Yusuf Arakkal and Bikash Bhattacharya welcome guests alongside locally crafted bronze and brass sculptures, terracotta and traditional murals. The artistic vibe luckily continues in the hotel's three restaurants – try Saffron for contemporary Indian cuisine par excellence – and in-house bars. Namaste.

WWW.DESIGNHOTELS.COM /
PARKNEWDELHI

ADDRESS
15 PARLIAMENT STREET
NEW DELHI 110 001
INDIA

ROOMS
220

RATES
INR 14000 –
INR 50000

OPEN
11/1987

INDIA
NEW DELHI

# THE PARK
# NEW DELHI
## *New Delhi*

---

Inspired by ancient Hindu philosophies that strive for harmony between man and nature, the renowned British design firm Conran & Partners has used the elements of earth, water, fire, air and space as the core concepts for The Park New Delhi, successfully balancing Indian visual traditions and contemporary minimalism. The arced lobby plays with air and space: white-glass facades bathe the interior in natural light, and a sheer glass-bead curtain winds its way towards the marble reception. Meanwhile, hot pink sculptural sofas, rugs and lighting introduce India's signature celebratory colour to the all-white décor. The purity is further offset by elements of fire and water in the hotel restaurants: leather and limestone furnishings and a glass-bead curtain framing a palette of blues that segues into the hotel's spectacular outdoor pool. Upstairs, private arced corridors lead guests to sleek rooms that vary in size according to the curved architecture; on the two Residence floors, private Jacuzzis and a 24-hour butler assure every traveller the best in Indian service and comfort. Effortlessly shifting between yesterday's majesty and today's sleek simplicity, the hotel's elemental feel might just be a mirror of modern India as a whole.

# THE PELHAM HOTEL
## *London*

---

On Cromwell Place in London's posh South Kensington neighbourhood, a small white portico ushers guests into this distinctive terrace house, where renowned interior designer Kit Kemp has translated the English country-house style into smart city living. In the lobby, large oil paintings, antique writing desks and upholstered chairs transport guests into a zone of both cosy creature comforts and subtle luxury. In the drawing room and library, guests can unwind in front of period fireplaces that crackle well into the night or just smell the lovely, generous arrangements of fresh flowers. Guestrooms also offer deliciously welcoming warmth and light, along with playful quirks: Kemp's innovative use of fabric for walls, headboards and soft furnishings introduces bold patterns. In one fetching example, a fabric-covered headboard with broad vertical stripes in magenta, orange, brilliant red and chocolate brown provides a visually unique, warm contrast to the Rococo-patterned red-and-white bedspread below. En-suite bathrooms featuring cast-iron oversize bathtubs are done in sumptuous mahogany and granite. Never settling for the tried and true, Kemp forges a surprising yet always grounded elegance in a trendsetting urban environment.

WWW.DESIGNHOTELS.COM/
PELHAM

ADDRESS
15 CROMWELL PLACE
LONDON SW7 2LA
UNITED KINGDOM

ROOMS
52

RATES
GBP 180 –
GBP 610

OPEN
09/1989

UNITED KINGDO
LONDON

WWW.DESIGNHOTELS.COM /
PURE

ADDRESS
NIDDASTRASSE 86
60329 FRANKFURT AM MAIN
GERMANY

ROOMS
50

RATES
EUR 100 –
EUR 460

OPEN
09/2005

GERMANY
FRANKFURT
AM MAIN

# THE PURE
## *Frankfurt am Main*

---

A completely renovated loft in the heart of Frankfurt, The Pure captures the city's cosmopolitan spirit. "It's all in white – which sets the focus on the person inside," says hotelier and local impresario Micky Rosen. A harmonic public space containing lobby, breakfast room, bar and lounge lets guests take centre stage amidst exclusively light-coloured materials such as white leather, Thassos marble, white lacquer and light grey floors. Yet the experience is far from sterile. The mostly black-clad staff is attentive and friendly, a bountiful breakfast buffet stays fresh until noon, and lighting and music add a dash of flavour that changes throughout the day. Soft illumination and tunes create a calm ambience in the morning; by night the hotel is an energetic oasis underscored by vibrant orange visual effects. Outfitted with oversize Fatboy beanbags, fountains and bamboo, The Pure's patio effortlessly extends the communicative space. It's all reduced and clear, even if the guestrooms' clean-lined furnishings, light fabrics and high ceilings are given a dash of warmth by glossy African zebrawood and oak parquet. And just around the corner, The Pure Basement is a new gargantuan loft-like event space featuring a chic atmosphere for any occasion.

WWW.DESIGNHOTELS.COM/
THEROCKWELL

**ADDRESS**
181 CROMWELL ROAD
LONDON SW5 0SF
UNITED KINGDOM

**ROOMS**
40

**RATES**
GBP 120 –
GBP 200

**OPEN**
01/2006

**UNITED KINGDOM**
LONDON

# THE
# ROCKWELL
## *London*

---

Guests hoping to be just a hop from Harrods will find this intimate, understated and luxurious four-storey Victorian terrace house an ideal home base during any stay in London. Architects Squire and Partners took advantage of the space's original English charm by restoring the intricate wrought-iron banisters, sweeping stone staircases and Victorian mosaic floor. Then they set off these conservative elements with splashes of contemporary design. The meticulously restored façade might appear to be classical, but vivid green window sashes and elegant glass balustrades offset original mouldings. Once inside, guests can settle into cosy comfort by the lounge's inviting open fireplace, walnut bookshelves and lush burgundy draperies. Or they can dine in the One-Eight-One restaurant overlooking a lush landscaped garden with teak garden benches. Inside this rare urban oasis, nature provides a calming motif with oak furnishings and wallpaper with palm designs; a traditional English floral-wallpaper theme in the guestrooms. The rooms' atmosphere is nevertheless ultramodern, thanks to clean, pure furnishings, glazed power showers, and Hansgrohe bathroom fittings by Philippe Starck. A perfect fusion of contemporary luxury with charm from the past, the Rockwell's unpretentious design has already attracted a decidedly elegant, fashion-forward clientele.

ADDRESS
TESVIKIYE STREET NO 41-41 A
3436/7 ISTANBUL
TURKEY

ROOMS
82

RATES
EUR 200 –
EUR 1000

OPEN
03/2006

TURKEY
ISTANBUL

# THE SOFA
# HOTELS & RESIDENCES
## *Istanbul*

---

Oriental indulgence meets hip Occidental design to create a unique experience at the Sofa Hotels & Residences Istanbul. Created by renowned Turkish architect Sinan Kafadar and located in the heart of the city's super fashionable Nisantasi quarter, the seven-storey Sofa boasts 82 spacious rooms (including 17 executive suites) with clean design and comfort-conscious service. The hotel's "Anytime, Anything" button connects to staff 24 hours a day to arrange everything from concert tickets to one of the numerous pampering wraps, scrubs, massages and more at the Taylife spa downstairs. The peaceful Patika Bookstore is amply stocked with rare reads for sophisticated global nomads, who can also enjoy long coffees or international fare at the Café Sofa from morning till night. Or they can dine at the striking Longtable restaurant, where guests walk to their tables along a 14-metre catwalk, parallel to a bar just as long, to partake of delicious New Mediterranean cuisine. The adjacent terrace is as lush as the garden of Babylon; in the penthouse, the Art*8 Lounge offers views of both international contemporary art and the Bosphorus. There's even a vast event space. It all adds up to a wonderful reflection of the spirit that reigns at the crossroads of Europe and Asia.

WWW.DESIGNHOTELS.COM /
THREESISTERS

ADDRESS
PIKK 71 / TOLLI 2
10123 TALLINN
ESTONIA

ROOMS
23

RATES
EUR 195 –
EUR 899

OPEN
10/2003

ESTONIA
TALLINN

# THE THREE SISTERS
## *Tallinn*
---

Merging a maze of three multi-level 14th-century buildings into a fluid design concept was a compelling challenge for architect Martinus Schuurman and designer Külli Salum. The interconnecting galleries, walkways, staircases and 23 hotel rooms that emerged from their collaboration underscore the design's organic inspiration and evoke atmospheres that never fail to fascinate. Working within Estonia's legal limits on the use of chrome, glass and plastic and also aiming to create unique spaces for each of the conjoined units, local carpenters crafted wood staircases, window shutters and doors entirely by hand. Salum was eager to retain the integrity of their separate identities by developing a distinct personality for each of the three spaces. Thus, one of the buildings has been conceived as a bohemian youngest sister, characterised by vintage and cutting-edge photography. In stark contrast is the older sister's classic chic, expressed in Casamilano and Le Corbusier furnishings, and the antique furnishings which dominate the décor of the middle sister. Together, The Three Sisters presents a perfect setting for Tallinn's smart and stylish society in all of its intriguing complexities.

WWW.DESIGNHOTELS.COM /
VINCENT

ADDRESS
98 LORD STREET
SOUTHPORT PR8 1JR
UNITED KINGDOM

ROOMS
60

RATES
GBP 140 –
GBP 695

OPEN
05/2008

UNITED KINGDOM
SOUTHPORT

# THE VINCENT
## *Southport*

---

William Sutton, otherwise known as the Mad Duke, established the genteel northwestern English resort of Southport in the late 18th century. It's said that after his brief exile here, Napoleon returned to France and based his remodelling of Paris on the architecture of Lord Street. It is on this august thoroughfare that the new Vincent hotel is located, its impressive glass and limestone façade sheltering a dignified modern interior of bright walls, dark timber and treacherously comfortable armchairs, with quirky touches such as a wooden floor which climbs dramatically up one lobby wall. The cool and contemporary theme continues in the 59 guestrooms, where unlikely textures and dashes of colour break up soft shades of ecru and brown, Wenge wood panelling contrasts with bespoke art-print carpets, and Omni baths soothe mind and body with a high-concept Japanese soak. Convivial socialising is the province of a members' bar that showcases a stunning black granite counter, while the Grand Galleria room spans the width of the hotel and has a terrace overlooking Lord Street. At the heart of England's golf coast, The Vincent captivates sportsmen, design enthusiasts and business travellers alike – and might even have tempted Napoleon back into exile.

PORTUGAL
MADEIRA

OPEN
12/2008

RATES
EUR 220 –
EUR 740

ROOMS
79

ADDRESS
RUA DOS ARANHAS 27-A
9000 – 044 FUNCHAL
MADEIRA, PORTUGAL

WWW.DESIGNHOTELS.COM/
VINEHOTEL

# THE VINE
## *Madeira*

---

A visit to the "Island of Eternal Spring" wouldn't be complete without a luxurious stay at The Vine, located in the heart of Funchal, the picturesque capital of Madeira. Generous space and pared-down sophistication are the trademarks of the property, which takes its name and inspiration from the island's world-famous Madeira wine. Interiors reflect the vision of award-winning Portuguese designer Nini Andrade Silva, whose 79 rooms and suites offer the ideal blend of soothing neutral colour palettes and breathtaking city or harbour views. A limousine service, in-room check-in and welcome massage assure that guests can immediately start rejuvenating. Vinotherapy treatments at the spa will detox and revitalise the body while relaxing and refreshing the mind. Meanwhile, tantalising culinary creations envisioned by three-star Michelin chef Antoine Westermann at the rooftop restaurant UVA (Portuguese for "grape") tickle the palate with a fusion of French cuisine complemented by the use of savoury local ingredients. Social life at the hotel revolves around a lobby lounge offering all-day dining, and the popular 360° – an open-air bar with heated rooftop swimming pool – which has, as its name suggests, spectacular panoramic views.

WWW.DESIGNHOTELS.COM / UMAPARO

ADDRESS
PO BOX 222
PARO
KINGDOM OF BHUTAN

ROOMS
29

RATES
USD 300 –
USD 1800

OPEN
2004

BHUTAN
PARO

# UMA PARO
## *Paro*
---

Perched on a hill in one of the most untouched countries on earth, Uma Paro is a dramatic inland resort enveloped by snow-capped mountains, blue-pine forests and an ancient mountain culture. The Bhutanese king's policy of protecting the country from tourism has helped keep the Himalayan nation refreshingly pristine, and the designers of Uma Paro embraced this unspoiled quality. Visitors really feel as if they've taken a trip backwards in time. The resort was designed in collaboration with traditional Bhutanese artisans: indigenous detailing adorns interiors, walls are hand-painted by local artists, and the entire complex is arranged to resemble a traditional Bhutanese village speckled with orchards, lawns and flower gardens. The 20 rooms and nine villas provide dazzling views of the Paro Valley below, including the rice paddies that sustain the resort's Bukhari restaurant. Facilities include a yoga studio, hot stone bathhouse, indoor pool with outdoor sundeck, steam rooms, treatment rooms and a gym. All areas incorporate as much sunlight and visible nature as possible so that guests can easily access the magical mountain kingdom that surrounds them. And the nearby town of Paro offers the chance to experience first hand the country's thriving Buddhist culture.

WWW.DESIGNHOTELS.COM/
UMAUBUD

**ADDRESS**
JALAN RAYA SANGGINGAN,
BANJAR LUNGSIAKAN,
KADEWATAN, UBUD
80571, GIANYAR BALI
INDONESIA

**ROOMS**
29

**RATES**
USD 260 –
USD 525

**OPEN**
2004

**INDONESIA**
BALI

# UMA UBUD
## *Bali*

---

Designed to feel like a luxuriously comfortable rural home in the Balinese hills, Uma Ubud merges indoor spaces with the outside world, yet always assures guests all the secluded privacy they could want. In the town of Ubud, the resort is an almost magical place where visitors can both escape and embark on new adventures. Each day starts with a guided tour through misty rice paddies and ends with a soothing yoga class. In the resort's 29 rooms and suites, garden terraces overflow with tropical fauna; three Uma Pool Suites also include a private infinity-edge pool, and the Shambhala Suite has its own spa treatment area. All rooms open to the outdoors, allowing easy access to sunlight and chirping birds. In some rooms, open-air walkways lead to elegant bathrooms. The lobby, 25-metre jade green pool and bar are also open-air, as are the yoga pavilions and main restaurant, Kemiri. Whether dining on locally sourced dishes or breathing through the downward dog, guests are immersed in the spirit of Balinese culture. Four treatment rooms, a reflexology area, meditation bale, a gym, steam room and sauna provide plenty of spots to drink in the tranquil atmosphere in a breathtaking setting.

WWW.DESIGNHOTELS.COM/
VIGILIUS

ADDRESS
VIGILJOCH
39011 LANA
ITALY

ROOMS
41

RATES
EUR 225 –
EUR 620

OPEN
09/2003

ITALY
SOUTH TYROL

# VIGILIUS MOUNTAIN RESORT
## *South Tyrol*
---

Among the soaring peaks and crisp Alpine air of South Tyrol, architect Matteo Thun has created an eco-inclined mountain hideaway where awareness co-exists with aesthetics, and everything revolves around nature and landscape. Accessible only by cable car and almost invisible from the outside, the vigilius mountain resort offers the tranquillity of altitude and panoramic views over beautiful mountain scenery and a larch forest. The principle of "organic architecture" is expressed in elements such as a grass-covered roof, the use of natural larch wood throughout, and internally heated clay walls in 41 rooms and suites. It's around these rooms and public spaces that guests can meet and mingle in a kind of high-altitude private community. The reception area is a gentle glow of orange, the Parlour Ida features a cosy tiled stove from the original 19th-century structure, and 300-year-old timbers were used in the Restaurant 1500. Everywhere are views, from the sunrises and sunsets of the guestrooms facing east and west, to the enormous picture window and terraces of the hedonistic spa. Exquisite Alpine and North Italian cuisine round off the respite from cares and worries which, along with traffic and noise, are left behind far below.

WWW.DESIGNHOTELS.COM /
VILLABEIGE

ADDRESS
70/1 MOO 3
TUMBON TALING NGAM
KOH SAMUI 80410 SURATHANI
THAILAND

ROOMS
4

RATES
EUR 1100 –
EUR 2300

OPEN
11/2006

THAILAND
KOH SAMUI

# VILLA BEIGE
## *Koh Samui*

---

Perched above a private beach, surrounded by coconut trees and ensconced within a lush jungle, the Villa Beige estate offers the ultimate seclusion on the island of Koh Samui. A cream and white colour scheme gives the property its name, but the emphasis remains on the ocean's marvellous blues, turquoises and aquamarines. Each of the four luxury suites has stunning floor-to-ceiling windows, Bisazza mosaics and aluminum-sculptured furniture designed by Quasar Khanh. A white marble pool, onsite spa and recreational gym entice, but a personal chef, spa therapist and concierge take the indulgent service even further. The attentive manageress even brings local culture in: think local dancers or even Thai boxing. At first, visitors might find it hard to tear themselves away from such extravagant pampering, but Koh Samui's wonders include natural waterfalls and coral reefs to explore. The gorgeous island didn't even have roads until the early 1970s and is still largely unspoiled. A knowledgeable staff is on hand to arrange everything from elephant trekking expeditions and private boat trips to the islands to made-to-order meals of Thai cuisine. A secluded hideout for those who don't want to follow the crowds, Villa Beige is a peaceful jewel in a fast-disappearing paradise.

WWW.DESIGNHOTELS.COM /
LOISIUMHOTEL

ADDRESS
LOISIUM ALLEE 2
3550 LANGENLOIS
AUSTRIA

ROOMS
82

RATES
EUR 134 –
EUR 290

OPEN
10/2005

AUSTRIA
LANGENLOIS

# WINE & SPA RESORT
## LOISIUM HOTEL
### *Langenlois*

---

It's an innovative concept: a spa for wine-lovers. Built over an underground labyrinth of 900-year-old wine cellars and set amid rolling vineyards in Austria's most popular white wine region, the hotel, designed by American architect Steven Holl, seems to float on pillars and glass. Cork as material, form and texture is woven into the hotel's space – from the light fixtures in the restaurant to the lobby staircase and concrete walls. The 82 guestrooms follow the cork theme with cork-shaped lamps, and a map of the cellars is a motif used throughout the hotel, even on textiles. Airy rooms have large windows overlooking extensive vineyards and the wonderfully rural surrounding villages. The hotel has a lovely outdoor swimming pool in the vineyards, and guests – many of whom blissfully wander through the hotel in white bathrobes – can indulge in a full array of Aveda spa treatments in an award-winning spa. They can also sample intriguing local treatments involving grape and wine products before settling down to a wine-themed meal in the spectacular restaurant. Another main attraction is a trip to the educational (and Holl-designed) wine centre next door. Cheers.

2

OF RELAXED GRAND

PREVIOUS PAGE
*Justine Ashbee / Iconoclastic Reverb*
*www.justineashbee.com*

THIS PAGE
*Photo:Fabrice Bouquet*
*fabricebouquet@schierke.com*

# Relaxed Grandeur

TIMELESS ELEGANCE
MEETS MODERN DESIGN.
TRADITIONAL HOSPITALITY
MEETS THE INNOVATIVE
AND NEW.

# *Tradition & Craftsmanship*

## COMBINED WITH THE ULTIMATE IN CONTEMPORARY CHIC

There's another kind of experience to be had within Design Hotels'™ world; one with the trappings of a classic grand hotel, but with an underlying character of casual, contemporary sophistication. Time-less elegance meets modern design. Traditional hospitality meets innovation.

Envision a brand-new twist to a classic Hermès scarf, or exquisitely constructed tall boots from an Italian leather purveyor like Gucci. Imagine a painting by art-world star John Currin, who uses old master techniques to create surreal, modern portraits that go for blue-chip prices in galleries and at auction (and always lands in New York society pages with his young good looks). Tradition and crafts-manship are combined with the ultimate in contemporary chic. An exquisite legacy effortlessly mixes with new modern ease.

THIS PAGE
*Photo: Mattias Tiedermann*
*Mattias Tiedermann/agentmolly.com*

# EXCEPTIONAL LOCATIONS, EXTRAVAGANT PRIVACY AND PERSONALISED PAMPERING

Whether housed in grand old palaces or in modern new constructions, these hotels are infused with an air of elegance, but one in which it's just as okay to wear trainers as wingtips. These properties could be seen as three-dimensional expressions of post-luxury consumerism in an era in which luxury goods are less interesting because they've gone mainstream. What *is* interesting is the smell of old leather, the feel of custom-made luggage, the taste of heirloom ingredients used in innovative cuisine, the hand-stitched wallet with a lifetime guarantee.

An exquisite update of a legendary name: Think Hedi Slimane and Dior. Or a hotel with the patina of the past mixed with today's luxury. In these properties, guests are transported to a bygone era in restored palaces and peaceful gardens. A soaring lobby allows long views of the sea through arched colonnades. Dark wood walls and leather lounge furniture hug patrons in bespoke extravagance. But there's a markedly modern thread running through it all at the same time. These are places where anyone would be tempted to leisurely read the *International Herald Tribune* or the latest issue of *Monocle* all morning. What could be better than feeling steeped in history in updated spaces flooded with light, with someone quietly offering you a coffee or a bite at just the right moment?

There's the quietly classy and almost spiritual feel of a blue-chip lobby art gallery. Or a labyrinth of historical buildings linked together with innovative architecture and whimsical personal touches. Curl up in cashmere blankets, admire hand-painted wallpaper, breathe easy in enormous guestrooms and truly relax in Turkish baths.

Beyond creature comforts, today's rarest commodities might be time, silence, discretion and privacy. These properties appreciate the value of these commodities, and provide them in ways that go far beyond the obvious. Glide in unnoticed through separate entrances. Move into an absolutely secluded, perfectly appointed apartment with breathtaking views of the Eiffel Tower and a private chef.

Each element creates an extraordinary atmosphere that's certainly luxe, never too formal, and preferable to whatever else is out there. It's a bit like an incident that Antonio Pérez Navarro mentions in his Made by Originals story on page 90: former U.S. President Bill Clinton mentioned on a particular evening that he'd rather stay and relax in the Hospes Maricel hotel than attend an exclusive dinner on a yacht.

From well-stocked libraries for the mind to explore, to intimate spas to rejuvenate even the most ravaged bodies and souls; from the aromatherapy oils in the bathroom to just being left alone, these properties give guests looking for an unusually fine experience exactly what they want and need: rare grandeur in an utterly relaxing atmosphere.

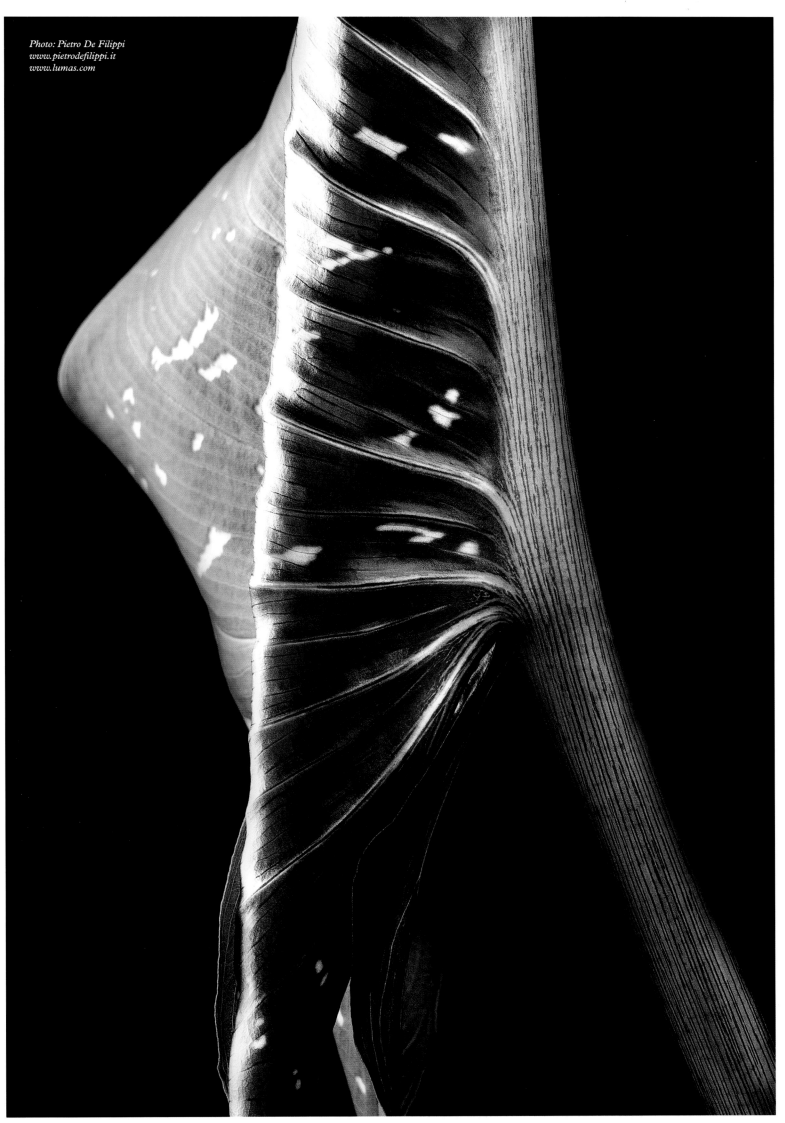

Photo: Pietro De Filippi
www.pietrodefilippi.it
www.lumas.com

# INDEX

WWW.DESIGNHOTELS.COM/
CHARLOTTESTREET

ADDRESS
15 CHARLOTTE STREET-
LONDON W1T 1RJ-UNITED
KINGDOM

ROOMS
52

RATES
GBP 220 –
GBP 1150

OPEN
06/2000

UNITED KINGDOM
LONDON

# CHARLOTTE
# STREET HOTEL
## *London*

---

At the Charlotte Street Hotel, individually decorated guestrooms, intimate drawing rooms and an array of priceless modern art inspire guests to make Kit Kemp's converted warehouse their home away from home. A sensual Botero sculpture and alluring abstract landscapes by Roger Cecil welcome arriving guests and lure them towards wood-panelled drawing rooms, where they can lounge in overstuffed furniture flanked by stone fireplaces and handpicked artwork of the famed Bloomsbury school. The Bloomsbury aesthetic extends to sumptuous guestrooms where period paintings, handmade furniture and even a vintage dressmaker's doll serve as eye-catching centrepieces. Kemp's signature use of patterned fabrics as a decorative language brilliantly combines function with sophistication. Although history is brilliantly presented throughout the space, business travellers' professional needs are satisfied in a state-of-the-art private screening room, fully equipped with the latest modern conveniences. Such compelling contrasts between postmodern practicality and old-fashioned allure are embodied by the tableau Kemp commissioned for the bar and restaurant from Alexander Hollweg, which updates Roger Fry's 1916 fresco *Scenes of Contemporary London Life* with a treasure trove of scenes from today.

WWW.DESIGNHOTELS.COM / COVENTGARDEN

ADDRESS
10 MONMOUTH STREET
LONDON WC2H 9HB
UNITED KINGDOM

ROOMS
58

RATES
GBP 235 –
GBP 1150

OPEN
04/1996

UNITED KINGDOM
LONDON

# COVENT GARDEN HOTEL
## *London*

---

In the midst of London's famed entertainment district, the Covent Garden Hotel's dramatic design commands centre stage. In the reception area, guests pass grand curtains festooned with English roses before entering a world of aged woods, dignified architecture and head-turning interiors by designer Kit Kemp. Kemp's signature mix of abstract and figurative upholstery patterns, demi-canopies, decorative headboards, flowing drapes and matching wallpaper envelop guests in archetypical English charm. Kemp taps into the surrounding theatrical energy by highlighting dignified stone stairs, maple panelling in the generously sized drawing room, eye-popping upholstery and stunning inlaid wood details on the furnishings. Guests in search of an intimate retreat can withdraw offstage into Tiffany's Library, which provides a radiant fireplace and honour bar. The gym, beauty spa, two private dining rooms and a private screening room provide all of the most modern amenities, while Brasserie Max, with its pewter-paned mirror, cosy banquettes and tucked-away corners, earns widespread applause as a pre- or post-theatre retreat.

WWW.DESIGNHOTELS.COM /
GALLERYHOTELART

ADDRESS
VICOLO DELL'ORO 5
50123 FLORENCE
ITALY

ROOMS
74

RATES
EUR 300
EUR 1550

OPEN
05/1999

ITALY
FLORENCE

# GALLERY HOTEL ART
## *Florence*
---

True to its name, Gallery Hotel Art is a temple to contemporary art and culture. Sitting pretty on a tiny square just steps from the Ponte Vecchio, it is Florence's first contemporary boutique hotel, a constantly evolving project for lovers of art and good living and a feast for all the senses. Courtesy of the illustrious Ferragamo family, the hotel provides an atmosphere of chic, contemplative cosmopolitanism. *Objets d'art* ranging from paintings and photography to sculptures accent the walls of the multifunctional lobby, which is home to regularly changing exhibitions. The hotel sees itself as a dynamic engine of cultural exchange, a concept exemplified by the Fusion Bar & Restaurant, where Mediterranean and Japanese cultures meet in an expression of culinary panache. Likewise, the guestrooms exude subtle sophistication, decorated with black and white studies of Florentine monuments. The seventh-floor penthouse suites offer unrivalled views over Florence's rooftops, where guests can wrap themselves in fine linen sheets and cashmere blankets, an example of the hotel's successful balance of aesthetic beauty and physical well-being. A Mecca for aficionados of good taste.

**UNITED KINGDOM** LONDON

**OPEN** 05/2007

**RATES** GBP 250 – GBP 3000

**ROOMS** 50

**ADDRESS** 1 SUFFOLK PLACE LONDON SW1Y 4BP UNITED KINGDOM

WWW.DESIGNHOTELS.COM / HAYMARKETHOTEL

# HAYMARKET HOTEL
## *London*

---

Fusing contemporary and classical references in an ultra central London location, Haymarket Hotel asserts itself as a bold step away from cookie-cutter minimalism. Originally designed by John Nash, the master architect responsible for most of Regency London including Buckingham Palace, Trafalgar Square and the adjoining Haymarket Theatre, the hotel's exterior greets guests with rows of dramatic columns running the length of Suffolk Place. Yet even as the noble lineage of Nash's building is preserved, guests are invited to luxuriate in co-owner Kit Kemp's "modern English" interior design. Art lovers will appreciate the verve with which the airy sepia-grey lobby, filled with marigold and oak furniture, showcases a large stainless steel Tony Cragg sculpture and paintings by British treasure John Virtue. Aesthetes will also admire how the colour schemes in the library and conservatory frame hand-picked antiques. Physical and visual pleasures merge in guestrooms overflowing with inviting pillows, luscious textures, cloth-covered walls and custom-made furniture such as Shagreen coffee tables with ivory wood-toned details. Modern English with a classic pedigree: Haymarket Hotel is timeless.

WWW.DESIGNHOTELS.COM /
AMERIGO

**ADDRESS**
RAFAEL ALTAMIRA, 7
03002 ALICANTE
SPAIN

**ROOMS**
80

**RATES**
EUR 115 –
EUR 795

**OPEN**
09/2003

**SPAIN**
ALICANTE

# HOSPES AMÉRIGO
## *Alicante*

---

In the centre of Alicante, close to La Esplanada avenue and El Postiguet beach, the grand façade of Hospes Amérigo draws your attention upward to its Juliet balconies and arched neo-Gothic windows. Other hints of previous lives as Dominican convent, office complex and apartment block emerge in the salvaged stones that form parts of the walls on each floor and in the wrought-iron work surrounding the balcony above the modern polished-marble, light-filled lobby. Guests are sent back to a luscious past but can also bask in a luxe present in guestrooms decorated with a warm and cosy palette of neutral colours and simple textures that would have likely thrilled even the site's 19th-century residents. A sensual aesthetic suffuses every intimate corner and gleaming surface of this truly exceptional property. Guests inspired by the romance can repair to the roof terrace, where striking views of Alicante's castle can be enjoyed while languishing in the heated pool, savouring a dinner under the stars or relaxing over a natural treatment in the crystal Bodyna Spa.

WWW.DESIGNHOTELS.COM /
LASCASAS

ADDRESS
C/ SANTIAGO, PLAZA JESÚS
DE LA REDENCIÓN Nº2
41003 SEVILLA
SPAIN

ROOMS
41

RATES
EUR 140 –
EUR 500

OPEN
01/2001

SPAIN
SEVILLE

# HOSPES LAS CASAS DEL REY DE BAEZA
## *Seville*

---

Mingling elements of Moorish and European design from the two cultures that have shaped the Andalusian capital over centuries, the Hospes Las Casas del Rey de Baeza is a relaxed, sophisticated fusion of past and present. Bright, whitewashed walls are embellished with the ochres and reds of southern Spain's bullrings in the hotel's courtyards. These are shaded by arcaded walkways that tempt those who wander them into conspiratorial moments amid a forest of salvaged wooden posts and stone columns, both painted and untouched. Ah, the passion of Seville. Once inside, cool terracotta flooring and natural tones lead guests to the 41 guestrooms, where a gracious modernity takes over. Dark chocolate-coloured furnishings, sisal mats, wooden beds from Indonesia, extravagant floor cushions and soft lighting set the scene for a retreat from the sultry city outside in interiors surprisingly reminiscent of urban apartments. Natural light shines through slim passages formed by columns, bouncing off free-standing bowl sinks, water jugs and other ornaments from bygone eras, but ready to be enjoyed in all their glory today.

ADDRESS
PLAZA DE LA
INDEPENDENCIA, 3
28001 MADRID
SPAIN

ROOMS
41

RATES
EUR 199 –
EUR 510

OPEN
10/2007

SPAIN
MADRID

# HOSPES MADRID
## *Madrid*

---

Originally an affluent apartment house designed in 1883 by architect José María de Aguilar, the handsome red-brick Hospes Madrid is an icon of Bourbon Restoration period architecture. So the Hospes Design Team needed to take special care that their modern additions were in harmony with the building's historic elements. Guests eager to experience the landmark in its original glory will be relieved that despite a clean, contemporary style, the original mouldings, columns, wrought iron and woodwork remain intact. The lobby's high ceiling and magnificently restored wooden door offer a grand welcome through the former carriage entrance. This gracious sense of hospitality extends throughout the hotel, where a tranquil, opulent ambience is achieved through white marble and gold details offset by dark fine wood. The Bodyna Spa is ensconced in the former stables; the Senzone Restaurant offers a formal dining room with an oak-coffered ceiling and stucco work – in contrast to the luminous interior patio, where guests can relax on comfortable sofas and listen to whispering water as they drink at the hotel bar. Hospes Madrid's imaginative array of modern additions accentuate an overall sense of permanent privilege and eternal elegance.

# HOSPES
# MARICEL
## *Mallorca*
---

Formerly a notorious haunt of the old-school jet set, this proud and palatial building once hosted parties that kept the paparazzi snapping. The atmosphere now is more leisurely, but today's international travellers can still savour a hint of those decadent days in the retained details – a Neo classical entrance, large windows, neo-Gothic pillars – of a 1949 building. Otherwise, a revamp by the Hospes Design Team has returned traditional Balearic elements of the original structure – archways and arcades, columns in marble and local stone – while modern accents supply a beautifully contemporary flair. The 24 rooms and five suites fulfil modern priorities with design that maximises comfort, space and light and uses neutral colours to complement brilliant views of the Mediterranean. The seafront arcade and grand terraces send guests straight to another era – or to a state of relaxed bliss. So does the refined, subtle service. Whether they arrive by private yacht or automobile, visitors can sample an array of open-air spa treatments in the grotto-like alcoves above the waves, savour local seafood in the Senzone Restaurant or float in the stunning infinity pool, which seems to dissolve into the ... yes ... infinite blue of the sea.

WWW.DESIGNHOTELS.COM /
MARICEL

ADDRESS
CARRETERA D'ANDRATX, 11
07184 CALVIA
MALLORCA
SPAIN

ROOMS
51

RATES
EUR 189 –
EUR 1700

OPEN
03/2003

SPAIN
MALLORCA

WWW.DESIGNHOTELS.COM / PALACIOPATOS

ADDRESS
SOLARILLO DE GRACIA, 1
18002 GRANADA
SPAIN

ROOMS
42

RATES
EUR 125 –
EUR 990

OPEN
05/2005

SPAIN
GRANADA

# HOSPES
# PALACIO DE LOS PATOS
## *Granada*
---

Converted from a late 19th-century palace in Granada's historic centre, the Hospes Palacio de los Patos is an urban oasis combining dramatic classical design with equally stunning modern architecture. The Hospes Design Team has retained the splendour of such original elements as the grand staircase, while 42 well-appointed guestrooms and suites ensure that guests feel at home within an environment of vivid, sultry contrasts fusing the city's Moorish influence with a Spanish-Iberian flavour. Guests can settle into modernist comfort in two buildings – a classical part in the palace's heart and a new construction housing 12 rooms, plus restaurant and spa. The subterranean area connecting the two structures is ingenuously covered with water tanks, allowing natural light to shimmer through. A lush Moorish garden showcases the sensuality of history, while guests can sample contemporary Andalusian flavours in the Senzone restaurant before they head back into the rooms. From the cuisine to the landscaping, authenticity and originality were the guiding principles for creating a sensory experience that brings the rich cultural history of Granada into the future.

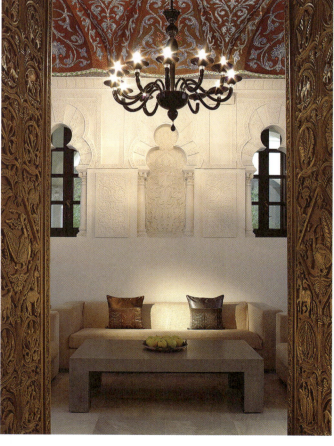

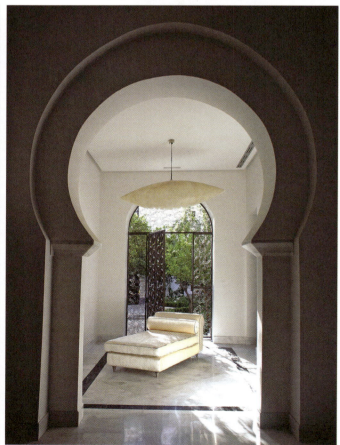

WWW.DESIGNHOTELS.COM/
PALACIOBAILIO

ADDRESS
RAMIREZ DE LAS CASAS
DEZA, 10-12
14001 CORDOBA
SPAIN

ROOMS
53

RATES
EUR 145 –
EUR 655

OPEN
10/2006

SPAIN
CORDOBA

# HOSPES
# PALACIO DEL BAILÍO
*Cordoba*

— — —

Built between the 16th and 18th centuries, this traditional Andalusian agrarian estate, now in the historical heart of Cordoba, has been meticulously restored and finely balanced with contemporary design. Guests move among original detailing such as wrought-iron railings, cool terracotta tiles, Moorish embellishments and a lavishly painted ceiling – all artfully enhanced with understated modern touches. Rich fabrics and textures in champagne and copper are offset by dark walnut and light polished marble floors throughout. Solid slabs of black local stone lure guests to the lush, flowery gardens outside, the perfect place to linger over a drink, a book or a loved one. The estate is composed of several buildings – the palace itself, designated a "place of cultural interest," along with its coach houses, stables and granaries – arranged around a mosaic of five patios. In the spectacular main patio, traditional paving has been replaced with a dramatic glass floor to reveal Roman ruins 4.5 metres below. The restored frescoes further reflect a care for cultural detail, while a sense of serene luxury invites guests to be revitalised by history, just as history itself has been so subtly revitalised.

**SPAIN**
VALENCIA

**OPEN**
02/2006

**RATES**
EUR 125 –
EUR 700

**ROOMS**
66

**ADDRESS**
NAVARRO REVERTER, 14
46004 VALENCIA
SPAIN

**WWW.DESIGNHOTELS.COM /**
**PALAUDELAMAR**

# HOSPES
## PALAU DE LA MAR
*Valencia*

---

Two adjacent 19th-century palaces in the heart of Valencia have been transformed into this welcoming "palace of the sea." Under a stained-glass skylight, the grand loggia stairway with its intricately carved wooden banister is rendered all the more striking by stark, ivory white surroundings. On the wood floor of the vaulted foyer, guests can feel as if they're strolling the deck of a boat; the sexy contemporary interior patio pairs well with the stately historicism. Covered by sails and a glass-and-steel balcony, the patio's raised boxes are lushly filled with fragrant Mediterranean vegetation. The Bodyna Spa offers both serenity and indulgence on the balcony leading to guestrooms, where visitors find peace amid calm modernity. In some rooms, guests can bask in light from ceiling windows; in others they can stretch out in spacious bathrooms, where extravagant tubs are either sectioned off from or opened up to the main space via a folding wooden screen. Elsewhere, the intimate library invites creativity and quiet conversation, while the restaurant tempts with Valencian savours and fine local ingredients.

WWW.DESIGNHOTELS.COM/
HOSPES_VILLA_PAULITA

ADDRESS
AV. PONS I GASCH 15
17520 PUIGCERDÀ (GIRONA)
SPAIN

ROOMS
36

RATES
EUR 105 –
EUR 225

OPEN
07/2007

SPAIN
PUIGCERDÀ

# HOSPES
# VILLA PAULITA
## *Puigcerda*

—  —  —

This majestic Catalan villa and spa is an ideal retreat from the urban fray. Originally built as a private summer residence equidistant from Toulouse and Barcelona, the three-storey red mansion with fairytale-like turreted octagonal tower has a dollhouse quality that never fails to charm guests looking for a mix of history and modern creature comforts. Many of the 19th-century building's original features – such as forged iron balustrades, grilles and balconies – have been preserved, and antiques have been renovated: the former proprietor's late 19th-century wooden chairs, which the Hospes Design Team painted white and cushioned with shimmering grey velvet, are just one example. Guests will find particular pleasure in the rustic allure of sloped ceilings exposing original wood beams, warm wood floors, a soft grey palette and the unique black-and-white Catalan artworks hanging over each guest bed's canopy. With its serene lakeside setting, the outdoor environment has been integrated as an additional space for socialising and relaxation. Glass pyramids are spaced throughout the manicured gardens; the light-flooded Bodyna Spa is located on the resort's lower level. The indulgence continues at Senzone L'Estany, a gourmet restaurant offering cuisine balanced between sophistication and tradition, just like the rest of this stunning property.

**ADDRESS**
301, ROUTE DE LAUSANNE
1293 GENÈVE BELLEVUE
SWITZERLAND

**ROOMS**
102

**RATES**
CHF 600 –
CHF 1000

**OPEN**
01/2003

**SWITZERLAND**
GENEVA

# LA RÉSERVE GÈNEVE HOTEL & SPA
## *Geneva*

---

In a magnificent park on the shores of Lake Geneva, La Réserve whisks guests away on a whimsical global safari. Parisian designer Jacques Garcia has transformed the 1970s hotel into a playful explosion of extravagant colour, secluding shrubbery and revealing glass galleries. A gold leaf trim courses the lobby's upper wall, below which a frieze quotes a line from philosopher and Geneva native Jean-Jacques Rousseau: "Back to Nature." Perched on standing and mounted lamps are colourful plastic cutouts of parrots and peacocks. A band of leopard-print fabric cuts a horizontal line across lipstick-red chairs. The entrance to the Loti restaurant is guarded by a lifelike plaster elephant, and a copper elephant's head originally commissioned for the 1931 Paris Colonial Exhibition is mounted within. Whether visiting on business or indulging in pure leisure, guests will find La Réserve a feast for the eyes as well as an exotic haven of creative relaxation. The outdoor pool, tranquil spa and elegant Venetian water taxi used for trips into the city make this hideaway even more fun for travellers before they retire into the soft velvets and black granite of their guestrooms.

WWW.DESIGNHOTELS.COM/
LARESERVEPARIS

ADDRESS
10 PLACE DU TROCADERO – 3,
AVENUE D'EYLAU
75116 PARIS, FRANCE

ROOMS
10

RATES
EUR 2150 –
EUR 4330

OPEN
01/2005

FRANCE
PARIS

# LA RÉSERVE PARIS
*Paris*

---

Situated directly across from the Eiffel Tower, La Réserve Paris stays true to its name through interior architect Remi Tessier's refined take on discreet affluence. La Réserve prides itself on the soft lighting and subdued monochromatic aesthetic, which invite guests to relish the noble grace of rosewood, ebony, sycamore, stone and slate. Here the emphasis is on privacy, and many of the ten multilevel apartments boast private office, dining and landscaped garden areas. La Réserve's sleek furniture suits the Parisian preference for natural colour palettes such as contrasting shades of black and ecru. Tessier, who has collected accolades for luxury yacht designs, demonstrates an iron grasp of the linkage between functional design and clean elegance. Guests can imagine soaring away on sublimely modernist furnishings by Andrée Putman, Maxalto, Flos and Vitra. And with the exception of the sumptuous four-poster beds and the high double windows, everything from the plush Flexform chairs to the twin marble sinks in the bathrooms is symmetrically aligned. A sofa or a nightstand is never without its mate, making this ultra modern space an ode to old-fashioned romance.

WWW.DESIGNHOTELS.COM/
THEFRANKLIN

ADDRESS
22-28 EGERTON GARDENS
LONDON SW3 2DB
UNITED KINGDOM

ROOMS
40

RATES
GBP 210 –
GBP 1500

OPEN
2009

UNITED KINGDOM
LONDON

# THE FRANKLIN
*London*

---

Spanning four Victorian townhouses in London's Knightsbridge, The Franklin has been designed to combine its English heritage with contemporary European style. A feeling of space and tranquillity is immediate upon entering the open lobby with direct access to the tree-lined garden. Overlooking the garden, the dining room, lounge and bar mix timeless and elegant pieces in a palette of warm minks and soft greens. Polished nickel Brandt van Egmond chandeliers alongside a floor-to-ceiling etched glass wall in the bar complete the design. A rare Chantilly pattern used in the wood floor surfaces is echoed in the stone floor. While every public aspect is designed to maximise function and aesthetic delight, the real marvels await guests in their rooms. Each room is filled with unique handcraftsmanship, and the wall finish created exclusively for the Franklin by Create is a mix of plaster and pigment with a pearlescent coating - a kind of attention to detail that is also reflected in the 40-room hotel's personal, gracious service.

WWW.DESIGNHOTELS.COM /
SOHO

ADDRESS
4 RICHMOND MEWS
LONDON W1D 3DH
UNITED KINGDOM

ROOMS
91

RATES
GBP 235 –
GBP 1150

OPEN
09/2004

UNITED KINGDOM
LONDON

# THE SOHO HOTEL
## *London*

---

A style feast awaits any guest at The Soho Hotel, the flagship and largest property in Tim and Kit Kemp's London style empire. Holding court in the bubbling borough of Soho, the hotel was formerly a multi-storey car park before Britain's interior design individualists created it within the original red-brick structure. In this shrine to eclecticism, guests luxuriate in unusually large rooms with floor-to-ceiling warehouse-style windows. Lovingly designed and furnished by Kit Kemp, the 91 rooms boast exciting creative tension between their design components. Kemp's contemporary British style is firmly founded on top-notch furnishings and materials deployed in an artful combination of a plethora of styles, colours and patterns. "'Eclecticism' means being interested in a lot of things: creating living interiors that aren't boring," explains the designer, whose private art collection also enriches the distinguished personal flavour of the guestrooms and public spaces. An especially commissioned mural in the hotel's Refuel Bar & Restaurant pays homage to the building's humble beginnings, but it will struggle for pride of place with the very contemporary ten-foot-high Botero sculpture nearby in the lobby. A feast for the eyes, indeed.

# WIDDER HOTEL
## *Zurich*

---

Widder Hotel is a hamlet of nine historical residences, many dating back to the Middle Ages, expertly renovated and subtly linked with staircases and porticoes to create a feeling of home-scale intimacy and exclusive luxury. Swiss architect Tilla Theus preserved not only the individual façades, but also the internal floor plans and structures, giving rise to a somewhat labyrinthine hotel that has often been hailed as Switzerland's finest. High-tech construction techniques merge seamlessly with age-old building elements. A case in point is a glass roof atop a 12th-century stone house, or the integration of nine elevator banks, including one of glass and chrome that rises alongside a wall of river stones. Delightful original features like exposed wooden beams and frescoes are mixed with classics of modern furniture design in steel and glass. Each guestroom has its own layout and interior design, with some refreshing surprises, such as leather bedspreads, not to mention the latest modern amenities from Bang & Olufsen. Living proof that the ancient and the modern can coexist in perfect harmony, the Widder is worth a trip to Zurich in its own right.

**3**

ALTERNATIVE
EXPERIMENTAL
JUST A LITTLE

04

01

02

03

THIS PAGE
01 *Zoren Gold & Minori*
*www.mi-zo.com*

02 *BLESS book frames and*
*n°28 fur hammock*

03 *Jerszy Seymour / Diesel*
*www.jerszyseymour.com*

OPPOSITE PAGE
04 *Julia Pfaller / Purple Haze*
*www.juliapfaller.de*

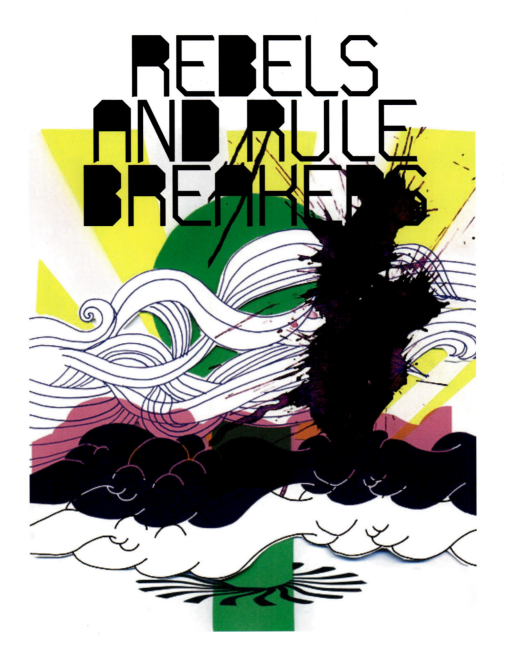

**REBELS AND RULE BREAKERS**

### NOT YOUR USUAL HOTEL EXPERIENCE: BOUNDARY-PUSHING PROPERTIES LET YOU KNOW YOU'RE NOT AT HOME

There's more – another movement in our portfolio that we see as a microcosm of the bigger world. Made for guests with a sense of adventure by designers, architects and owners who take their signature concepts to new heights, some hotels know no limits.

They remix and mash up old hospitality concepts – such as combining a hostel and hotel. They push boundaries, especially visual ones. They create the worlds of the future, which is the direction they're always looking towards. Design Hotels™ sees them as the epitome of the experimental, extreme and eccentric.

Groundbreaking and rule breaking, these idiosyncratic hotels can stir the imagination just as much as a consciousness-altering art exhibition, a revolutionary film or even a book. Neo-pop art by Takashi Murakami, non-narrative, crazy films by Matthew Barney or cyberpunk literature by Neal Stephenson, anyone? Ron Arad, the eccentric designer behind the duoMo hotel in Rimini, Italy (along with some of the world's most sculptural and expensive chairs), perhaps best captures their spirit when he says, "I don't want to make people feel at home. Because they're *not* at home."

# INSPIRATION IN OUT OF THE ORDINARY LOCATIONS

**DESIGN SURPRISES AND SERVICE FLOURISHES SHOW LIFE AND STYLE FROM OTHER ANGLES**

These hotels lead you into other worlds, like the high-concept retail spaces and hanging lamps made of neon slime by award-winning industrial designer Jerszy Seymour (see previous page). Familiar objects, materials, colours, smells and sounds are cast in a new light.

In a balmy neighbourhood in a major Asian urban hub, a sweeping lobby with a curvy staircase and 1920s raw ceiling might make you think of a Busby Berkeley showgirl extravaganza. Elsewhere, you might get two rooms across the hall from each other instead of just one – lie in the sitting room's hammock; then head downstairs to grab a snack any time of day, instead of relying on room service. Or sleep in a birdcage of a bed under the gables of a restored Dutch cottage, then wake up to picture-window river views as you slip into mega-designer Marcel Wanders's sleek white tub with a room of its own – just after acclaimed chef Peter Lute himself delivers a breakfast box to your door.

Sometimes the locations are just as offbeat as the hotels. Experience lifestyles, traditions and even climates you never knew Earthy Mediterranean life abounds on a 40-hectare working farm on the Sicilian island of Pantillera, where old whitewashed buildings dot the unusual volcanic landscape. In the Arctic tundra, be greeted with polarised clothing, then bond with other intrepid travellers in spaces sporting cuddly furs and warm fireplaces. Where else could you go midnight-sunbathing in summer, see the Northern Lights in winter or hang out with real reindeer?

These experimental hotels challenge, excite and inspire anyone who visits them. They're a mischievous, fun or dramatic escape from everyday life. They like to fly in the face of convention and, with a wink and a smile, invite you to discover places where assumptions are turned on their heads.

Nobody is exactly the same all the time. Neither is Design Hotels™. We see these three loose categories as guidelines that travellers can use to sample the different experiences they find in the rest of their worlds: in art, in fashion, in business, at the events they attend, in the publications and books they read, in the music they listen to – and, of course, in their own personalities. Each of our members has its own distinctive personality, too. It's an invitation to feel comfortable everywhere. Welcome to our worlds, and we'd love it if you tried them all.

# INDEX

ADDRESS
PAUL-DESSAU-STRASSE 2
22761 HAMBURG
GERMANY

ROOMS
128

RATES
EUR 105 –
EUR 155

OPEN
11/2003

GERMANY
HAMBURG

# 25HOURS HOTEL
## *Hamburg*
---

Unsparingly stylish, 25hours Hotel invites guests to feel at home amid chic and playful sixties and seventies-inspired design details. At the entrance, 420 convex chrome mirrors stud the black, curved reception desk, and turn each guest's arrival into a brilliantly presented event. Go beyond and be charmed by hand-tufted pile rugs from Kasthall, mod Brionvega television sets and spun-metal table lamps from Flos, which can be purchased directly from 25hours. Usual divisions between a hotel and one's home are further erased in the chilled-out pink, red and orange communal rooms designed to encourage young guests to meet and mingle. Thus, the guests-only ground-floor "living room" offers low lounge seats by Alfa for stretching out in front of a cosy fireplace and a giant flat-screen TV. Defined by pale blues or frothy greens, the equally groovy guestrooms sport white fringe curtains, retro chairs and desks that double as seats. Across the street you can make yourself comfortable at the 25hours guesthouse, which offers 3 M-rooms and 2 XL-rooms with hardwood floors, designed mainly in white, red and black colours. The fashionable communal kitchenette is just as inviting as the main building's living and dining rooms.

WWW.DESIGNHOTELS.COM / 25HOURSFRANKFURT

ADDRESS
NIDDASTRASSE 58
60329 FRANKFURT AM MAIN
GERMANY

ROOMS
76

RATES
EUR 100 –
EUR 180

OPEN
07/2008

GERMANY
FRANKFURT
AM MAIN

# 25HOURS HOTEL FRANKFURT TAILORED BY LEVI'S
## *Frankfurt am Main*

---

Young, urban and infinitely stylish: these are the adjectives that come to mind after stepping into the new 25hours Hotel Frankfurt Tailored by Levi's. The unlikely-yet-exciting collaboration between the chic German hotel group and the classic American brand is the result of Frankfurt real-estate fate – the two companies independently leased adjacent buildings in the city's Main Station district. And as good neighbours are wont to do, they started talking. From these conversations, a lifestyle hotel began taking shape. *Au courant* designers Michael Dreher and Delphine Buhro and architect Karl Dudler were brought in to seamlessly integrate the two brands, and, before long, 76 unique guestrooms (fittingly sized M, L and XL) were kitted out in inviting shades of indigo and blue. Quirky decorative elements evoke different decades of the 20th century, with an emphasis on the freewheeling era most often associated with the iconic jeans brand: rock 'n' roll. Urban nomads can rock out in the hotel's fully equipped Gibson music jam room or relax on the spectacular rooftop lounge. An iMac workstation and the organic snack bar Red Tab by Nykke & Kokki round out 25hours' commitment to making guests feel absolutely comfortable … as if they've slipped into the perfect pair of jeans.

WWW.DESIGNHOTELS.COM / AZUCAR

ADDRESS
CARRETERA FEDERAL NAUTLA –
POZA RICA KM 83.5, MONTE GORDO,
93588, TECOLUTLA, VERACRUZ
MEXICO

ROOMS
20

RATES
USD 120 –
USD 235

OPEN
12/2005

MEXICO
VERACRUZ

# AZÚCAR
## *Veracruz*

---

From the founders of ultrahip Mexican hotels Condesa *df* and Deseo comes Azúcar, named for the sugar cane grown in the state of Veracruz, where this hideaway is located. The "sweet" resort is effortlessly elegant, featuring 20 low-lying whitewashed *palapas* (bungalows), each topped with a thatched roof. "I wanted to recuperate a lifestyle gone by," explains hotelier Carlos Couturier. "To give guests the pleasures of simple things." Thus chairs are reproductions of those his grandparents had in their 1930s ranch, and each bungalow is named after a Veracruz sugar mill. A back-to-basics white-on-white aesthetic offers an authentic style that both hearkens to the past and fulfils the modern traveller's aesthetic demands. A locally made hammock stretches across the private patio featured in every *palapa*, inviting guests to swing as the Gulf breezes blow; the airy ease makes the resort a haven for those weary of mass tourism. Highlights include a relaxing *biblioteca* (library) where guests can lounge in wicker chairs under an open thatched ceiling, as well as an outdoor spa that features a yoga space and an array of holistic spa services. True to its name, Azúcar is like a sweet treat that keeps guests coming back for more.

# BÁSICO
## *Playa del Carmen*
---

Located steps from the ocean in the bustling centre of Playa del Carmen, Básico attracts a style-savvy young crowd with 15 quirky rooms distributed over four floors. Here, traditional ideas of everyday Mexico are brought to life: references to public schools, "cantinas" and the petroleum industry permeate the property, imbuing the hotel with an exciting local feel. Básico's first two storeys house air-conditioned guestrooms whose pink neon lamps, intentionally exposed plumbing and subdued lighting create an almost sexual tension, punctuated with surprises like floating beds and whimsical objects such as autographed footballs, floating tyres for swimming and even beach club passes. In the top floor's Azotea Bar and pool area, two petroleum water tanks act as pools, offering superb views of the Caribbean and the vibrant beach town below. On steamy evenings, guests can enjoy sea breezes and the sounds of local DJs from customised truck fronts that serve as cabanas with built-in mattresses. Speckled with amusing popular accents and made mostly from recycled materials that challenge preconceived notions of what a design hotel should be, Básico updates Mexican nationalism and makes it something for the world to enjoy.

WWW.DESIGNHOTELS.COM/
BÁSICO

ADDRESS
5A AVENIDA Y CALLE 10
77710, PLAYA DEL CARMEN
QUINTANA ROO, MEXICO

ROOMS
15

RATES
USD 178 –
USD 278

OPEN
10/2001

MEXICO
PLAYA
DEL CARMEN

# BOCA CHICA
## *Acapulco*

---

Just steps from an idyllic cove, Boca Chica is a grand addition to Acupulco's new era. Once the playground of the Hollywood elite, this upscále area first came to prominence when Orson Welles filmed *The Lady from Shanghai* in the old city centre in the late 1940s. Located in the district of Caleta, the 36-room hotel was constructed in the late 1950s next to the glamorous Club de Yates and famed Los Flamingos Hotel. Today, the vintage exterior looks like it's straight out of a 1950s movie set, but inside, the reinvigorated interior has been chicly remodeled by designers Frida Escobedo and José Rojas. Vintage pieces were curated by Mexican contemporary artist Claudia Fernández, and the spacious tropically designed rooms come with large hammocks, outdoor living rooms and private gardens. Guests can venture downstairs to get a massage or chill out with a frozen margarita at the happening in-house disco, or hang out on a pool terrace and order 24-hour sushi room service. Welcome back, Acapulco. You've still got it.

WWW.DESIGNHOTELS.COM/
BOCACHICA

**ADDRESS**
PUNTA CALETILLA,
FRACCIONAMIENTO LAS PLAYAS
39390, ACAPULCO, GUERRERO
MEXICO

**ROOMS**
36

**RATES**
USD 125 –
USD 275

**OPEN**
03/2009

**MEXICO**
ACAPULCO

# CASA CAMPER
## *Barcelona*
---

"*Camper* means *peasant* in Catalan, and we believe everything we do should still be connected to the land," says Miguel Fluxá of Casa Camper, the Mallorca-based shoe company's first hotel. Located in the city centre, nestled in a side street of Barcelona's trendy El Raval district, the 25-room hotel offers urban nomads a space that keeps perfect step with Camper's philosophy. There's a 24-hour lobby food-service area available on a complimentary basis, and a new restaurant concept carried out by Albert Raurich (former chef du cuisine of Ferran Adrià's El Bulli Restaurant) that proposes to unify the philosophy behind the Spanish tapas with the "tapas" of Asian gastronomy. Each standard room actually has two spaces: a completely furnished bedroom in red and white as well as a comfortable mini-lounge with a second TV, sofa, table and a relaxing hammock across the corridor, both furnished by the Vinçon design store. A pioneer in environmentally friendly actions, Casa Camper is as unique and as groovy as its shoes … but also keeps things simple. The secret to luxury lies in simplicity, after all.

**WWW.DESIGNHOTELS.COM/ CASACAMPER**

**ADDRESS** CARRER ELISABETH N°11 08001 BARCELONA SPAIN

**ROOMS** 25

**RATES** EUR 184 – EUR 320

**OPEN** 01/2005

**SPAIN** BARCELONA

**ADDRESS**
5A AVENIDA Y CALLE 12
PLAYA DEL CARMEN
QUINTANA ROO 77710,
MEXICO

**WWW.DESIGNHOTELS.COM/
DESEO**

**ROOMS**
15

**RATES**
USD 178 –
USD 278

**OPEN**
10/2001

**MEXICO**
PLAYA
DEL CARMEN

# DESEO
# [HOTEL + LOUNGE]
## *Playa del Carmen*

---

A glowing white two-storey structure in the mellow fishing village of Playa del Carmen, the Deseo has become one of the hottest spots on the Yucatán Peninsula. Created by the groundbreaking Mexican Grupo Habita, the hotel evokes the charm of the Caribbean coast while offering a level of sophistication aimed directly at the discerning international style connoisseur. The hotel's focal point is the lounge area, which combines the functions of lobby, restaurant, bar and pool. Set on a raised open-air platform, it is furnished with comfortable Belize chairs, generous daybeds and breezy linen curtains that provide a relaxed Caribbean flavour and encourage social interaction. The DJ's chilled-out tunes add the perfect sonic backdrop to the comfortable setting. Each of the 15 rooms and suites provides a literally and emotionally cool retreat from the heat with the help of marble floors and a natural colour palette designed to soothe both the eye and mind. Comfortable, visually striking guestrooms boast fun details like sliding wood doors, beach fiesta kits and hammocks. More traditional style elements, like the imposing stone entrance modelled on a Mayan temple, manage to ground the design concept with local tastes.

Jademansarde

WWW.DESIGNHOTELS.COM/
DIETRAEUMEREI

ADDRESS
OBERE PFARRGASSE 3
64720 MICHELSTADT
GERMANY

ROOMS
4

RATES
EUR 95 –
EUR 145

OPEN
08/2008

GERMANY
MICHELSTADT

# DIE TRÄUMEREI
## *Michelstadt*

---

Standing as a landmark site in the pastoral German town of Michelstadt im Odenwald since 1623, the newly opened boutique hotel Die Träumerei is a brilliantly executed project by German film actress Jessica Schwarz and her sister Sandra Schwarz, both of whom grew up admiring the historic building from afar. Now converted into four spacious and impeccably designed rooms, the re-imagined timbered house with cosy café fully retains the whimsical charm of its shingled predecessor, with many aesthetic bonuses added to the new incarnation. Quirky design touches abound, such as movie-row seats and individual room themes of hollyhock, ivory, jade and gold. Die Träumerei (which translates as "The Dreamery") thus wordlessly taps into the attic-dwelling nostalgia of many people in creative professions. The artistic use of the original dark wood beams will make guests feel as if they're stepping into a fantastical hautedesign tree house. And the guestrooms' intimacy and comfort is a dream come true for couples in need of a getaway. Let your latent childhood desires run rampant, for a weekend.

**WWW.DESIGNHOTELS.COM /**
**DUOMOHOTEL**

**ADDRESS**
VIA GIORDANO BRUNO 28
47900 RIMINI
ITALY

**ROOMS**
43

**RATES**
EUR 198 –
EUR 440

**OPEN**
05/2006

**ITALY**
RIMINI

# DUOMO HOTEL & NOMI CLUB
## *Rimini*

---

Situated on a narrow street in Rimini, one of Italy's long-standing seaside resorts, the duoMo hotel underwent a flashy transformation in 2003, when celebrated designer Ron Arad injected it with his own brand of eccentric, futuristic style. Immediately distinguishable by its shining, metallic façade, duoMo makes no attempts to blend in with its more traditional surroundings. Oversize accents, dramatic angles, daring colours and adventurous shapes create an unconventional atmosphere for the hotel's hip clientele. Arad's use of light and shadow evokes duoMo's signature theme of infinite spaces, while individual bathroom pods in each room give the feeling of otherworldly comfort. World-renowned DJs regularly play at the hotel's Sunday beach parties, already popular among the local in-crowd, and often spin at the much-hyped noMi club, where guests can make eyes at each other off any of the bar's myriad, albeit distorted, reflective surfaces. On balmy summer nights, the bar's walls literally open and the party spills out onto the streets of the town's lively historical centre, helping spur the transformation of Rimini from a somewhat forgotten beach resort into a trendy destination for a new generation of jet-setters.

# ESTALAGEM DA PONTA DO SOL
## *Madeira*
---

This stark white getaway is all simplicity and straight edges, framing the raw magnificence of its clifftop setting high above the Portuguese village of Ponta do Sol. Layering itself down a slate cliff, the hotel is cut into the rocky landscape in a series of thick stone wall terraces. Here, walkways let visitors explore the meticulously manicured grounds and drink in the endless blue of the breathtaking ocean views – which they also are privy to from private balconies. Inside, interior designer Carvalho Araújo created a monochrome look using white walls adorned with classic black-and-white photography, black stone floors strewn with grey rugs, and minimalist furnishings in light wood. Outside, the swimming pool's infinity edge makes the vast Atlantic seem just a dive away. The restaurant is completely stripped of any superfluous décor, emphasising the vista across the coastline of Madeira, extensive banana plantations and the village below. It all adds up to an utterly relaxing retreat in a sophisticated atmosphere … perfect for couples looking to connect, singles looking to recharge or anyone looking for all-round beauty.

WWW.DESIGNHOTELS.COM/
PONTADOSOL

**ADDRESS**
QUINTA DA ROCHINHA,
9360 – 529 PONTA DO SOL
PORTUGAL

**ROOMS**
54

**RATES**
EUR 90 –
EUR 132

**OPEN**
04/2001

PORTUGAL
MADEIRA

WWW.DESIGNHOTELS.COM / EV

ADDRESS
TÜRKBÜKÜ
BODRUM
TURKEY

ROOMS
48

RATES
EUR 150 –
EUR 600

OPEN
05/2005

TURKEY
BODRUM

# EV HOTEL
*Bodrum*

---

You might have to look twice at architect and designer Eren Talu's holiday resort overlooking Türkbükü Bay in order to shake the feeling that it's nothing more than a shimmering mirage. Eight buildings, in a shade of white quite blinding under the Turkish sun, cascade down a hillside overlooking the bay near the town of Bodrum. Described as "eight giant steps towards heaven," they are home to 48 separate residences; their stark geometry offers a sharp contrast to the rolling landscape. Talu's use of the colour white throughout acts as a backdrop against which guests can add their own personality to the design. The layout, including a pool for each building, ensures privacy while at the same time creating a loose sense of community. Talu has taken the white motif through every room, aiming to create a lush serenity as well as a cool sanctuary from the hot sun. Terry-cloth linens and curtains provide a feeling of soft comfort, and well-positioned mirrors give the impression of endless space. Carefully chosen mood lighting and brightly coloured furnishings seemingly scattered at whim are the only vivid accents – apart from those you provide yourself, of course.

WWW.DESIGNHOTELS.COM /
GOLDMAN25HOURS

ADDRESS
HANAUER LANDSTRASSE 127
60314 FRANKFURT AM MAIN
GERMANY

ROOMS
49

RATES
EUR 90 –
EUR 135

OPEN
12/2006

GERMANY
FRANKFURT
AM MAIN

# GOLDMAN
# 25HOURS HOTEL
## *Frankfurt am Main*

---

A repurposed hotel in Frankfurt's bustling Ostend district, Goldman 25hours is both a hideaway and a local hot spot. Influenced and inspired by the Frankfurt nightclub scene, designers Delphine Buhro and Michael Dreher created a flowing, funky space where lounge, southern European restaurant, bar and living room flow into and out of each other, giving a constant low-level buzz of activity that soothes and stimulates. Atop the latter is an outdoor terrace that offers a South Seas feel on balmy summer nights. Each of the seven floors has its own consistent colour scheme, and the 49 guestrooms are individually designed around local celebrities – or "godfathers" – whose personal stories are expressed in the room. Guests get a never-ending variety of vintage eclecticism, and the themed rooms – like the Princess, Paris and Casino rooms – add to the sense of fun. Goldman Restaurant provides the perfect social outlet as well as a Mediterranean-influenced menu that has already put the hotel on the culinary map. Frankfurt's burgeoning cosmopolitanism is here to see, bright and clear, 25 hours a day.

WWW.DESIGNHOTELS.COM/
HOTELDANIEL

ADDRESS
EUROPAPLATZ 1
8020 GRAZ
AUSTRIA

ROOMS
107

RATES
EUR 59 –
EUR 149

OPEN
06/2005

AUSTRIA
GRAZ

# HOTEL DANIEL
*Graz*

---

A prime example of slick modular modernity by award-winning Berlin architectural firm Studio Aisslinger, Hotel Daniel is only a few minutes' walk from Graz's historic old town, the convention centre and the eye-popping Kunsthaus. Visitors are instantly put at ease by the composed atmosphere of simple elegance and warm functionality. Modern furniture-design classics are featured against a background of sleek planes of oak and natural stone. The 107 guestrooms stylishly emphasise compact multifunctionality and a warm simplicity. With a large public area, an Internet corner and a meeting room for up to 70 people, executives have everything they need. So do more spontaneous guests, who can mix and mingle with the local scene in the open-plan bar and restaurant. While the breakfast terrace, fireside lounge and library cater to the more leisurely at heart, the espresso bar with tapas counter offers guests a flexible range of modern cuisine before they hop onto one of the house Vespas for a self-guided tour of this lovely Austrian city. It's the perfect "trend-proof" place for well-travelled culture vultures and business travellers alike.

# HOTEL
# GREULICH
## *Zurich*
---

In a residential area of Zurich, Hotel Greulich is a hotel of only 18 rooms, sparsely finished with simple furniture and a neutral colour scheme by Swiss painter Jean Pfaff. Architects Franz Romero and Markus Schaefle created the property by combining several buildings dating to the 1930s, and gave the façade a sensuous, slate blue curve ending at an inconspicuous entrance. Guests arrive in an intimate lobby before journeying to their rooms over dark grey terrazzo floors, past natural cedar walls and across the glass-covered courtyard. Here, the shimmering grey tones of a grove of silver birch trees frame the space, and a calming water trough underlines the Zen atmosphere. The Japanese-influenced guestrooms feature sleeping areas with low beds, separated from the adjoining bathrooms by frosted glass panels. A shared terrace overlooking the courtyard enhances the introspective mood, a crackling fireplace glows invitingly in the cigar room, and the "slow food" restaurant offers a meditative approach to sophisticated, organic gastronomy. Wonderfully personal, aesthetically pleasing and reservedly Swiss, the Greulich offers a rare bit of nourishment to the soul.

WWW.DESIGNHOTELS.COM/
GREULICH

ADDRESS
HERMAN-GREULICH-STRASSE 56
8004 ZÜRICH
SWITZERLAND

ROOMS
18

RATES
CHF 220
CHF 400

OPEN
2009

SWITZERLAND
ZURICH

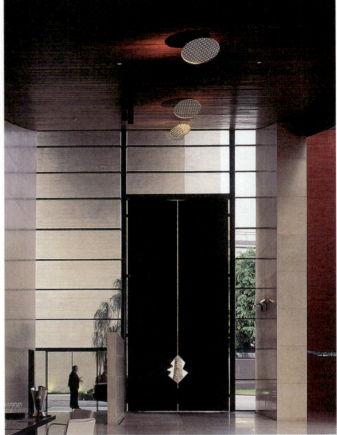

WWW.DESIGNHOTELS.COM /
UNIQUE

ADDRESS
AVENIDA BRIGADEIRO
LUIS ANTONIO, 4700
01402-002 SÃO PAULO
BRAZIL

ROOMS
95

RATES
USD 395 –
USD 7000

OPEN
12/2002

BRAZIL
SÃO PAULO

# HOTEL UNIQUE
## *São Paulo*
---

Rising proudly above São Paulo like a graceful ocean-liner, the Unique is sculptural architecture at its most original – and a must for savvy architecture fans and well-travelled urbanites alike. The spacey, green-weathered copper that adorns the façade stretches across the building's unusual shape, a large inverted arch with circular windows like oversize portholes. The effect of the geometric forms, dark glass and desert gardens is nothing less than spectacular, nor does the interior disappoint. There, the curvilinear theme continues in a choreographed spectrum of circles, squares, ellipses and sine curves that flow into and out of each other. Nothing is superfluous, and no space is wasted; the harmony is palpable. In guestrooms, high-tech details are combined with natural elements to create an otherworldly effect that still manages to seem welcoming. Unusual accessories from around the globe add to the ultra cool, something-special feel that's only accented by the staff's coolly impeccable service. Upstairs, what is perhaps São Paulo's finest rooftop terrace offers amazing views of the city: that is, if guests can take their eyes off the fascinating crimson swimming pool that runs along its edge. A night at the Unique is definitely a singular experience.

WWW.DESIGNHOTELS.COM /
KNIGHTSBRIDGEHOTEL

ADDRESS
10 BEAUFORT GARDENS
LONDON SW3 1PT
UNITED KINGDOM

ROOMS
44

RATES
GBP 170 –
GBP 595

OPEN
05/2002

UNITED KINGDOM
LONDON

# KNIGHTSBRIDGE HOTEL
## *London*

—–—

On a quiet leafy street not far from Harrods and Harvey Nichols, designer Kit Kemp has added another chic bauble to her collection of London luxury properties. As admirers of Kemp's classically British aesthetic well know, she pays careful attention to each room, filling it with modern English style featuring clean neutrals and bold colours. In this eponymous Knightsbridge gem, the drawing room, library and lobby are adorned with original works by significant British artists. Art lovers will adore the Carol Sinclair sculpture that rises like stalagmites from the floor. But the art does not overshadow Kemp's signature harmonious mixture of patterns, fabrics and furniture styles. Setting this location apart from her other hotels are the African sculpture and fabrics, mixed with tasselled curtains and the blue neon rungs of a ladder in the library, which add adventuresome touches to the stately interior. First-floor guests gaze through floor-to-ceiling windows onto one of London's most charming areas, while the upper floors reveal tantalizing glimpses of Harrods' rooftops. Although the guestrooms' cosy cushions and pretty fabrics could be considered quaint, the jazzy contrast of stripes, florals and geometric shapes injects a thrilling jolt of modernity to their comforting charm.

WWW.DESIGNHOTELS.COM /
KUBE

ADDRESS
1–5, PASSAGE RUELLE
75018 PARIS
FRANCE

ROOMS
41

RATES
EUR 250
EUR 900

OPEN
11/2005

FRANCE
PARIS

# KUBE HOTEL
## *Paris*
---

Tucked into a tiny, quiet street at the summit of Paris's multicultural Montmartre district is a retro-future hotel that defies the city's classical clichés. Upon entering Kube, visitors will be forgiven for thinking they've walked onto the set of an achingly smart 1960s sci-fi film. A glowing Plexiglass cube serves as Kube's reception area, while at the heart of the hotel is a spacious lounge-restaurant-bar: a futuristic, low-lit space with high ceilings, stainless steel accents and a state-of-the-art sound system camouflaged in red ceiling lanterns. The ultratrendy "Ice Kube" bar on the mezzanine features an icy blue-lit igloo, Eero Aarnio's 1968 Bubble Chairs and a Grey Goose vodka-only drinks menu. The 31 sleek guestrooms and 10 suites are arranged around an open courtyard and accessed via colourful elevators. This gives a hint of the playful features in store, including faux-fur, cubic bathtubs and beds lit from beneath. Biometric fingerprint technology controls room access, and each room is fitted with integrated computer equipment that serves as a DVD and CD player as well as television screen. Welcome to the future!

WWW.DESIGNHOTELS.COM/
LIMESHOTEL

**ADDRESS**
142 CONSTANCE STREET
FORTITUDE VALLEY, BRISBANE
QLD 4006
AUSTRALIA

**ROOMS**
21

**RATES**
AUD 289 –
AUD 319

**OPEN**
06/2008

**AUSTRALIA**
BRISBANE

# LIMES HOTEL
## *Brisbane*
---

Travel-savvy urbanites will appreciate the simple sophistication and contemporary energy abuzz at the Limes Hotel in Fortitude Valley – the heart of Brisbane's nightlife and entertainment. Award-winning Argentinean designer Alexander Lotersztain, a true global nomad, explains that he conceived the hotel as a holistic "design experience ... stripped of the associated design ideals of something unattainable. I shifted the design focus to make the guest feel special, yet not afraid of jumping into the bed like it was their own." His close attention to detail is reflected in all the hotel's facets, from each of the cosy 21 rooms to the hip rooftop lounge bar and seasonal open-air cinema. Guests are welcomed with handcrafted Dello Mano brownies and fresh fruit, an iPod music system, wireless and broadband Internet, L'Occitane toiletries and finest linens, not to mention a kitchenette and either balcony or courtyard. The eye-catching façade reproduces the hotel's limestone logo on a grand scale, making the Limes a design statement as well as an urban landmark, while the sleek, modern interior, with its rich textures and finishings, contributes to an intimate ambience unencumbered by excessive ornamentation.

WWW.DESIGNHOTELS.COM/
LUTESUITES

ADDRESS
AMSTELDIJK ZUID 54-58
1184 VD OUDERKERK AAN DE AMSTEL
NETHERLANDS

ROOMS
7

RATES
EUR 285 –
EUR 395

OPEN
01/2005

NETHERLANDS
AMSTERDAM

# LUTE SUITES
## *Amsterdam*

---

It all began in 2003 with Dutch chef Peter Lute's eponymous restaurant colonising a portion of a reclaimed 18th-century gunpowder factory and making culinary history. But not long after, he joined forces with megadesigner Marcel Wanders and transformed the seven adjacent two- and three-level cottages into Lute Suites, making the landmark location an unforgettable gastronomic and hospitality experience. Just a few minutes outside Amsterdam on the river Amstel, the restaurant's sophisticated French-oriented cuisine melds into the guestrooms' true design eclecticism: each suite's look is completely different, but what every guest can depend on are modern kitchenettes, a private wine cabinet, sleek baths and breakfast delivered to the door. Little design quirks abound, but like the river framed by the suites' ten-foot windows, water is an interior centrepiece, showcasing Wanders's work with Italian manufacturers Bisazza and Boffi. In two suites, the bedroom is a tent-like nest beneath the roof, connected to the mezzanine via a narrow staircase. The result of a dream-team effort that's also a warm friendship that guests can feel, Lute Suites is true to the unapologetically earnest philosophy of Wanders's design studio: "Here to create an environment of love, live with passion, and make our most exciting dreams come true."

# LUX 11
## *Berlin*
---

Just steps from the famous TV tower that soars over trendy Berlin-Mitte, Lux 11 is the perfect place for individualists who like just the right balance of pampering, style and autonomy. Behind the 19th-century residential building's sparkling white façade, the ground level's lobby, avant-garde boutique, Aveda salon and contemporary Japanese restaurant give way to quiet privacy in the hotel's 72 quirky guestrooms above. That's where concrete and wood meld with tactile textiles in intimate, open floor plans. "The interiors play with opposites: warm and cold, smooth and rough," says London-based architect Giuliana Salmaso, who, with Claudio Silvestrin, conceived the hotel's design to match the city it is part of. Also following Berlin's ethos is a focus on independence: Lux 11's apartment-hotel concept means that rooms are equipped with sleek kitchenettes. Urban-lifesit livestyle mavens who like having their fingers on the pulse of the action – more than a few celebrities have thrown parties here – prefer staying at Lux 11 for extended stays, as if they'd temporarily moved to Berlin's most vibrant neighbourhood and made it their very own.

WWW.DESIGNHOTELS.COM /
LUX11

ADDRESS
ROSA-LUXEMBURG-STRASSE 9-13
10178 BERLIN
GERMANY

ROOMS
72

RATES
EUR 165 –
EUR 295

OPEN
07/2005

GERMANY
BERLIN

WWW.DESIGNHOTELS.COM/
NEWMAJESTIC

**ADDRESS** 31–37 BUKIT PASOH ROAD
089845
SINGAPORE

**ROOMS** 30

**RATES** SGD 400 –
SGD 800

**OPEN** 02/2006

**SINGAPORE**
SINGAPORE

# NEW
# MAJESTIC HOTEL
## *Singapore*
---

It has a certain glamour, this revamped historic hotel on a Chinatown street once notorious for housing wealthy men's mistresses. The shop-house façade blends perfectly with the neighbourhood, while inside, the juxtapositions of antique and modern, interior and exterior, provide a theatrical environment where guests can indulge their imaginations. The 30 guestrooms are individually crafted visions by a diverse group of creatives enlisted by Colin Seah of Ministry of Design. His core crew came up with four room "typologies." In the Hanging Bed Room, larger-than-life murals span whole walls. The sensuous Loft Room's vintage twin tubs look up on an attic-area sleeping space that appears to float. And a glass-encased bathtub is placed centre stage in the Aquarium Room. In the hotel's restaurant, ceiling portholes open on to the floor of the outdoor pool, and swimmers cast shadows onto the tables below. The high-ceilinged lobby provides a grand space to make an entrance: vintage chairs from owner Loh Lik Peng's personal collection can be rearranged to suit any drama, while the sensuously curved white staircase seems to invite a line of chorus girls, like something from a classic Hollywood musical. Majestic, indeed.

WWW.DESIGNHOTELS.COM/
NUMBERSIXTEEN

ADDRESS
16 SUMNER PLACE
LONDON SW7 3EG
UNITED KINGDOM

ROOMS
42

RATES
GBP 120 –
GBP 270

OPEN
06/2000

UNITED KINGDOM
LONDON

# NUMBER SIXTEEN
## *London*

---

A white-stucco Victorian terrace situated steps from London's major museums and even Harrods; only the corresponding house number suggests that Number Sixteen is a hotel and not an upscale private residence. Like the other Kit Kemp properties in town, the designer's custom textiles are a study in elaborate detail and dramatic patterns in each of the 42 individually outfitted guestrooms. Guests can mingle in the hotel's handsome drawing rooms, and some guestrooms have private areas overlooking the hotel's stunning English garden. One drawing room is romantically adorned with rose prints and oil paintings, while the lobby greets guests with a more austere ambience. The eclectic furnishings – a mix of antique, modern and ethnic accents – keep the aesthetic fresh and elegantly eccentric. The attentive service, however, might have guests wondering whether this accommodation weren't a gracious private home after all. Number Sixteen's sense of subdued, relaxed modernity is brought to its apex in its conservatory and exquisite private garden, whose reflecting pool, fountain and lush foliage offer the kind of seclusion that is all too rare in this bustling cosmopolitan capital.

WWW.DESIGNHOTELS.COM /
PURO

ADDRESS
MONTENEGRO 10
07006 PALMA DE MALLORCA
SPAIN

ROOMS
26

RATES
EUR 188 –
EUR 515

OPEN
04/2004

SPAIN
MALLORCA

# PUROHOTEL OASIS URBANO
## *Mallorca*

---

Madrid-based architect Alvaro Planchuelo has extensive experience restoring historic buildings in Spain and West Africa, but this time a Swedish hotelier wanted a transformation that would make way for the 21st century by fusing global elements from Asia, Africa and Arabia. Located in Palma de Mallorca's old Muslim neighbourhood, this 18th-century town mansion retains its signature arches and inviting courtyard but rejects past notions of decorative prestige. The result is a kind of global bohemian feel that is nothing less than sexy. Anyone entering Erik and Katarina van Brabant's interiors will be soothed yet inspired by the prevailing white, cushions made from hand-selected Rajasthani saris and other hand-worked materials and fascinating details from just about everywhere. Above the beds are pale sculptural spheres of feathers that are actually ceremonial hats worn by Bandjon tribes in Cameroon; even pushing aside the room's massive hand-carved doors from Burma evokes an otherworldly feeling. In the spacious bathroom, simply lying in a spa-size square black bath is transformed into a luxurious, perhaps even spiritual, activity – as is a stay transformed simply by embracing time and enjoying the cultural wealth all around.

WWW.DESIGNHOTELS.COM /
ROCKHOUSE

ADDRESS
WEST END ROAD
NEGRIL, WESTMORELAND
JAMAICA, W.I.

ROOMS
34

RATES
USD 160 –
USD 425

OPEN
12/1994

JAMAICA
NEGRIL

# ROCKHOUSE HOTEL
## *Negril*

---

Hexagonal thatched-roof buildings, volcanic Jamaican coastline and sparkling turquoise waters give the Rockhouse Hotel a look and feel that's straight out of a Robinson Crusoe fantasy. The truth is not far off: the resort designers sought to mimic the seamless merging of man and nature so beautifully exemplified by African village life. Together, the hotel's bar and restaurant constitute the central square of this Rockhouse "village," perched on a gorgeous deck suspended above the Pristine Cove. A stunning infinity pool set in a clifftop rock garden perfects the back-to-nature atmosphere, while ubiquitous references to the Caribbean Sea and surrounding Jamaican countryside complete the picture of an island getaway. But the true highlights are the generous timber bungalows overlooking either glowing Caribbean waters or the hotel's expansive, lush tropical gardens. Rockhouse also offers a number of studios, whose breezy linen curtains and custom-made furniture of local wood add to the overall in-tune-with-nature ambience. Throughout the property, ladders and stairs carved into the rock provide easy access to the water, while a new temple-like spa pavilion – complete with Massage Cabana, Caribbean Drench Hut and yoga room – rounds out this laid-back haven of relaxation.

WWW.DESIGNHOTELS.COM /
SANCTUMSOHO

ADDRESS
18-20 WARWICK STREET
LONDON, W1B 5NF
UNITED KINGDOM

ROOMS
30

RATES
GBP 145 –
GBP 1250

OPEN
03/2009

UNITED KINGDOM
LONDON

# SANCTUM SOHO
## *London*
---

Paying homage to Soho's history as a centre of artistic activity and bohemia, London's Sanctum Soho is a celebration of edgy glamour that fluidly integrates art and individuality into its design. The lobby is decorated with paintings and vintage light fittings; two elegant fireplaces provide a touch of welcoming warmth. Once the sun sets, the hotel transforms into a local hot spot – the members' bar bustles and the exclusive in-house cinema hosts screenings for up to 40 people. Those exhausted after a night of partying in the hotel, an evening of exploring Soho's bars or a day checking out its boutiques will be grateful for the rooftop bar, secret garden and hot tub, as well as the variety of personalised rejuvenation and beauty treatments on offer in the rooms. Individual attention doesn't stop there: each of the hotel's 30 rooms was designed on the basis of four mood schemes – Silver Bullet, Espresso Deco, Naked Baroque and Purple Haze. No two rooms look the same, and each is opened by a proper, tasselled key as opposed to the standard electronic card. Whether relaxing in their rooms or clinking glasses in the hotel bar, Sanctum Soho guests can be sure that they're doing it in style.

WWW.DESIGNHOTELS.COM/
SANTATERESA

ADDRESS
CONTRADA SIBÀ
91017 PANTELLERIA (TP)
SICILY
ITALY

ROOMS
18

RATES
EUR 110 –
EUR 392

OPEN
04/2006

# SANTA TERESA RESORT
## *Pantelleria*

---

Set amid breathtaking natural beauty on the volcanic island of Pantelleria, Santa Teresa Resort offers travellers a rustic simplicity and a perfect sense of the true and untouched. Situated over 40 hectares of vineyards, olive trees and lush flora, four mini-villages consist of 18 beautifully restored *dammusi* – ancient bungalows of local cut stone dotting a rugged black landscape. Once home to Pantelleria's native inhabitants and infused with the area's Arabian past, the unique dammusi were transformed into modern abodes, some by architect Gabriella Giuntoli. Whitewashed walls frame minimalist interiors in white and light grey – some interiors feature colourful touches such as yellow, soft blue and green – and the arched ceilings and narrow windows lend the serenity of a cool, calm sanctuary after a day spent splashing in hidden ocean coves, golfing or relaxing by one of the beautiful resort's pools. Pantelleria is just 70 kilometres from the North African coast, and the weather, food and culture all reflect its location at this continental crossroads. After delicious couscous, fresh fish or Arabian sweets, enjoyable at one of Pantelleria's restaurants, guests can relax over a drink on the resort's terrace and reflect on the revitalising combination of privacy, ancient tradition and slow, simple living.

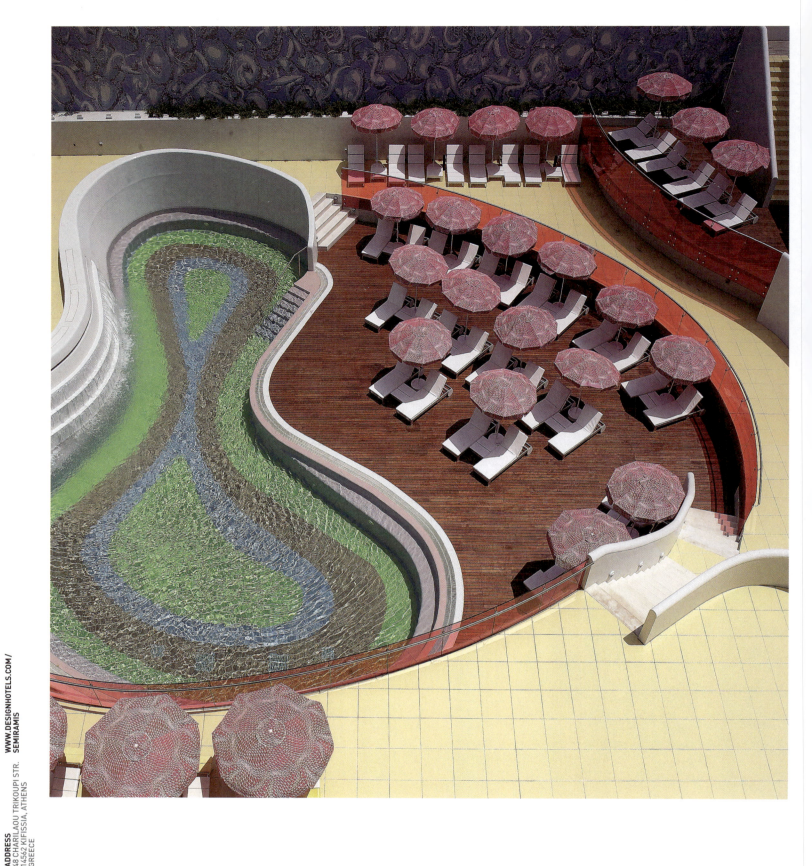

**WWW.DESIGNHOTELS.COM /**
SEMIRAMIS

**ADDRESS**
48 CHARILAOU TRIKOUPI STR.
14562 KIFISSIA, ATHENS
GREECE

**ROOMS**
51

**RATES**
EUR 220 –
EUR 550

**OPEN**
08/2004

**GREECE**
ATHENS

# SEMIRAMIS HOTEL
## *Athens*

---

Athens's Semiramis Hotel is what happens when you give a hot designer control over every aspect of a building and its interior. Design star Karim Rashid's dazzling display of lollipop colours and organically shaped furniture play happily alongside a rotating collection of contemporary fine art, hand-picked by owner and art collector Dakis Ioannou. Situated in Athens's leafy, posh Kiffisia district, it's a feast for the eyes for any guest. The hotel's rotating art collection, which might include works by Tim Noble, Sue Webster or Jeff Koons, presents the best of contemporary art, while Rashid's juicy pinks, oranges, greens and yellows bathe lobby couches, transparent glass partitions and other surfaces. It all adds up to an atmosphere – and almost exuberant service culture – that positively pulses with energy. With an extra element of cheekiness, guests are encouraged to play with Rashid's device for communicating with the outside world. Instead of the boring "Do Not Disturb" signs, he offers electronic message boards, which guests can personalise from their in-room keyboards. Rashid suggests invitations such as, "Hello, I'm single. Please come in."

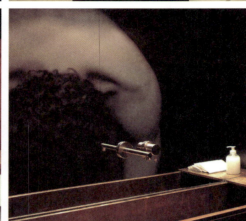

WWW.DESIGNHOTELS.COM / STRAF

ADDRESS
VIA SAN RAFFAELE, 3
20121 MILANO
ITALY

ROOMS
64

RATES
EUR 297 –
EUR 704

OPEN
12/2003

ITALY
MILAN

# STRAF
## *Milan*

---

The Straf began its life as a 19th-century palazzo a few steps from Milan's Duomo Cathedral and La Scala opera house before it spent years as a "normal" hotel. But now the hotel is a mesmerising monument to the deconstructivist design aesthetic of Milanese architect/artist/fashion designer Vincenzo de Cotiis. With bare cement floors and stairs, rooms featuring oxidised copper and split slate, scratched mirrors, burnished brass and torn, aged gauze captured between sheets of glass, the Straf forges an atmosphere of warmth and well-being from scrappy, hard-edged materials. The 64 guestrooms come in either a light or dark colour palette and exude intimacy despite (or perhaps because of) the hints of industrial design. Guests can bask under colour-therapy light panels in some rooms; all offer tactile pleasures in fine textiles, decadent bathrooms and mirrored surfaces. Public areas are slightly unfinished odes to fashion and relaxation: a reading area invites guests to a couch formation under a glass courtyard, and the slick Straf Bar has become a magnet for sunglassed fashion mavens from around the world. "The hotel is almost like an installation," says de Cotiis. An experience here is indeed nothing less than artistry.

WWW.DESIGNHOTELS.COM/
THEEMPEROR

ADDRESS
NO.33 QIHELOU STREET
DONGCHENG DISTRICT
BEIJING 100006
CHINA

ROOMS
55

RATES
EUR 129 –
EUR 599

OPEN
04/2008

CHINA
BEIJING

# THE EMPEROR
## *Beijing*
---

Just steps away from the Forbidden City - home to 24 emperors who reigned China over 500 years – The Emperor is a blend of ancient tradition and progressive modernity, just like 21st-century China. Beyond the traditional brick façade's modesty, the 55-room boutique hotel, conceived by the Berlin-based architecture firm Graft Labs, unfolds into a lively, even funky, dialogue between old and new. Sleek curves lead guests from the hallway to lounge sofas, beds, desks and closets in clean whites complemented by a different imperial colour on each floor. Room numbers have been replaced by icons; contemporary, grafitti-like wall murals of Chinese emperors stand guard at each suite entrance. Inside the guestrooms, the swooping rooftops of the Forbidden City skyline etched into the suede-lined walls and glass room-dividers surround guests with traces of the past, while classical Chinese operas waft through cosy hallway alcoves. The lower-level restaurant, Shi, enchants the palate with modern reinterpretations of traditional Chinese recipes in a playful curtained ambience, and on the top level, guests at the open-air bar and spa can relish unrivalled views of Beijing across the golden eaves of the Forbidden City and beyond.

WWW.DESIGNHOTELS.COM /
GRANDDADDY

ADDRESS
38 LONG STREET
CAPE TOWN 8001
SOUTH AFRICA

ROOMS
26

RATES
ZAR 945

OPEN
09/2008

SOUTH AFRICA
CAPE TOWN

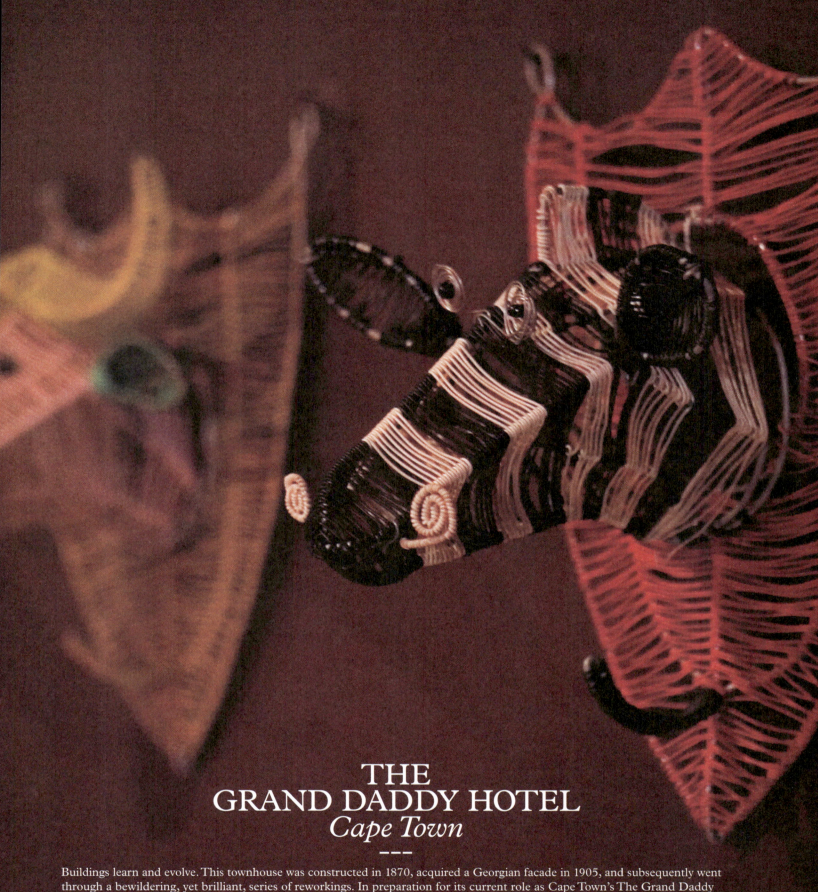

# THE
# GRAND DADDY HOTEL
## *Cape Town*
---

Buildings learn and evolve. This townhouse was constructed in 1870, acquired a Georgian facade in 1905, and subsequently went through a bewildering, yet brilliant, series of reworkings. In preparation for its current role as Cape Town's The Grand Daddy (formerly the Metropole), designer François du Plessis made the most of the existent funky mixture of retro, modern and classic, adding a vivacious touch of African chic. The lobby is served by South Africa's oldest working elevator, and dominated by the passion and decadence of the colour red. International guests can settle into the first-floor M-Bar & Lounge's plush, poppy hues, or be transported to the 1960s in the street-level M-Café, where chocolate and lime green reign. Even in the clean-lined Veranda restaurant, with its absorbing view of Long Street, bright colour juxtapositions remain the rule. The 25 guestrooms offer their visitors peaceful luxury brought up to the present day with a soothing, textured minimalism and high-tech appointments. The building might have all the character of maturity and experience, but the hotel that inhabits it boasts an undeniably youthful energy that sparkles exuberantly throughout its spacious chambers and broad corridors.

WWW.DESIGNHOTELS.COM/
THELIBRARY

ADDRESS
14/1 MOO 2, CHAWENG BEACH,
KOH SAMUI
SURATTHANI 84320
THAILAND

ROOMS
26

RATES
THB 10500
THB 16000

OPEN
01/2007

THAILAND
SURATTHANI

# THE LIBRARY
## *Koh Samui*
---

Distractions are kept to a minimum at this graceful hotel complex set in 6,400 square metres of lush Thai beachfront in Koh Samui. Group designer Tirawan Songsawat has created a minimalist structure, preserving a heritage property at the water's edge while intruding as little as possible on its ecology and aesthetics. The hotel's 26 suite-studio cabins are scattered discreetly around the grounds. These consist of a ground-floor suite space and a separate studio upstairs that offers fabulous views of both ocean and old-growth trees that have been spared the developer's bulldozer. Guests may lose (or find) themselves among vegetation interspersed with artwork and statuary, contrasting a bold colour scheme in which white, red, black and grey predominate: The Library's exterior is white, the swimming pool red, the restaurant grey. Interiors follow the same ultraminimalist palette and feature low-slung, rectilinear furnishings that invite visitors to stretch out and listen to the lapping of the waves – or, of course, to dive into the books in the exemplary namesake library. Plasma-screen televisions and broadband connections complement golden Buddhas and wooden shutters in a perfect balance of nature, comfort and art.

WWW.DESIGNHOTELS.COM /
THEOTHERSIDE

**ADDRESS**
9930 NEIDEN
NORWAY

**ROOMS**
20

**RATES**
EUR 260 –
EUR 600

**OPEN**
10/2009

**NORWAY**
NEIDEN

# THE
# OTHER SIDE
*Neiden*

---

The otherworldly allure of The Other Side embodies the shamanistic sensibility of Swedish/French design duo Birgitta Ralston and Alexandre Bau. Inspired by the indigenous aesthetic of Norway's Sámi people, Bau and Ralston married pure ultramodern luxury with the natural beauty of the Neiden plateau. Nestled in Norway's northernmost region on the border between Finland and Russia, the unusual resort provides exposure to the Northern Lights in winter and to summer's midnight sun. In 12 houses laid out in groups of three following a pattern based on a Sámi shaman drum, guests can curl up in furs by their fireplaces and witness a panoramic view of Barents Sea, the Neidenelven, and spot elk and reindeer roaming the surrounding tundra. The houses themselves are homages to their intense environs: the Wind House is raised into the air, the Water House is positioned over a pond and the Fire House overlooks an enormous ritual outdoor fireplace bathing the majestic setting in firelight. Each cluster of houses is joined by a multi-storey bathhouse. Contrasting creature comforts with a unique experience of all of the elements, The Other Side is an extreme-climate take on modern luxury.

WWW.DESIGNHOTELS.COM /
TOWNHOUSEHOTEL

ADDRESS
150 20TH STREET
MIAMI BEACH, FLA 33139
UNITED STATES

ROOMS
69

RATES
USD 115 –
USD 495

OPEN
09/2000

UNITED STATES
MIAMI BEACH

# TOWNHOUSE HOTEL
## *Miami Beach*
—––

According to its architect and designer India Mahdavi, Miami's high-energy Townhouse Hotel was created to reflect three things: "Sea, sex and sun." It does precisely that. Fun, flirtatious and affordable, the Townhouse fits perfectly into the South Beach landscape. The hotel's rooftop terrace overlooking the infamous beach ranks among the most original in Miami, which, given the local penchant for extravagance, is definitely not an accolade to be sniffed at. On it, bronzed bodies lounge on queen-size waterbeds under cardinal-red parasols, listening to the tunes emanating from the excellent sound system. Music, in fact, plays a vital role in the hotel's overall concept, resounding in the wide corridors on every floor. Because public spaces were designed to encourage social interaction, hallways are dotted with benches, stocked with reading material and even equipped with gym machines. Minimalist guestrooms are light and airy – white-on-white spaces dotted with playful touches like red plastic beach balls and clunky old-fashioned phones. Each also features an inviting L-shaped sofa, the ideal impromptu spot for an extra overnight guest. "Sea, sex and sun," indeed.

WWW.DESIGNHOTELS.COM/
X2KOHSAMUI

ADDRESS
442 MOO 1, HUA THANON,
TUMBOL MARET,
UMPHUR KOH SAMUI
84310 SURATTHANI
THAILAND

ROOMS
27

RATES
THB 5200 –
THB 23280

OPEN
06/2008

THAILAND
KOH SAMUI

# X2 KOH SAMUI
## *Koh Samui*

———

Thailand's X2 (pronounced "cross-to") resorts are about soul, freedom and simplicity. These credos add up to an earthy philosophy that beautifully continues at X2 Koh Samui, on the Hua Thannon beach on the southeastern coast of Koh Samui island. The newly built resort's 27 villas rest on a largely undeveloped beach surrounded by old tree growth; the buildings' sleek, horizontally oriented design seems to meld into nature. With interiors in calm neutral tones that stand in sharp contrast to the Gulf of Thailand's brilliant turquoise waters, most have their own swimming pools and terrace gardens. There's plenty to do and even excellent fusion food on offer all day at the resort's 4K ("fork") restaurant, but the resort admits that its main activity is, well, relaxation. For this reason, perhaps the huge outdoor massage pavilion best captures X2 Koh Samui's true essence. With just two beds on which to be pampered by expert hands, the coolly modernist building has an entire acre of land and 30 metres of beachfront all to itself. This, dear traveler, is a place to really *feel* that the most desirable luxuries of today are infinite time, endless space and the sweet sound of silence.

WWW.DESIGNHOTELS.COM/
X2RESORT

ADDRESS
52 MOO 13, AO NOI MUANG
77210 PRACHUAP KHIRI KHAN
THAILAND

ROOMS
23

RATES
THB 5200 –
THB 28800

OPEN
12/2007

THAILAND
HUA HIN

# X2 KUI BURI
*Hua Hin*

---

Extending over several beachfront hectares on the Gulf of Thailand, X2 Kui Buri enfolds its lucky visitors in just a little paradise on earth. It relaxes the eyes with uninterrupted sea views and engages the senses with a combination of indigenous materials and modern lines. This is feng shui meets utopian community in a design by Duangrit Bunnag, for whom simplicity means spatial economy and a lack of complication. Guests can absolutely unwind in 23 villas. These are largely identical with understated furnishings and floor-to-ceiling glass doors that open onto the beach, yet a certain individuality lies in their proximity to the bordering terrace, adjacent pool and neighbouring garden areas. The resort makes use of invisible wall design – what's a craggy stone wall to one villa appears as a fence partition to another. Common areas include a large pool, indulgent spa, a fusion restaurant and roof terrace bar that overlooks the sparkling waters of the gulf and a tranquil white-sand beach untouched by development. A smooth wooden boardwalk meanders like a maze through the resort, each twist and turn revealing a new panorama in an environment of unfussy luxury and natural peace.

# EXPERIENCE
# *DESIGN HOTELS*™
# CALL TO MAKE
# YOUR RESERVATION

---

## INTERNATIONAL TOLL FREE RESERVATION NUMBERS

### AMERICAS
| | |
|---|---|
| USA | 1 800 337 46 85 |
| CANADA | 1 800 337 46 85 |
| BRAZIL | 0021 800 37 46 83 57 |
| ARGENTINA | 00 800 37 46 83 57 |

### EUROPE
| | |
|---|---|
| AUSTRIA | 00 800 37 46 83 57 |
| BELGIUM | 000 800 37 46 83 57 |
| DENMARK | 00 800 37 46 83 57 |
| FINLAND | 990 800 37 46 83 57 |
| FRANCE | 00 800 37 46 83 57 |
| GERMANY | 00 800 37 46 83 57 |
| GREECE | 00 800 49 12 90 54 |
| HUNGARY | 06 800 1 22 36 |
| IRELAND | 00 800 37 46 83 57 |
| ITALY | 00 800 37 46 83 57 |
| NETHERLANDS | 00 800 37 46 83 57 |
| NORWAY | 00 800 37 46 83 57 |
| PORTUGAL | 00 800 37 46 83 57 |
| RUSSIA | 810 800 20 74 10 49 |
| SPAIN | 00 800 37 46 83 57 |
| SWEDEN | 00 800 37 46 83 57 |
| SWITZERLAND | 00 800 37 46 83 57 |
| UNITED KINGDOM | 00 800 37 46 83 57 |

### AFRICA
| | |
|---|---|
| SOUTH AFRICA | 09 800 37 46 83 57 |

### ASIA/PACIFIC
| | |
|---|---|
| AUSTRALIA | 0011 800 37 46 83 57 |
| CHINA | 00 800 37 46 83 57 |
| HONG KONG | 001 800 37 46 83 57 |
| JAPAN | 0041 800 37 46 83 57 |
| NEW ZEALAND | 00 800 37 46 83 57 |
| SINGAPORE | 001 800 37 46 83 57 |
| THAILAND | 001 800 37 46 83 57 |

## TERMS AND CONDITIONS APPLY

## GENERAL CONTACT DETAILS
| | |
|---|---|
| RESERVATIONS | +49 30 884 94 00 40 |
| WEBSITE | WWW.DESIGNHOTELS.COM |
| E-MAIL | RES@DESIGNHOTELS.COM |
| GDS CODE | DS |

SHOULD YOUR COUNTRY NOT BE LISTED PLEASE USE
THE GENERAL RESERVATION NUMBER, BUT BE AWARE
THAT INTERNATIONAL CALL CHARGES WILL APPLY.

### PLEASE NOTE:
THE TELEPHONE NUMBERS FOR THE COUNTRIES
LISTED ARE FOR CALLS MADE FROM WITHIN THAT
COUNTRY ONLY.

---

## FOR GENERAL ENQUIRIES ABOUT DESIGN HOTELS™
DESIGN HOTELS AG
CORPORATE HEADQUARTERS
STRALAUER ALLEE 2C
10245 BERLIN
GERMANY

PHONE +49 30 884 94 00 00
FAX +49 30 257 698 96
E-MAIL RECEPTION@DESIGNHOTELS.COM

# IMPRINT

---

**PUBLISHED BY**
DESIGN HOTELS AG
STRALAUER ALLEE 2C
10245 BERLIN, GERMANY
WWW.DESIGNHOTELS.COM
PUBLISHING@DESIGNHOTELS.COM

**INTERNATIONAL DISTRIBUTION**
GESTALTEN
BERLIN, GERMANY
WWW.GESTALTEN.COM
SALES@GESTALTEN.COM

**PROJECT MANAGEMENT**
BERND NEFF

**CREATIVE DIRECTORS**
MICHAEL SCHICKINGER
JOHANNES SCHWARK

**ART DIRECTOR**
ANNE PRINZ

**EDITORIAL DIRECTOR**
PATRYCJA PAPPELBAUM

**EDITOR-IN-CHIEF**
KIMBERLY BRADLEY

**CONTRIBUTING WRITERS**
ERIK ANDERSEN
RACHEL DOYLE
ANA FINEL HONIGMAN
KYLE JAMES
ALISA LIEU ANH KOTMAIR
JENNA KRUMMINGA
SUSANA SEIJAS
ANDREAS TZORTZIS

**CONTRIBUTING EDITORS**
ANA FINEL HONIGMAN
EVE HURFORD
JENNA KRUMMINGA
DAVID RIMMER
EMILIE TRICE

**COPY EDITORS**
GINGER A. DIECKMANN
LILAN PATRI
KARI RITTENBACH

**LAYOUT**
EVA RÖHRIG

**PRE-PRESS**
GREGOR ORLOWSKI

**PHOTOGRAPHY "MADE BY ORIGINALS"**
KERSTIN ZU PAN
PETER LANGER

**PRODUCTION MANAGEMENT**
STEFANIE SANDL

**PRODUCTION ASSISTANTS**
PETER BARTON
FABIA STUTZER

**MEMBERSHIP RELATIONS**
ASTRID BACHMANN

**PRINTED IN GERMANY BY**
DRUCKHAUS SCHÖNEWEIDE
BALLINSTRASSE 15
12359 BERLIN
GERMANY

ISBN: 978-3-89955-238-6

---

TO MAKE YOUR
**RESERVATION**